The Menaechmus Twins

AND

Two Other Plays

LIONEL CASSON is Professor of Classics and Comparative Literature at New York University and Director of the summer session of the American Academy in Rome. He has contributed widely to literary and scholarly journals, and is author, editor, and translator of many works in the Classics. His translations of *"Amphitryon" and Two Other Plays* and *"The Menaechmus Twins" and Two Other Plays* by Plautus and *Selected Satires of Lucian* are all published in the Norton Library.

The Menaechmus Twins

AND

Two Other Plays

By Plautus

Edited and Translated by LIONEL CASSON

The Norton Library

W · W · NORTON & COMPANY · INC ·

NEW YORK

To Nan *and* Milt

This book was previously published as part of a volume entitled *Six Plays of Plautus*. The companion volume, *"Amphitryon" and Two Other Plays,* is also available in the Norton Library (N601).

Lionel Casson's translation of *The Rope* first appeared in *Masters of Ancient Comedy,* published by The Macmillan Company in 1960, and is reprinted here by arrangement with The Macmillan Company. The translation has been slightly revised.

First published in the Norton Library 1971 by arrangement with Doubleday & Company, Inc.

Published simultaneously in Canada by George J. McLeod Limited, Toronto

Books That Live

The Norton imprint on a book means that in the publisher's estimation it is a book not for a single season but for the years. W. W. Norton & Company, Inc.

SBN 393 00602 6

PRINTED IN THE UNITED STATES OF AMERICA

1 2 3 4 5 6 7 8 9 0

PREFACE

Plautus wrote upwards of fifty plays, of which twenty have survived more or less in their entirety.[1] In making my choice for this anthology, I tried not only to include his best but to give some idea of his range. His forte was farce, and my selections exemplify at least two of his favorite farcical devices: mistaken identity (*The Menaechmus Twins*) and the scheming servant (*Pseudolus*). *The Rope* is an example of his more romantic style; the plot is as important to the play as the purely comic scenes, and these, in line with the general tenor of the work, are of a somewhat higher order than the unabashed tomfoolery of the *Pseudolus*.

I have arranged the plays alphabetically by their Latin titles (*Menaechmi, Pseudolus, Rudens*), as is traditional in editions of Plautus. In spite of many learned attempts, no one has yet succeeded in demonstrating convincingly the chronological order of his work (see p. xvi).

In these translations I have followed the same principles I did in my *Masters of Ancient Comedy*, and I can do no bet-

---

[1] I say "more or less" because all but one of the preserved manuscripts of his work derive from a single manuscript of the eighth century A.D. which was, unfortunately, in a mutilated condition, and, as a consequence, there are gaps in the text that range from a few lines (see, e.g., *Casina*, ll. 889, 890) to whole scenes (see, e.g., *Amphitryon*, l. 1035).

ter than repeat what I wrote there (p. viii) to explain what my procedure has been:

"All Greek and Roman drama was in verse. Moreover, . . . Plautus [was], in a sense, writing musical comedy: a considerable portion of [his] plays is not dialogue to be spoken but lyrics to be sung. These by their very nature called for translation in verse. Everywhere else I have used prose.

"The usual purpose of a verse translation is to retain the style and spirit of the original at the expense, if necessary, of literal accuracy; and, of a prose translation, precisely the opposite. What I have done is to reverse this usual state of affairs: I have chosen prose in order to retain the spirit, if not the style, of the original, and my prose is, if anything, more free than many a translation in verse.

"There have been many periods in the history of drama when verse was the only accepted vehicle for comedy. To-day, of course, playwrights writing in the vein of . . . Plautus use normal colloquial speech. My aim was to make these ancient plays sound as much like contemporary comedy as I could—and still remain a translator and not an adapter. That meant not only using prose, but prose that reflected the vocabulary and rhythms of contemporary speech. Every line I translated I subjected to a simple test: I read it aloud and asked myself whether it sounded the way a person would express himself in the given situation today. Frequently the original lent itself to a rendering that satisfied this requirement and was at the same time a close translation; more often, close translation was impossible and I rendered the general sense of a passage with no attempt to reproduce the meaning of the individual words; at times I frankly paraphrased. All references that would make sense only to ancient audiences or modern scholars I replaced with some sort of current equivalent. For the ubiquitous oaths and exclamations that invoke the names of ancient deities I substituted modern expressions; I converted drachmas and talents into dollars (allowing for current inflation has made my figures considerably higher than those in earlier translations); I replaced ancient geographical names with modern equivalents; I doc-

tored the jokes where necessary to make them intelligible to
today's audiences. Moreover, in line with my aim to make
living theater of these plays, I added full stage directions,
just as a modern playwright would."

The lyric portions of the originals are extremely fluid and
flexible, characterized by lines of unequal length and by
frequent changes of meter. My renderings reproduce only the
metrical pace, as it were. Where the mood was comic, I used
rhymed verse; where more serious, unrhymed.

Plautus chose the names he assigned his characters with
great care. A number are not actually names but pure comic
inventions, and for these I used English equivalents (e.g.,
Sponge, the scrounger in *The Menaechmus Twins,* is in the
original *Peniculus,* literally "brush"). For other characters, he
(or the author of the Greek original he adapted) used common Greek names which were somehow especially apt, just
as a playwright of today will emphasize a female character's
nature by giving her a name such as Faith or Grace; in these
cases I kept the original name but explained its aptness in the
stage directions.

Plautus wrote his plays to be performed without breaks.
Subsequently, editors introduced act divisions. Since these
have become traditional, and serve a useful purpose as well,
I have retained them.

I am indebted to The Macmillan Company of New York
for permission to reproduce from *Masters of Ancient Comedy*
my translation of *The Rope;* I have corrected some minor
errors in the prose portion and redone some of the lyrics in
rhymed verse.

As always, I owe a large debt of gratitude to my most
careful and helpful critic, my father. The introduction and
stage directions have everywhere benefited from his rigorous
insistence on accuracy in language, and the dialogue from his
keen ear for accuracy in idiom. My wife contributed many a
well-turned phrase and gave brightness to many a lackluster
line. And I am grateful to the John Simon Guggenheim Me-
morial Foundation for providing in an indirect way the free

time that made this volume possible—in an indirect way because these translations were largely done as daily relaxation after hours of close research on the topic for which I had actually received my fellowship.

Lionel Casson

Rome
September 1962

CONTENTS

INTRODUCTION

Sometime around 250 B.C., in the tiny mountain village of Sarsina high in the Apennines of Umbria, ancient Rome's best-known playwright was born.

We know so little about his life that we're not even sure of his full name; probably—but only probably—it was Titus Maccius Plautus. We can only guess how a backwoods country boy managed to leave his village, to learn Latin so well he achieved effects with it no later writers ever matched (the native tongue of Sarsina was not Latin but Umbrian, a relative of Latin), to learn the literary language of the day, Greek (see below, p. xvii), to crack the world of the theater at the capital, and through it to fight his way to reputation and money. According to one of the stories told about him years after he died, he got his start in the theater as an actor in native farces. This could very well be true: Plautus' plays show unmistakably that their author knew what went on behind the stage as well as on it. Moreover, what easier way was there for a boy with the appropriate talent to escape the shackles of a small town than by joining an itinerant theatrical troupe? Once Plautus achieved fame, he never lost it: when he died, in 184 B.C., he was the dean of Rome's writers of comedy.

Comedy itself was only three centuries or so older than he was. It had achieved definite form where so much else of Western culture had, in Athens of the fifth century B.C.: the first recorded performance of a comedy took place in March 486 B.C., in the Theater of Dionysus on the south slope of Athens' Acropolis.

But the type of comedy that flourished in fifth-century Athens, Greek "Old Comedy" as it has been called, neither lasted very long nor started any important trends. When its best-known exponent, Aristophanes, died, it more or less died with him. Old Comedy was, essentially, topical satire, and Aristophanes' plays, full of withering, uproarious jibes at contemporary Athenian politics and politicos, education and educators, writings and writers, did not interest subsequent generations to whom all this was just so much ancient history, and whose taste in comedy ran in different directions.

Toward the end of his life, however, Aristophanes started to mine a comic vein that, being more universal in appeal, lasted a good deal longer, right through Plautus down to our own times, in fact. He shifted the emphasis from satire to humor, and began to write about people as a class, not specific personalities, and to poke fun at men's ways in general, not at their behavior as citizens in a given place at a given time.

By 300 B.C., this form of comedy, Greek "New Comedy" as it has been called, had come to maturity and was providing the principal and preferred theatrical fare of the day. Aristophanes was a thing of the past; audiences jammed the theaters to see the latest works of the masters of New Comedy, of Diphilus, Philemon, Apollodorus of Carystus, and, above all, Menander. They wrote about ordinary people, mocking—Menander gently, the others more boisterously— human foibles and crotchets, the laughable things people are prone to do, the silly behavior certain circumstances almost invariably call forth. The world these playwrights chose to portray is small: they deal almost exclusively with the doings of upper middle-class households. The dramatis personae are equally limited: the father of the household, irascible or stupid as plot requires; his formidable wife; their idler of a son; scheming servants; dull-witted servants; longwinded cooks; gold-digging courtesans; famished hangers-on; flint-hearted pimps. The plot often revolves about, or at the very least includes, a love affair, and there was an unfortunate tendency (we haven't overcome it to this day) to tell—with variations, to be sure—the story of the boy who meets the girl, can't marry her because she has no money or comes from the wrong side of the tracks, but ends up living happily ever after since she turns out to be the rich neighbor's long-lost daughter.

According to the ancient critics, Menander and the other great names in Greek New Comedy wrote consummate masterpieces. We today are in no position either to confirm or contest this judgment for, of the hundreds of these works that were staged, all that has survived is one complete play and that a rather poor specimen, half of another, and one third each of two more.[1]

New Comedy was immensely popular. The latest productions of Diphilus and Menander, after opening in Athens, went to theaters all over the Greek-speaking world, in Asia Minor, on the Aegean Isles, along the coast of North Africa, and—most important for comedy's subsequent history—in South Italy.

As early as 700 B.C., the lower part of Italy, from Naples south through Sicily, had been largely taken over by Greeks. The area was dotted with their populous and well-to-do cities, each of which by 300 B.C. had its theater where not only local farces and skits were put on but also the latest imports of New Comedy from Athens.

To the north lay Rome. Until just a few decades before Plautus was born, Rome was relatively obscure and provincial, with no pretensions to culture, a nation of hard-fisted farmers and hard-fighting soldiers. However, by the time Plautus was an adult, she had extended her power southward and was the acknowledged mistress of the Greek cities of southern Italy. Her soldiers, statesmen, and merchants came into contact with, and got eye-filling glimpses of, a new, far more sophisticated and gracious way of life. Among other things, they were exposed to the delights of the Greek stage

[1] For translations of these, see my *Masters of Ancient Comedy*, pp. 65–175.

and, in no time at all, developed a healthy appetite for it. This was a milestone in the history of comedy: it was responsible for the creation of Latin comedy, and Latin comedy is the direct ancestor of much of the comedy of later Western literature.

The Romans, to be sure, had some theatrical fare of their own. Their village fiestas featured several types of short, boisterous farce, including one in which song and dance played an important part; if Plautus actually did start his career as an actor, it must have been in pieces of this kind. But it was all rather primitive stuff. In 240 B.C., a Greek named Livius Andronicus translated and adapted a Greek New Comedy for a Roman audience and immediately started a vogue; he had filled a need. Latin versions of Greek plays quickly found a place on programs alongside the local fare, and, in larger communities, easily outstripped it in popularity. Livius was followed by Gnaeus Naevius (ca. 270–201 B.C.), Rome's first native playwright, who, in addition to adapting Greek works, inaugurated true Roman comedy by writing original plays in Latin. He apparently was a talented author, but unfortunately only fragments of his work have been preserved. The distinction of having produced the earliest Latin plays to survive goes to his gifted younger contemporary, Plautus.

Plautus, in a very real sense, faced the same problems as a writer for Broadway today. He had to turn out pieces that would please a motley, more or less undiscriminating audience, and he had to sell them to tough, business-minded producers.

In the ancient world, plays were put on as part of the general entertainment given at public festivals. During Plautus' lifetime, Rome had four great annual festivals whose programs included drama, and special events such as the funerals of great men or victory celebrations provided still further opportunities for the playwright. Plays were never lone features on these occasions; they shared the program with chariot races, horse races, boxing matches, and other similar entertainments. The theatrical troupes, small groups of five or six actors usually of Greek extraction, were managed by a *dominus gregis* or "leader of the troupe." He was producer and director combined: he entered into a contract with the officials in charge of a given festival to supply a certain number of performances, and, when the time came, staged them. The officials payed him a lump sum and furnished the facilities: for the actors a temporary wooden structure which was nothing more than a long, low, narrow stage with a backdrop showing two or three house fronts, and for the audience temporary wooden bleachers. It was the job of the *dominus* to find his troupe likely scripts, which he either bought himself or recommended for purchase to the officials.

These were the men Plautus had to deal with: the *domini,* the festival officials, and on occasion a Roman aristocrat who was footing the bill for a special event. For one reason above all others he had no trouble peddling his plays: he knew what his audiences wanted, and he gave it to them.

Plautus as a playwright is not original in the strictest sense. In writing a play, he began, following in the footsteps of Livius, with a Greek original, a work by one of the writers of New Comedy. But he quickly parts company with Livius, who more or less faithfully rendered his originals into Latin. Since a close translation of a play by, for example, Menander would have little appeal for the crowds at a Roman festival, Plautus generally took from the Greek only the outline of the plot, the characters, and selected segments of the dialogue, and then stepped out on his own. In a sense he worked the way playwrights of today do when they convert a "legitimate" comedy into a musical. Along with revamping the dialogue, he replaced the relatively simple metrical pattern of the original with one more complex and, perhaps as a carry-over from his youthful days as an actor in native farce, introduced frequent scenes in song and dance (the music and dance that accompanied these have disappeared without trace; we are left with only the bare lyrics). Furthermore, since he was writing not for intellectuals but for the people who patronized sporting events and circuses, and since his listeners were there to be amused, he did his level best to make them laugh from the belly. Without a second thought he would interrupt the flow of the action for a scene of pure slapstick or for a series of lowbrow jokes; he made up broadly comic names to label his characters; he explained every turn of the plot to make sure the slowest wits could follow it; he even explained the jokes to make sure everyone got them. At all costs he kept the pot of the action boiling, the stream of gags and puns and comic alliterations flowing. It is of no avail to find fault with him for not providing real endings for his plays, for introducing characters and then abruptly dropping them, for making, in a word, the most elementary blunders in playwrighting. He did not care—the play was not the thing, the laughs were.

None of the Greek plays he adapted has survived, and we consequently cannot be certain of the exact extent of his changes, but there cannot be much doubt that they were far-reaching. *The Rope,* for example, very likely has much less in common with the play by Diphilus from which it was taken than, say, *My Fair Lady* has with Shaw's *Pygmalion.*

Much scholarly effort has been expended in trying to work out the chronological order of Plautus' comedies and thereby trace his development as a playwright, but without much success. However, we can be fairly certain that the three included here belong to his mature years. In fact, we know definitely that the *Pseudolus* was one of his latest works.

Plautus has been as popular after death as he was during his lifetime. If he owes a debt to his Greek predecessors, later playwrights of the highest stature have evened the account by being indebted to him, from Shakespeare in the sixteenth century (*The Comedy of Errors* is based on *The Menaechmus Twins*) through Molière in the seventeenth (e.g., *l'Avare* is based on *The Pot of Gold*) to Giraudoux in the twentieth (*Amphitryon 38* is an adaptation of the *Amphitryon*). Along with his younger contemporary, Terence, Plautus kept the spirit of Greek New Comedy alive and enabled it to make its great contributions to later literature.

Dickens' Sam Weller, Wodehouse's Jeeves, the girls in the movies who come from the wrong side of the tracks and then turn out to be the long-lost daughters of eminently eligible parents—these and countless others are the lineal descendants of Pseudolus, Trachalio, Palaestra, and others of Plautus' dramatis personae. Nor is he merely a disembodied literary influence; he is still living theater. *A Funny Thing Happened on the Way to the Forum,* which was a success on Broadway some years ago, was a pastiche of *Pseudolus, Casina,* and others, and before that, the last of a long line of adaptations of *The Menaechmus Twins,* Richard Rodgers' and Lorenz Hart's *The Boys from Syracuse,* was a smash hit as a musical comedy and a motion picture. Probably no other single writer has had so profound and continuing an influence on the history of comedy.

BIBLIOGRAPHICAL NOTE

For anyone interested in studying further Plautus' plays and their influence, or any phase of Roman comedy, George Duckworth's monumental *The Nature of Roman Comedy* (Princeton University Press, 1952) provides a useful starting point. It covers, with extensive bibliography, just about every phase of the subject.

THE MENAECHMUS TWINS

DRAMATIS PERSONAE

SPONGE (PENICULUS), *hanger-on of Menaechmus of Epidamnus, who makes his way by scrounging from him and other well-to-do people*

MENAECHMUS OF EPIDAMNUS, *a well-to-do young married man, resident in Epidamnus*

LOVEY (EROTIUM), *a courtesan with whom Menaechmus of Epidamnus has been having an affair*

ROLL (CYLINDRUS), *her cook (slave)*

MENAECHMUS OF SYRACUSE, *twin brother of Menaechmus of Epidamnus, resident in Syracuse*

MESSENIO, *his servant (slave)*

MAID OF LOVEY (*slave*)

WIFE OF MENAECHMUS OF EPIDAMNUS

FATHER-IN-LAW OF MENAECHMUS OF EPIDAMNUS

A DOCTOR

[DECIO, *servant of Menaechmus' wife*]

SERVANTS

SCENE

A street in Epidamnus. Two houses front on it: stage left Menaechmus', stage right Lovey's. The exit on stage left leads downtown, that on stage right to the waterfront. The time is noon or a little after.

PROLOGUE

(The actor assigned to deliver the prologue enters, walks downstage, and addresses the audience.)

PROLOGUE First and foremost, ladies and gentlemen, health and happiness to all of—me. And to you, too. I have Plautus here for you—not in my hands, on my tongue. Please be kind enough to take him—with your ears. Now, here's the plot. Pay attention, I'll make it as brief as I can.

Every comic playwright invariably tells you that the action of his piece takes place entirely at Athens; this is to give it that Greek touch. Well, I'm telling you the action takes place where the story says it does and nowhere else. The plot, as a matter of fact, *is* Greekish. Not Athensish, though; Sicilyish. But all this is so much preamble. Now I'll pour out your portion of plot for you. Not by the quart, not by the gallon, by the tankload. That's how big-hearted a plot-teller I am.

A certain man, a merchant, lived at Syracuse. His wife presented him with twin sons, two boys so alike that no one could tell them apart, neither the woman who nursed them, nor the mother who bore them. I got this from someone who'd seen them—I don't want you to get the idea I saw them myself; I never did.

Well, when the boys were seven years old, their father filled a fine freighter full of freight and put one twin aboard to take with him on a business trip to Tarentum. The other he left home with the mother. As it turned out, they arrived at Tarentum during a holiday, and—the usual thing during holidays—a lot of people had come to town, and son and sire got separated in the crowd. A merchant from Epidamnus happened to be on the spot; he picked the boy up and carried him off to Epidamnus. At the lad's loss, alas, the love of life left the father; a few days later, there at Tarentum, he died of a broken heart.

[A] message about all this—that the boy had been carried off and the father had died at Tarentum—was brought back to Syracuse to the grandfather. When he heard the news, he changed the name of the boy who'd been left at home. The old man was so fond of the kidnaped twin that he transferred this one's name to his brother: he called the twin still left Menaechmus, the same name as the other had. (It was the old man's name too—I remember it so well because I heard it so often when his creditors dunned him.) To keep you from getting mixed up later I'm telling you now, in advance, that both twins have the same name.

Now, in order for me to make the whole story crystal clear for you, I have to retrace my steps and get back to Epidamnus. Any of you got some business you want me to take care of for you at Epidamnus? Step up, say the word, give me your orders. But don't forget the wherewithal for taking care of them. Anyone who doesn't give me some cash is wasting his time—and anyone who does is wasting a lot more. But now I'm really going back to where I started, and I'll stay put in one place.

[The man from Epidamnus, the one I told you about a few seconds ago who carried off the other twin, had no children of his own—except his moneybags. He adopted the boy he had kidnaped, made him his son, found him a wife with a good dowry, and left him his whole estate when he died. You see, the old fellow happened to be going out to his country place one day after a heavy rain; a short way out of town he began fording a stream that was sweeping along, the sweeping current swept him off his feet the way he had once swept off that boy, and away to hell and gone he went.]

So a handsome fortune dropped into his adopted son's lap. He—I mean the twin who was carried off—lives here (*pointing*). Now, the other, the one who lives in Syracuse, will arrive just today, along with a servant; he's searching for his twin brother. This (*gesturing toward the backdrop*) is Epidamnus—but only so long as our play is on the boards; when some other play goes on, it'll be some other city. It changes just the way the actors do—one day they're pimps, next day paupers; next youngsters, next oldsters; next beggars, kings, scroungers, cheats. . . .

ACT I

(*Enter Sponge* [Peniculus, *literally "brush"*], *stage left, a man in his thirties with a protruding paunch and a general down-at-the-heels look.* He is a parasitus, *"free-loader," the character, standard in ancient comedy, who, to fill his belly, runs errands and acts as general flunky and yes-man to anyone willing to issue an invitation to a meal.* He walks downstage and addresses the audience.)

SPONGE   The boys call me Sponge. Because, when I eat, I wipe the table clean.

It's stupid to put chains on prisoners or shackles on runaway slaves, at least to my way of thinking. This misery on top of all their others just makes the poor devils more set than ever on breaking out—and breaking the peace. Prisoners get out of the chains somehow or other, and slaves saw through the shackle or smash the pin with a rock. No, bolts and bars are the bunk. If you really want to keep someone from running away, chain him with dishes and glasses. Belay him by the beak to a groaning board. You give him all he wants to eat and drink daily and, so help me, he'll never run away, not even if he's up for hanging. Holding on to him is a cinch once you chain him with *that* kind of chain. And belly bonds are so firm and flexible—the more you stretch them, the tighter they get.

For example, I'm on my way to Menaechmus' house here (*pointing*). I sentenced myself to his jail years back: I'm going now of my own free will so he can put the irons on me. This Menaechmus is a man who doesn't just feed a man; he bloats the belly for you, he restores you to life— you won't find a finer physician. He's a fellow like this: he's as big an eater as they come himself, so every meal he serves looks like a thanksgiving day banquet: he overloads the tables, he piles up the plates like pyramids; you have to stand on your chair if you want something from on top. But it's been quite a while since my last invitation. I've had to be homebound with all that's dear to me—you see, whatever I eat that I pay for is dear, very dear. And there's this: right now all that's so dear to me has broken ranks and deserted the table. So (*pointing again to Menaechmus' house*) I'm paying him a visit. Wait—the door's opening. There's Menaechmus himself; he's coming out.

(*Sponge moves off to the side. The door opens and Menaechmus of Epidamnus stomps out. He is a good-looking man in his middle twenties, whose grooming, clothes, and air all smack of a substantial income. His manifest irascibility is unusual: normally he is gay, an inveterate jokester, and always out for a good time. He is wearing a coat which he clutches tightly about him. He turns and addresses his wife who is visible in the doorway.*)

SONG

MENAECHMUS OF EPIDAMNUS (*angrily*)
> If you weren't so stupid and sour,
> Such a mean-tempered bitch, such a shrew,
> What you see gives your husband a pain,
> You'd make sure would give *you* a pain too.
>> From this moment henceforth,
>> You just try this once more,
>> And, a divorce in your hand,
>> You go darken Dad's door.
>
> Every time that I want to go out
> I get called, I get grabbed, I get grilled:
>> "Where are you going to go?"
>> "Why are you going outside?"
>> "What are you going to do?"
>> "What are you going to get?"
>> "What have you got in your hand?"
>> "What were you doing downtown?"

Why, the way I declare every act of my life,
It's a customs official I wed, not a wife!
Oh, you're spoiled, and I did it myself. Listen, you—
I'll explain here and now what I'm planning to do.

I've filled your every need:
The clothes you've on your back,
Your servants, food, and cash—
There's nothing that you lack.

(If you only had some sense,
You'd watch what you're about.
You'd let your husband be,
And cut the snooping out.)

And what's more, so your snooping's not lost
And the time you put in not a waste,
I'll be off to go find me a girl
Who can join me for dinner someplace.

SPONGE (*to the audience, in anguish*)
He pretends to be hard on his wife—
But it's *me* that he's giving the knife!
Eating out! Do you know who he'll hurt?
It's yours truly he'll hurt, not his wife.

MENAECHMUS OF EPIDAMNUS (*to himself, wonderingly, as his wife disappears inside*)
Well, I finally gave her what for—
And I drove the old bitch from the door!

(*To the audience, triumphantly*)

What's happened to the husbands who've been keeping mistresses?

What's holding up their plaudits and their cheers for what I've done?

They *all* owe me a medal for the fight I fought and won!

(*Throws his coat open to reveal a woman's dress he has on over his clothes*)

I stole this dress from her just now—I'll bring it to my girl.
Now *that's* the way to operate—outfox a foxy guard!
A beautiful piece of work it was, a feat to shout about,
A lovely piece of work it was, superbly carried out.

(*Losing his jubilation suddenly as realization dawns*)

I snitch from the bitch at *my* expense—and my downfall gets it all.

(Cheering up again)

But the enemy's camp's been looted, and we've safely made
our haul!

SPONGE *(calling as Menaechmus starts marching toward Lovey's door)* Hey, mister, any share in that swag for me?

MENAECHMUS OF EPIDAMNUS *(stopping and closing his coat,
but not turning around; to himself)* Ambushed! I'm lost!

SPONGE Saved, you mean. Don't be afraid.

MENAECHMUS OF EPIDAMNUS *(still not turning)* Who is it?

SPONGE Me.

MENAECHMUS OF EPIDAMNUS *(turning)* Hi, friend-in-need
and Johnny-on-the-spot.

SPONGE Hi.

MENAECHMUS OF EPIDAMNUS What are you doing these
days?

SPONGE *(grabbing Menaechmus' hand and pumping it)* I'm
shaking the hand of my guardian angel.

MENAECHMUS OF EPIDAMNUS You couldn't have timed it
better to meet me.

SPONGE I'm always like that—I know Johnny-on-the-spotitude
down to the last dotitude.

MENAECHMUS OF EPIDAMNUS You want to see a brilliant
piece of work?

SPONGE *(smacking his lips)* Who cooked it? One look at the
leftovers and I can tell in a minute if he slipped up anywhere.

MENAECHMUS OF EPIDAMNUS Tell me, have you ever seen
those famous pictures they hang on walls? The eagle
carrying off Ganymede or Venus with Adonis?

SPONGE *(testily)* Lots of times. But what have those pictures got to do with me?

MENAECHMUS OF EPIDAMNUS *(throwing open his coat to reveal the dress)* See this? Do I look like one?

SPONGE *(staring)* What have you got on there, anyway?

MENAECHMUS OF EPIDAMNUS (*slyly*) Tell me I'm the nicest guy you know.

SPONGE (*suspiciously*) Where do we eat?

MENAECHMUS OF EPIDAMNUS (*pretending to be annoyed*) First tell me what I told you to.

SPONGE All right, all right. You're the nicest guy I know.

MENAECHMUS OF EPIDAMNUS (*as before*) How about adding something on your own, please?

SPONGE (*grudgingly*) And the most fun to be with.

MENAECHMUS OF EPIDAMNUS Go on.

SPONGE (*exploding*) God damn it, no going on till I know what for. You're on the outs with your wife, so I'm watching my step with you.

MENAECHMUS OF EPIDAMNUS (*sensing his teasing has gone far enough, gaily and conspiratorially*) Let's you and I, without letting my wife know a thing, kill off this day—

SPONGE (*interrupting*) Well, all right! That's something like! How soon shall I start the funeral? The day's already half dead, all the way down to the waist.

MENAECHMUS OF EPIDAMNUS (*with a great show of patience*) Interrupt me, and you just hold things up for yourself.

SPONGE (*hurriedly*) Menaechmus, poke my eye out if I utter another word. Orders from you excepted, of course.

MENAECHMUS OF EPIDAMNUS (*tiptoeing away from his house with anxious glances over his shoulder at the door*) Come on over here. Away from that door.

SPONGE (*following*) Sure.

MENAECHMUS OF EPIDAMNUS (*tiptoeing farther, with more glances*) Even more.

SPONGE (*following*) All right.

MENAECHMUS OF EPIDAMNUS (*now far enough away to give up tiptoeing—but still glancing*) Come on, step along. Farther from that lion's den.

SPONGE I swear, if you ask me, you'd make a wonderful jockey.

MENAECHMUS OF EPIDAMNUS   Why?

SPONGE   The way you look behind every second to make sure your wife's not catching up.

MENAECHMUS OF EPIDAMNUS   I want to ask you a question.

SPONGE   Me? The answer's Yes, if you want yes; No, if you want no.

MENAECHMUS OF EPIDAMNUS   If you smelled something, could you tell from the smell—

SPONGE   (*with one type of smell in mind, interrupting*)   Better than a board of prophets.

MENAECHMUS OF EPIDAMNUS   All right, then, try this dress I have. What do you smell? (*He hands Sponge part of the skirt, Sponge sniffs, then jerks his nose away*)   What did you do that for?

SPONGE   You've got to smell a woman's dress at the top. Down there there's an odor that never washes out, and it's death on the nose.

MENAECHMUS OF EPIDAMNUS   (*moving the upper part toward him*)   Smell here then. (*Laughing as Sponge sniffs gingerly*) You do a wonderful job of wrinkling up your nose.

SPONGE   I had good reason.

MENAECHMUS OF EPIDAMNUS   Well? What does it smell from? Tell me.

SPONGE   Loot, lechery—and lunch.

MENAECHMUS OF EPIDAMNUS   (*clapping him on the back and leading him toward Lovey's door*)   Right you are. Now it goes right to my lady friend Lovey here. And I'll have her fix up a lunch for me, you, and her.

SPONGE   (*smacking his lips*)   Fine!

MENAECHMUS OF EPIDAMNUS   (*gaily*)   We'll pass the bottle from now till the crack of dawn tomorrow.

SPONGE   (*as before*)   Fine! Now you're talking. Should I knock on the door?

MENAECHMUS OF EPIDAMNUS   Knock away. (*As Sponge races*

up to Lovey's door and raises a fist to deliver a lusty bang)
No, wait!

SPONGE (*bitterly*) You just passed that bottle back a mile.

MENAECHMUS OF EPIDAMNUS Try a tiny tap.

SPONGE What are you scared of? That the door's made of bone china? (*Turns to knock.*)

MENAECHMUS OF EPIDAMNUS (*excitedly*) Wait! Wait, for god's sake! See? She's coming out. Look how the sun grows gray 'gainst the glory of that gorgeous figure!

(*The door opens and Lovey* [Erotium, *literally "little love"*] *comes out, a good-looking girl in a brassy sort of way, flashily dressed and heavily made up.*)

LOVEY Menaechmus, darling! How nice to see you!

SPONGE How about me?

LOVEY (*witheringly*) You don't count.

SPONGE (*unruffled*) I do so. I'm in this man's army too. Rear guard.

MENAECHMUS OF EPIDAMNUS (*seeing a chance to tease her, slyly*) Orders from headquarters, Lovey: invite Sponge and me to your house today. For a duel.

LOVEY All right. (*Throwing a baleful look at Sponge*) Just for today.

MENAECHMUS OF EPIDAMNUS (*as before*) A duel of drinks to the death. Whichever's the better man with the bottle becomes your bodyguard. You be referee, you decide which you'll sleep with tonight. (*Abruptly dropping his teasing as he notices her begin to sulk*) Honey, one look at you and, oh, do I hate that wife of mine!

LOVEY (*not yet mollified—and catching sight of the dress, frigidly*) In the meantime, you can't even keep from wearing her clothes. What is this, anyway?

MENAECHMUS OF EPIDAMNUS (*throwing his coat open, gaily*) Embezzled from her to embellish you, my flower.

LOVEY (*magically thawed out*) You always win out over all

the other men who run after me. You have such winning ways.

SPONGE (*aside*) That's a mistress for you: nothing but sweet talk so long as she sees something to get her hands on. If you really loved him, you'd be kissing his mouth off this minute.

MENAECHMUS OF EPIDAMNUS (*taking off his coat*) Sponge, hold this. I want to carry out the dedication ceremony I scheduled.

SPONGE Hand it over. (*Taking the coat and eying Menaechmus in the dress*) Since you're in costume, how about favoring us with a bit of ballet later?

MENAECHMUS OF EPIDAMNUS Ballet? Me? Are you in your right mind?

SPONGE You mean are *you* in your right mind. All right, if no ballet, get out of costume.

MENAECHMUS OF EPIDAMNUS (*taking the dress off and handing it to Lovey*) I took an awful chance stealing this today. Riskier, if you ask me, than when Hercules helped himself to Hippolyta's girdle. It's all for you—because you're the only person in the whole world who's really nice to me.

LOVEY What a lovely thought! That's the way all nice lovers should think.

SPONGE (*aside*) You mean if they're hell-bent to get to the poorhouse.

MENAECHMUS OF EPIDAMNUS (*to Lovey*) I paid a thousand dollars last year for that dress you have there. Got it for my wife.

SPONGE (*aside*) Using your own figures, that works out to a thousand dollars down the drain.

MENAECHMUS OF EPIDAMNUS (*to Lovey*) You know what I'd like you to do?

LOVEY I know one thing: I'll do whatever you like.

MENAECHMUS OF EPIDAMNUS Then have your cook prepare lunch for the three of us. Send him to the market for some gourmetetitious shopping. Have him bring back the pig family: the Duke of Pork, Lord Bacon, the little Trotters, and any other relatives. Things that, served roasted, reduce me to ravenousness. Right away, eh?

LOVEY   But of course!

MENAECHMUS OF EPIDAMNUS   Sponge and I are on our way downtown but we'll be back in a few minutes. We can have drinks while the things are on the fire.

LOVEY   Come back whenever you like. Everything will be ready.

MENAECHMUS OF EPIDAMNUS   Just hurry it up. (*Turning and striding off, stage left; to Sponge*) Follow me.

SPONGE   (*running after him*)   I'm not only following you, I'm not letting you out of my sight. Today is the one day I wouldn't lose you for all the treasures of heaven!

(*As Menaechmus and Sponge leave, Lovey walks to the door of her house.*)

LOVEY   (*calling through the door to her maids inside*)   Tell Roll, the cook, to come out here right away. (*A second later, Roll* [Cylindrus], *a roly-poly cook, races out and stands attentively in front of her.*) You'll need a shopping basket and some money. Here's fifteen dollars.

ROLL   Yes, ma'am.

LOVEY   Go do the marketing. Get just enough for three—not a bit more and not a bit less.

ROLL   What people are you having?

LOVEY   Menaechmus, his parasite, and myself.

ROLL   (*thoughtfully*)   That makes ten—a parasite can do for eight. Easily.

LOVEY   Now you know who'll be there; you take care of the rest.

ROLL   (*importantly*)   Right. Consider lunch cooked. Tell your guests to go in and sit down. (*Races off, stage left.*)

LOVEY (*calling after him*)   Come right back!

ROLL (*over his shoulder*)   Be back in a flash.

   (*Roll dashes off, Lovey enters her house, and the stage is now empty.*)

ACT II

(*Enter, stage right, Menaechmus of Syracuse and his servant Messenio carrying a satchel; behind them, loaded down
with luggage, is a pair of rowers from the skiff that brought
them ashore. These two move off to the side of the stage and
put their burdens down.*
[*In appearance Menaechmus of Syracuse is identical with
his twin. But there the likeness ends. Menaechmus of Epidamnus is gay, generous, and fun loving; his brother is
shrewd, calculating, and cynical. Messenio, about the same* ✳
*age as his master, is the long-faced type who worries easily
and takes himself very seriously.*)]

MENAECHMUS OF SYRACUSE Messenio, if you ask me, the
greatest joy a sailor can have is to sight land from the open
sea.

MESSENIO (*pointedly*) I'll be honest with you: it's even
greater when the land you come near and see is your homeland. Will you please tell me why we're here in Epidamnus?
Are we going to do like sea water and go around every
island there is?

MENAECHMUS OF SYRACUSE (*grimly*) We're here to look for
my brother. My twin brother.

MESSENIO (*exasperated*) When are we going to put an end
to looking for that man? We've been at it six years! Austria,
Spain, France, Jugoslavia, Sicily, every part of Italy near
salt water, up and down the Adriatic—we've made the
rounds of all of them. Believe me, if you were looking for a
needle, and it was anywhere to be found, you'd have found
it long ago. We're looking for the dead among the living.
Because, if he was alive to be found, you'd have found
him long ago.

MENAECHMUS OF SYRACUSE (*as before*) Then I'm looking
for someone who can prove it, someone who'll tell me he
knows for certain my brother is dead. Once I hear that,

I'll never look for him again. But until I do, so long as I
live, I'll never stop. *I* know how much he means to me.

MESSENIO (*grumbling*)   You're looking for hens' teeth. Why
don't we turn around and go home? Or maybe you and I
are going to write a travel book?

MENAECHMUS OF SYRACUSE (*sharply*)   You do what you're
told, eat what you're given, and stay out of trouble! Don't
annoy me now; we're doing things my way, not yours.

MESSENIO (*aside*)   Ho-ho! That's telling me who's the slave
around here. Couldn't have put things plainer with fewer
words. But I can't hold this in, I've got to speak up. (*To
Menaechmus*) Listen, Menaechmus. I've been looking over
our finances. So help me, we're traveling with a summer-
weight wallet. If you want my opinion, either you head
for home, or you'll be mourning your long-lost money
while you look for your long-lost brother. Let me tell you
what kind of people live in these parts. The hardest drink-
ers and worst rakes are right here in Epidamnus. Besides,
the town's full of crooks and swindlers. And they say the
prostitutes here have a smoother line of talk than anywhere
else in the world. That's why this place is called Epidamnus:
nobody stays here without a damned lot of damage.

MENAECHMUS OF SYRACUSE (*unperturbed*)   I'll keep my eyes
open. You just hand over the wallet.

MESSENIO (*suspiciously*)   What do you want with it?

MENAECHMUS OF SYRACUSE   After what you've been telling
me, I'm scared to leave it with you.

MESSENIO   Scared of what?

MENAECHMUS OF SYRACUSE   That you'll do me a damned lot
of damage in Epidamnus. You're a big man with the
women, Messenio, and I'm a man with a big temper, the
explosive type. If I keep the money, I avoid trouble both
ways: you don't lose your head and I don't lose my temper.

MESSENIO (*handing over the wallet*)   Here it is. You keep it.
Glad to have you take over.

(*Enter Roll, stage left, lugging a loaded shopping basket.*)

ROLL (*to himself*)   No trouble at all with the shopping. I got just what I wanted. I'll serve the diners a delicious dinner. Hey—who's that I see there? Menaechmus! Heaven help my poor back! The guests already at the door before I'm even back from the market! Well, I'll say hello. (*Walking up to Menaechmus*) Good afternoon, Menaechmus.

MENAECHMUS OF SYRACUSE (*surprised but cordial*)   Good afternoon to you—whoever you are.

ROLL (*taken aback*)   Whoever I am? You don't know who I am?

MENAECHMUS OF SYRACUSE   Of course not.

ROLL (*deciding to overlook the exchange as just another of Menaechmus' jokes*)   Where are the rest of the guests?

MENAECHMUS OF SYRACUSE   Guests? What guests are you looking for?

ROLL   That parasite of yours.

MENAECHMUS OF SYRACUSE (*blankly*)   Parasite of mine? (*To Messenio, sotto voce*) The man's daft.

MESSENIO (*sotto voce to Menaechmus*)   Didn't I tell you the place was full of swindlers?

MENAECHMUS OF SYRACUSE   Now, mister, who is this parasite you're looking for?

ROLL   Sponge.

MESSENIO (*digging into the satchel he is carrying*)   Got it safe right here in the satchel. See?

ROLL (*apologetically*)   Menaechmus, you're too early. Lunch isn't ready. I just got back from the shopping.

MENAECHMUS OF SYRACUSE (*with exaggerated concern*)   Tell me, mister, what were fresh fish selling for today?

ROLL   Dollar apiece.

MENAECHMUS OF SYRACUSE   Here's a dollar. Buy some for yourself; it's on me. The food'll do your brains good. Because there's one thing I'm dead sure of: you're out of your senses, whoever you are. Otherwise why would you make such a nuisance of yourself to a total stranger?

ROLL (*smiling indulgently*)   You don't know *me*? You don't know Roll?

MENAECHMUS OF SYRACUSE (*testily*)   I don't care if you're roll or loaf. Go to the devil! I don't know you, and, what's more, I don't want to!

ROLL (*with an I'll-play-along-with-your-little-joke smile*) Your name's Menaechmus, isn't it?

MENAECHMUS OF SYRACUSE (*anger giving way to curiosity*) To the best of my knowledge. And when you call me "Menaechmus" you talk sense. Where do you know me from, anyway?

ROLL (*chuckling*)   You're carrying on an affair with my owner Lovey (*gesturing toward the house*), and you have to ask *me* where I know you from?

MENAECHMUS (*tartly*)   I'm not carrying on any affairs, and I haven't the slightest idea who you are.

ROLL (*as before*)   You don't know who *I* am? Me? Your glass-filler all the times you come over to our house for drinks?

MESSENIO (*to the world at large*)   Damn! Here I am without a thing to split that skull of his in half!

MENAECHMUS OF SYRACUSE   You my glass-filler? When I've never set foot in Epidamnus, never set eyes on the place in my life till today?

ROLL   You mean you deny it?

MENAECHMUS OF SYRACUSE   I certainly do deny it!

ROLL (*pointing to the house of Menaechmus of Epidamnus*) You mean to say you don't live in that house there?

MENAECHMUS OF SYRACUSE (*roaring*)   To hell with any and everyone who lives in that house there!

ROLL (*to the audience, smiling*)   Swearing at himself. *He's* the one who's daft. (*To Menaechmus*) Listen, Menaechmus.

MENAECHMUS OF SYRACUSE (*sourly*)   What do you want?

ROLL   You know that dollar you offered to give me a minute
ago? Take my advice and use it to buy fish for your own
brains. You swore at your own self just now, you certainly
can't be in your right mind.

MENAECHMUS OF SYRACUSE   God! Talk, talk, talk! He's getting on my nerves!

ROLL (*to the audience*)   He always kids around with me like
this. He's a real card—when his wife's not around. (*To
Menaechmus*) I say, Menaechmus. (*As Menaechmus stubbornly stands with his back to him*) I say there, Menaechmus! (*Menaechmus throws up his hands in despair
and turns around. Roll holds out the basket.*) Take a look.
You think I bought enough for you, your parasite, and your
lady? Or should I go back for more?

MENAECHMUS OF SYRACUSE (*wearily*)   What lady? What parasite are you talking about?

MESSENIO (*to Roll, truculently*)   What's the matter? Something on your conscience that's driving you out of your
mind? Is that why you're making a nuisance of yourself
to this man?

ROLL (*resentfully*)   What are *you* butting in for? I don't
know you. I'm talking to this man here. Him I know.

MESSENIO   There's one thing I know: you're stark-raving
mad, you are.

ROLL (*pointedly ignoring Messenio; to Menaechmus, reassuringly*)   I'll have everything cooked in a minute. You won't
have to wait. So please don't go too far from the house.
(*Turning to go*) Anything I can do for you before I go in?

MENAECHMUS OF SYRACUSE (*stalking away*)   Yes. Go to hell.

ROLL (*muttering*)   No, damn it, you go—(*as Menaechmus
whirls around*) and have a seat while I (*importantly*) ex-
pose all this to the flame's fiery fury. I'll go and tell my
mistress you're here so she can invite you in and not leave
you standing around outside. (*Goes into the house.*)

MENAECHMUS OF SYRACUSE (*to Messenio*)   Has he gone?

(*Hearing the door slam*) He's gone. So help me, now I know that what you said was no lie.

MESSENIO (*importantly*) You just watch your step. It's my theory that one of those prostitutes lives here. That's what that lunatic who just left said.

MENAECHMUS OF SYRACUSE (*puzzled*) What amazes me is how he knew my name.

MESSENIO (*with the air of an expert*) Nothing amazing about that. These girls have a system. They send their tricky little maids and houseboys down to the docks. Whenever a foreigner heads for a berth, they start asking the name and the home port. The next minute the girls are hanging around his neck and sticking to him like glue. And, if he once takes the bait, he goes home a goner. (*Pointing to Lovey's house*) Now, there's a privateer moored in this berth right here. My advice is, let's steer clear of her.

MENAECHMUS OF SYRACUSE Good advice. Messenio, you're on your toes.

MESSENIO I'll know I'm on my toes when I see you on your guard, not before.

MENAECHMUS OF SYRACUSE Sh! Quiet a minute. I hear the door opening. Let's see who's coming out.

MESSENIO I'll get rid of this in the meantime. (*Handing the satchel to one of the rower-porters*) Hey, oar-power, keep an eye on this, will you please?

(*Lovey appears in the doorway. She turns and addresses a maid who was about to close the door behind her.*)

SONG

LOVEY (*adjusting the door*)
        No, not closed. Just like this, open wide.
        Now go in and get going inside.
        See that everything's set in the room.
        Spread some cushions. And lots of perfume.

(*Turns and addresses the audience*)

> Sophistication—that's the way
> To bring a lover-boy to bay.
> Plus saying Yes—to men a curse,
> To girls a way to fill a purse.

(*Looks around and, at first, doesn't see Menaechmus*)

> Now, where's he gone? My cook reports
>   He's standing by the door.
> Oh, there he is—my useful and
>   Most profitable amour.

> He's lord and master in my house.
>   He's earned the right to be,
> And so I let him. Now I'll go
>   And let him talk to me.

(*Walks up to Menaechmus*)

> Sweetie-pie! You surprise me, you do,
> With this standing around outside here.
> Why, my door's open wider to you
> Than your own. This is *your* house, my dear.

> Not a thing that you asked to be done
> Have my servants forgotten, not one.
> They're all ready inside, honeybunch,
> They've made *just* what you ordered for lunch.
> So, whenever you'd like to come in,
> We can all take our seats and begin.

MENAECHMUS OF SYRACUSE (*to Messenio*)   Who's this woman talking to?

LOVEY (*with a dazzling smile*)   You, of course.

MENAECHMUS OF SYRACUSE   And just what have you, in the present or past, ever had to do with me?

LOVEY (*meltingly*)   So much! And just because Cupid told me to pick you out of all the men in the world and make you the most important man in my life. And it's no more than you deserve. I can't tell you how happy you've made

me, just you alone, by all the nice things you've done for
me.

MENAECHMUS OF SYRACUSE (*sotto voce to Messenio*) Messenio, this woman's either drunk or daft. She treats a total
stranger like a bosom friend.

MESSENIO (*sotto voce*) Didn't I tell you? That's the kind of
thing that goes on around here. But this is just the leaves
falling. Stay three days longer and see what you get then:
a tree trunk on your head. That's what prostitutes here are
like—gold diggers, every one of them. (*Tapping himself importantly on the chest*) You just let *me* talk to her. Hey,
lady! (*As Lovey looks at him blankly*) Yes, you.

LOVEY What is it?

MESSENIO Where do you know this man from?

LOVEY (*with a that's-a-silly-question air*) Same place he's
known me from, all these years. Epidamnus.

MESSENIO Epidamnus? When he never set foot in the place
till today?

LOVEY Tee-hee! You make such funny jokes. (*Taking
Menaechmus by the arm*) Menaechmus dear, why don't
you come inside? It's much nicer in here.

MENAECHMUS OF SYRACUSE (*extricating himself; sotto voce to
Messenio*) What the devil! This woman's called me by my
right name. I don't get it. What's going on here?

MESSENIO (*sotto voce*) She got a whiff of that wallet you're
carrying.

MENAECHMUS OF SYRACUSE (*sotto voce*) Darned good thing
you warned me. (*Handing over the wallet*) Here, you take
it. Now I'll find out whether it's me or my money she's so
passionate about.

LOVEY Let's go in and have lunch.

MENAECHMUS OF SYRACUSE It's awfully nice of you, but,
thank you, I really can't.

LOVEY (*staring at him in amazement*) Then why did you
tell me to make lunch for you a little while ago?

MENAECHMUS OF SYRACUSE   *I* told you to make lunch?

LOVEY   You certainly did. For you and that parasite of yours.

MENAECHMUS OF SYRACUSE (*peevishly*)   Damn it all, what parasite? (*Sotto voce to Messenio*) This woman must be out of her mind.

LOVEY   Sponge.

MENAECHMUS OF SYRACUSE   Sponge? What sponge? For cleaning shoes?

LOVEY (*accustomed to Menaechmus' jokes, patiently*)   The one who was here with you a little while ago, of course. When you brought me the dress you stole from your wife.

MENAECHMUS OF SYRACUSE (*clutching his head*)   What's this? I brought you a dress I stole from my wife? Are you crazy? (*Sotto voce to Messenio*) She's dreaming; she sure goes to sleep like a horse—standing up.

LOVEY (*starting to sulk*)   You always get such pleasure out of teasing me. Why do you say you didn't do what you definitely did do?

MENAECHMUS OF SYRACUSE (*slowly, emphasizing each word*)   Now, will you kindly tell me just what I did do that I say I didn't do?

LOVEY   Give me one of your wife's dresses today.

MENAECHMUS OF SYRACUSE (*helplessly*)   And I *still* say I didn't! Listen: I never had a wife, I don't have one now, and never, since the day I was born, have I set foot inside this city till this minute. I had lunch aboard ship, I came from there here, and I ran into you.

LOVEY (*tearfully*)   Well! Oh, this is terrible, this will be the end of me! What ship are you talking about?

MENAECHMUS OF SYRACUSE (*glibly*)   A wooden one. Been scraped, calked, and repaired time and again. More pine plugs patching the planks than pegs holding pelts at a furrier's.

LOVEY (*pleading*)   Please, dear, no more games. Come inside with me now.

MENAECHMUS OF SYRACUSE   Lady, it's not me you want. It's
some other man, I haven't the slightest idea who.

LOVEY (*with a let's-be-serious-now air*)   I know perfectly
well who you are. You're Menaechmus, your father's name
was Moschus, and I've heard say you were born in Syracuse in Sicily. (*Like a schoolgirl reciting—and getting most
of her lesson wrong*) The king of Syracuse was Agathocles,
then Phint-something, then Etna, and now Hiero. Etna gave
it to Hiero when he died.

MENAECHMUS OF SYRACUSE (*amazed—and amused; dryly*)
Absolutely right, lady, every word.

MESSENIO (*sotto voce to Menaechmus*)   By god, I bet she
comes from there, and that's how she knows all about you.

MENAECHMUS OF SYRACUSE (*sotto voce*)   Then I really don't
think I can turn down her invitation.

MESSENIO (*sotto voce*)   You do nothing of the sort! You go
through that door, and you're through.

MENAECHMUS OF SYRACUSE (*sotto voce, peevishly*) ⌈Shut up,
will you? Everything's going fine. I'm going to say yes to
whatever she says: maybe I can get myself some free entertainment. (*To Lovey*) My dear girl, I knew what I was
doing when I kept saying no to you up to now. I was
afraid that fellow (*gesturing toward Messenio*) would tell
my wife about the dress and our date. Since you'd like to
go in now, let's.⌋

LOVEY   You're not going to wait for your parasite?

MENAECHMUS OF SYRACUSE (*exploding*)   No, I am *not* going
to wait for my parasite, I don't give a damn about my parasite, and, if he shows up, I want him kept out.

LOVEY   It'll be a pleasure, believe me. (*Going up to him and
stroking his cheek*) Menaechmus, do you know what I'd
like you to do for me?

MENAECHMUS OF SYRACUSE   Just say the word.

LOVEY   I'd like you to take that dress you just gave me to the
dressmaker and have her make some alterations and add
some touches I want.

MENAECHMUS OF SYRACUSE (*enthusiastically*)   By god, you're right! That way nobody'll recognize it, and my wife won't know you have it on if she sees you in the street.

LOVEY   Then remember to take it with you when you leave.

MENAECHMUS OF SYRACUSE   I sure will!

LOVEY   Let's go in.

MENAECHMUS OF SYRACUSE   I'll be right with you; I want to have a last word with this fellow here. (*Lovey goes into the house; he turns to Messenio.*) Hey, Messenio, come over here.

MESSENIO (*angrily*)   What's going on? What do you have to do *this* for?

MENAECHMUS OF SYRACUSE   I have to. (*As Messenio opens his mouth*) I know all about it, you can save your breath.

MESSENIO (*bitterly*)   That makes it even worse.

MENAECHMUS OF SYRACUSE (*triumphantly*)   Initial operation proceeding according to plan. I'm practically looting the enemy camp. Now, get going as fast as you can and take these fellows (*gesturing toward the rower-porters*) to the hotel this minute. Be sure you come back for me before sundown.

MESSENIO (*pleading*)   Menaechmus, listen, you don't know these girls.

MENAECHMUS OF SYRACUSE (*sharply*)   Enough talk. If I do anything stupid it'll be my neck, not yours. The stupid one's this woman. She doesn't have a brain in her head. From what I saw just now, there's rich pickings in here for us. (*Goes into the house.*)

MESSENIO (*calling after him*)   Good lord, are you really going in? (*Shaking his head, to himself*) He's a dead duck. The privateer has our rowboat in tow and is hauling it straight to hell and gone. But I'm the one without a brain in my head for thinking I can run my master. He bought me to listen to what he says, not order him around. (*To the rower-porters*) Follow me. I have orders to get back here in time, and I don't want to be late.

(*Messenio and his men file out, stage right. The stage is now empty.*)

ACT III

(*Enter Sponge, stage left, in a mad hurry. The sight of Lovey's closed door brings him to an abrupt halt. He claps a hand to his brow, then turns and walks downstage to address the audience.*)

SPONGE I'm over thirty now, and never have I ever in all those years pulled a more damned fool stunt than the one I pulled today: there was this town meeting, and *I* had to dive in and come up right in the middle of it. While I'm standing there with my mouth open, Menaechmus sneaks off on me. I'll bet he's gone to his girl friend. Perfectly willing to leave me behind, too!

(*Paces up and down a few times, shaking his head bitterly. Then, in a rage*) Damn, damn, damn the fellow who first figured out town meetings! All they do is keep a busy man away from his business. Why don't people pick a panel of men of leisure for this kind of thing? Hold a roll call at each meeting and whoever doesn't answer gets fined on the spot. There are plenty of persons around who need only one meal a day; they don't have business hours to keep because they don't go after dinner invitations or give them out. They're the ones to fuss with town meetings and town elections. If that's how things were run, I wouldn't have lost my lunch today. He sure wanted me along, didn't he? I'll go in, anyway. There's still hope of leftovers to soothe my soul. (*He is about to go up to the door when it suddenly swings open and Menaechmus of Syracuse appears, standing on the threshold with a garland, a little askew, on his head; he is holding the dress and listening to Lovey who is chattering at him from inside. Sponge quickly backs off into a corner.*) What's this I see? Menaechmus—and he's leaving, garland and all! The table's been cleared! I sure came in time—in time to walk him home. Well, I'll watch what his game is, and then I'll go and have a word with him.

MENAECHMUS OF SYRACUSE (*to Lovey inside*) Take it easy, will you! I'll have it back to you today in plenty of time, altered and trimmed to perfection. (*Slyly*) Believe me, you'll say it's not your dress; you won't know it any more.

SPONGE (*to the audience*) He's bringing the dress to the dressmaker. The dining's done, the drinks are down—and Sponge spent the lunch hour outside. God damn it, I'm not the man I think I am if I don't get even with him for this, but really even. You just watch. I'll give it to him, I will.

MENAECHMUS OF SYRACUSE (*closing the door and walking downstage; to the audience, jubilantly*) Good god, no one ever expected less—and got more blessings from heaven in one day than me. I dined, I wined, I wenched, and (*holding up the dress*) made off with this to which, from this moment on, she hereby forfeits all right, title, and interest.

SPONGE (*straining his ears, to the audience*) I can't make out what he's saying from back here. Is that full-belly talking about me and my right title and interest?

MENAECHMUS OF SYRACUSE (*to the audience*) She said I stole it from my wife and gave it to her. I saw she was mistaking me for someone else, so I promptly played it as if she and I were having a hot and heavy affair and began to yes her; I agreed right down the line to everything she said. Well, to make a long story short, I never had it so good for so little.

SPONGE (*clenching his fists, to the audience*) I'm going up to him. I'm itching to give him the works. (*Leaves his corner and strides belligerently toward Menaechmus.*)

MENAECHMUS OF SYRACUSE (*to the audience*) Someone coming up to me. Wonder who it is?

SPONGE (*roaring*) Well! You featherweight, you filth, you slime, you disgrace to the human race, you double-crossing good-for-nothing! What did I ever do to you that you had to ruin my life? You sure gave me the slip downtown a little while ago! You killed off the day all right—and held the funeral feast without me. Me who was coheir under the will! Where do you come off to do a thing like that!

MENAECHMUS OF SYRACUSE (*too pleased with life to lose his temper*) Mister, will you please tell me what business you and I have that gives you the right to use language like that to a stranger here, someone you never saw in your life? You hand me that talk and I'll hand you something you won't like.

SPONGE (*dancing with rage*) God damn it, you already have! I know god damned well you have!

MENAECHMUS OF SYRACUSE (*amused and curious*) What's your name, mister?

SPONGE (*as before*) Still making jokes, eh? As if you don't know my name!

MENAECHMUS OF SYRACUSE So help me, so far as I know, I never heard of you or saw you till this minute. But I know one thing for sure: whoever you are, you'd better behave yourself and stop bothering me.

SPONGE (*taken aback for a minute*) Menaechmus! Wake up!

MENAECHMUS OF SYRACUSE (*genially*) Believe me, to the best of my knowledge, I am awake.

SPONGE You don't know me?

MENAECHMUS OF SYRACUSE (*as before*) If I did, I wouldn't say I didn't.

SPONGE (*incredulously*) You don't know your own parasite?

MENAECHMUS OF SYRACUSE Mister, it looks to me as if you've got bats in your belfry.

SPONGE (*shaken, but not convinced*) Tell me this: didn't you steal that dress there from your wife today and give it to Lovey?

MENAECHMUS OF SYRACUSE Good god, no! I don't have a wife, I never gave anything to any Lovey, and I never stole any dress. Are you in your right mind?

SPONGE (*aside, groaning*)   A dead loss, the whole affair. (*To Menaechmus*) But you came out of your house wearing the dress! I saw you myself!

MENAECHMUS OF SYRACUSE (*exploding*)   Damn you! You think everybody's a pervert just because you are? I was wearing this dress? Is that what you're telling me?

SPONGE   I most certainly am.

MENAECHMUS OF SYRACUSE   Now you go straight to the one place fit for you! No—get yourself to the lunatic asylum; you're stark-raving mad.

SPONGE (*venomously*)   God damn it, there's one thing no-body in the world is going to stop me from doing: I'm telling the whole story, exactly what happened, to your wife this minute. All these insults are going to boomerang back on your own head. Believe you me, you'll pay for eating that whole lunch yourself. (*Dashes into the house of Menaechmus of Epidamnus.*)

MENAECHMUS OF SYRACUSE (*throwing his arms wide, to the audience*)   What's going on here? Must everyone I lay eyes on play games with me this way? Wait—I hear the door.

(*The door of Lovey's house opens, and one of her maids comes out holding a bracelet. She walks over to Menaechmus and, as he looks on blankly, hands it to him.*)

MAID   Menaechmus, Lovey says would you please do her a big favor and drop this at the jeweler's on your way? She wants you to give him an ounce of gold and have him make the whole bracelet over.

MENAECHMUS OF SYRACUSE (*with alacrity*)   Tell her I'll not only take care of this but anything else she wants taken care of. Anything at all. (*He takes the piece and examines it absorbedly.*)

MAID (*watching him curiously, in surprise*)   Don't you know what bracelet it is?

MENAECHMUS OF SYRACUSE   Frankly no—except that it's gold.

MAID   It's the one you told us you stole from your wife's jewel box when nobody was looking.

MENAECHMUS OF SYRACUSE (*forgetting himself, in high dudgeon*)   I never did anything of the kind!

MAID   You mean you don't remember it? Well, if that's the case, you give it right back!

MENAECHMUS OF SYRACUSE (*after a few seconds of highly histrionic deep thought*)   Wait a second. No, I *do* remember it. Of course—this is the one I gave her. Oh, and there's something else: where are the armlets I gave her at the same time?

MAID (*puzzled*)   You never gave her any armlets.

MENAECHMUS OF SYRACUSE (*quickly*)   Right you are. This was all I gave her.

MAID   Shall I tell her you'll take care of it?

MENAECHMUS OF SYRACUSE   By all means, tell her. I'll take care of it, all right. I'll see she gets it back the same time she gets the dress back.

MAID (*going up to him and stroking his cheek*)   Menaechmus dear, will you do me a favor too? Will you have some earrings made for me? Drop earrings, please; ten grams of gold in each. (*Meaningfully*) It'll make me *so* glad to see you every time you come to the house.

MENAECHMUS OF SYRACUSE   Sure. (*With elaborate carelessness*) Just give me the gold. I'll pay for the labor myself.

MAID   Please, you pay for the gold too. I'll make it up to you afterward.

MENAECHMUS OF SYRACUSE   No, you pay for the gold. I'll make it up to *you* afterward. Double.

MAID   I don't have the money.

MENAECHMUS OF SYRACUSE (*with a great air of magnanimity*)   Well, any time you get it, you just let me have it.

MAID (*turning to go*)   I'm going in now. Anything I can do for you?

MENAECHMUS OF SYRACUSE   Yes. Tell her I'll see to both

things—(*sotto voce, to the audience*) that they get sold as quickly as possible for whatever they'll bring. (*As the maid starts walking toward the door*) Has she gone in yet? (*Hearing a slam*) Ah, she's in, the door's closed. (*Jubilantly*) The lord loves me! I've had a helping hand from heaven! (*Suddenly looks about warily*) But why hang around when I have the time and chance to get away from this (*jerking his thumb at Lovey's house*) pimping parlor here? Menaechmus! Get a move on, hit the road, forward march! I'll take off this garland and toss it to the left here (*doing so*). Then, if anyone tries to follow me, he'll think I went that way. Now I'll go and see if I can find my servant. I want to let him know all the blessings from heaven I've had.

(*He races off, stage right. The stage is now empty.*)

ACT IV

(The door of Menaechmus' house flies open and his wife bursts out, shrieking, with Sponge at her heels.)

WIFE Am I supposed to put up with a marriage like this? Look the other way while that husband of mine sneaks off everything in the house and hands it all over to his lady friend?

SPONGE *(looking around uneasily)* Not so loud, please! I'll see to it you catch him red-handed right now. Just follow me. *(Starting to walk off, stage left)* He was on his way to the dressmaker with that dress he stole from you today. Had a garland on his head and was dead drunk. *(Noticing the garland Menaechmus of Syracuse had thrown down)* Hey, look! The garland he had on! I wasn't lying to you, was I? There you are. That's the way he went if you want to follow his trail. *(Looking toward the wings, stage left)* Well, look at that! He's coming back. Perfect! *(Peering hard)* But he doesn't have the dress!

WIFE *(grimly)* What should I do to him this time?

SPONGE Same as usual: lace into him. That's what I'd vote for. *(Pulling her off to the side)* Let's go over here. Then jump on him from ambush.

(Enter Menaechmus of Epidamnus, hot, tired, and in a foul temper. He walks downstage and addresses the audience.)

SONG

MENAECHMUS OF EPIDAMNUS

>   What a custom we have! Bothersome, bad,
>   Stupid, silly, senseless, mad!
>   And practiced most by our leading lights:
>   They all adore,
>   They're passionate for
>   A flock of fawning satellites.

Whether good or bad never bothers them:
The fawner's funds they're bothered about.
How people regard his character—
    They leave that out.

Is he good as gold but rather poor?
    He's a bum.
Is he worthless but has lots of gold?
    The best they come!

A patron goes wild with worry and care
    Because of his charges' acts.
They know no truth or law or justice;
    They deny undeniable facts;

They're vicious, avaricious crooks
    Forever up for trial—
Through usury and perjury
    They've made their pile.

In summary, civil, or criminal court,
Whenever a case of theirs comes up,
    We patrons come up too—
Of course: we have to take the stand
    And defend what the dastards do.

(*Pauses, shakes his head despondently, then continues bitterly.*)

That's what *I* had to do just today.
One of mine simply held me at bay.
I couldn't do what I wished, nor with whom,
For he hung and he clung; it was doom.
I went up on the stand and I entered a plea
On behalf of this creature's chicanery.

I proposed the most twisted and tortuous terms;
    Here I'd skim, there go on for a while.
I was arguing to settle the case out of court;
    What does *he* do? Insist on a trial!

There were three solid citizens who'd witnessed each crime—
Most open-and-shut case since the beginning of time!

He ruined this day for me.
God damn that stupid clown!
And god damn me as well!
For setting foot downtown.

I told her to make me lunch;
She's expecting me, I know.
A perfect day set up—
And I had to ruin it so!

I left as soon as I could
And hurried back uptown.
She'll be sore at me, I'm sure—
But that dress will calm her down,
The one I sneaked today from my wife
And handed to Lovey, the light of my life!

SPONGE (*sotto voce to the wife, triumphantly*)   Well, what do you say?

WIFE (*sotto voce*)   That I'm the miserable wife of a miserable husband.

SPONGE (*sotto voce*)   You can hear what he's saying, can't you?

WIFE (*sotto voce, grimly*)   I can hear, all right.

MENAECHMUS OF EPIDAMNUS (*to the audience, gesturing toward Lovey's door*)   Now why don't I be smart and go right inside here where I can have myself a good time?

SPONGE (*springing out of his corner, shouting*)   Wait! You're going to have a bad one, instead.

WIFE (*following him, shrieking*)   You'll pay me and with interest, you burglar.

SPONGE (*gleefully*)   That's giving it to him!

WIFE   So you thought you could commit all these crimes and get away with it, eh?

MENAECHMUS OF EPIDAMNUS (*all innocence*)   My dear wife, what are you talking about?

WIFE (*witheringly*)   You ask *me*?

MENAECHMUS OF EPIDAMNUS (*acting puzzled, and gesturing*

toward Sponge)   Should I ask him? (*Walks toward her as if to put an arm about her.*)

WIFE   Don't you dare touch me!

SPONGE (*to the wife*)   Keep at him!

MENAECHMUS OF EPIDAMNUS (*switching from puzzlement back to innocence*)   What are you so mad at me for?

WIFE (*grimly*)   You ought to know.

SPONGE   He knows, all right, but he's pretending he doesn't, the dirty rat!

MENAECHMUS OF EPIDAMNUS (*to his wife, as before*)   What *is* this all about?

WIFE   That dress—

MENAECHMUS OF EPIDAMNUS (*quickly*)   Dress?

WIFE   Yes, dress. Which a certain person— (*Menaechmus begins to shake. She observes him with grim satisfaction.*) What are you so scared about?

MENAECHMUS OF EPIDAMNUS (*with a sickly attempt at nonchalance*)   Me? Nothing. Nothing at all.

SPONGE (*to Menaechmus, sneering*)   With one exception— dress distress. (*As Menaechmus looks at him startled and then begins to pass frantic nods and winks*) So you *would* eat lunch behind my back, would you? (*To the wife*) Keep at him!

MENAECHMUS OF EPIDAMNUS (*sotto voce to Sponge*)   Shut up, will you!

SPONGE (*answering Menaechmus' stage whisper in ringing tones*)   I most certainly will *not* shut up. (*To the wife*) He's making signs to me not to speak.

MENAECHMUS OF EPIDAMNUS   Me? I most certainly am not! I'm not winking, I'm not nodding, I'm not doing anything of the kind.

SPONGE (*to the wife, shaking his head incredulously*)   Of all the nerve! He actually denies what you can see with your own eyes!

MENAECHMUS OF EPIDAMNUS (*to the wife, solemnly*)   My

dear wife, I swear to you by all that's holy, I did *not* make any signs to (*jerking his head contemptuously in Sponge's direction*) that there. Now are you satisfied?

SPONGE All right, she believes you about that there; now get back to the point.

MENAECHMUS OF EPIDAMNUS (*with angelic innocence*) Get back where?

SPONGE Get back to that dressmaker, I say. Go ahead. And bring back the dress.

MENAECHMUS OF EPIDAMNUS (*as before*) What dress are you talking about?

SPONGE It's time for me to stop doing the talking. This lady is forgetting her duty.

WIFE (*responding promptly to the cue*) Oh, I'm a poor, unhappy woman!

MENAECHMUS OF EPIDAMNUS (*going over to her, solicitously*) Why are you so unhappy, dear? Please tell me. Has one of the servants done something wrong? Are the maids or the houseboys answering you back? (*Switching from solicitousness to righteous indignation*) You just let me know about it. They'll pay for it, they will!

WIFE (*witheringly*) Nonsense!

MENAECHMUS OF EPIDAMNUS (*tenderly, to himself—but aloud*) She's so out of sorts. This distresses me.

WIFE (*as before*) Nonsense!

MENAECHMUS OF EPIDAMNUS (*nodding with sympathetic understanding*) Yes, you must be angry at one of the servants.

WIFE (*as before*) Nonsense!

MENAECHMUS OF EPIDAMNUS (*chuckling, as if what he's going to say is a great joke*) You can't be angry at *me*, at any rate.

WIFE (*grimly*) Now you're making sense.

MENAECHMUS OF EPIDAMNUS I certainly haven't done anything wrong.

WIFE Hah! Back to nonsense again.

MENAECHMUS OF EPIDAMNUS (*going up and putting his arm about her*) My dear, *please* tell me what's troubling you so much.

SPONGE (*to the wife, sneering*) Your little bunny's buttering you up.

MENAECHMUS OF EPIDAMNUS (*over his shoulder to Sponge, exasperated*) Can't you lay off me? Who's talking to you?

WIFE (*suddenly screaming*) Take your hands off me! (*Menaechmus leaps back as if stunned.*)

SPONGE (*to the wife*) That's giving it to him! (*To Menaechmus*) So you'll hurry off to eat lunch without me, will you? And then get drunk and walk out the door with a garland on your head and make fun of me, eh?

(*Menaechmus grabs Sponge and yanks him over to the side.*)

MENAECHMUS OF EPIDAMNUS (*sotto voce*) So help me, I not only haven't eaten lunch, I haven't set foot inside that house today!

SPONGE (*sotto voce*) You mean you deny it?

MENAECHMUS OF EPIDAMNUS (*sotto voce*) Of course I deny it.

SPONGE (*sotto voce*) What a nerve! You mean to say I didn't see you a little while ago standing in front of the door there with a garland on your head? When you said I had bats in the belfry and that you didn't know me and that you were a stranger here?

MENAECHMUS OF EPIDAMNUS (*sotto voce, blankly*) How could I? I just this minute came back home after you and I got separated.

SPONGE (*sotto voce, sneering*) Oh, I know your type. Didn't think I could get even with you, did you? I told the whole story to your wife, that's what I did!

MENAECHMUS OF EPIDAMNUS (*sotto voce, anxiously*)   What did you tell her?

SPONGE (*sotto voce, blandly*)   I don't know. Ask the lady herself.

(*Menaechmus turns on his heel and hurries to where his wife is standing.*)

MENAECHMUS OF EPIDAMNUS (*nervously*)   My dear wife, what's going on here? What sort of story did this fellow hand you? What is it? Why don't you answer me? Why don't you tell me what's the matter?

WIFE (*witheringly*)   As if you don't know! (*Slowly, emphasizing each word*) A dress was stolen from me.

MENAECHMUS OF EPIDAMNUS (*with wide-eyed innocence*)   A dress was stolen from you?

WIFE (*as before*)   Do you have to ask?

MENAECHMUS OF EPIDAMNUS (*as before*)   If I knew, I certainly wouldn't ask.

SPONGE   Damn you! What a faker! But you can't cover up any longer—she knows the whole story; I told it to her myself down to the last detail.

MENAECHMUS OF EPIDAMNUS (*as before*)   What story?

WIFE (*grimly*)   Since you have such an unmitigated gall and refuse to confess of your own free will, listen and listen hard. Believe you me, you'll find out what I'm mad about and what this fellow told me. (*Looking him straight in the eye*) A dress was stolen from me.

MENAECHMUS OF EPIDAMNUS (*with histrionic astonishment*)   A dress was stolen from me?

SPONGE (*to the wife*)   Look at that! The dirty rat's trying to fool you! (*To Menaechmus*) Stolen from *her*, not you. Damn it all, if it had been stolen from *you*, then it really would be lost.

MENAECHMUS OF EPIDAMNUS (*to Sponge, savagely*)   You keep out of this. (*To his wife*) Now, what were you saying, dear?

WIFE (*tight-lipped*) I was saying that one of my dresses disappeared from the house.

MENAECHMUS OF EPIDAMNUS Who could have stolen it?

WIFE (*meaningfully*) I should think the man who made off with it knows the answer to that one.

MENAECHMUS OF EPIDAMNUS Who is he?

WIFE Some one named Menaechmus.

MENAECHMUS OF EPIDAMNUS (*thundering*) God in heaven, the man's a criminal! Who is this Menaechmus?

WIFE I'll tell you: *you.*

MENAECHMUS OF EPIDAMNUS Me?

WIFE You.

(*They stand in silence for a few seconds, eying one another.*)

MENAECHMUS OF EPIDAMNUS (*blustering*) Who says so?

WIFE I do.

SPONGE So do I. And I also say you gave it to your lady friend Lovey here.

MENAECHMUS OF EPIDAMNUS *I* gave it?

WIFE Yes, you. You yourself.

SPONGE What do you want us to do? Bring an owl here to keep saying "yoo yoo" to you? We're getting hoarse, the both of us.

MENAECHMUS OF EPIDAMNUS (*solemnly, one hand on heart, the other raised*) My dear wife, I swear to you by all that's holy, I didn't give it. Does that satisfy you?

SPONGE And, damn it all, we take the same oath that you're lying!

(*Menaechmus looks from one to the other. They glower back. He quails visibly.*)

MENAECHMUS OF EPIDAMNUS (*feebly*) Well, you see, I didn't *give* it away, I sort of lent it out.

WIFE (*exploding*) Good god in heaven! *I* don't lend out your coats or suits, do I? If there's any lending to do, the wife will see to her things and the husband to his. Now you get that dress back into this house, do you hear?

MENAECHMUS OF EPIDAMNUS (*meekly*)   I'll see you get it back.

WIFE (*grimly*)   And my opinion is, you'd better. Because you don't enter this house unless that dress is with you. I'm going in now. (*Turns her back on him and stalks off toward the door.*)

SPONGE (*calling after her, alarmed*)   Don't I get anything for all I've done for you?

WIFE (*pausing at the threshold, contemptuously*)   I'll do the same for you when something's stolen from your house. (*Slams the door behind her.*)

SPONGE (*to the audience, horror-stricken*)   My god! That means never—I don't have anything to steal! Husband, wife—to hell with the both of you! I'm off downtown in a hurry—one thing I know for sure: I've worn out my welcome with this household! (*Scuttles off, stage left.*)

MENAECHMUS OF EPIDAMNUS (*to the audience, gaily*)   My wife thinks she's giving me a bad time by shutting me out. As if I don't have another place to go into, lots better. (*Addressing the closed door*) You don't like me, eh? (*With a mock sigh*) I'll just have to put up with it. But Lovey here likes me. She's not going to shut me out, she's going to shut me *in*. (*Turning back to the audience*) I'll go see her and ask her to return the dress I just gave her. I'll buy her another one, even better. (*Walking up to Lovey's door and knocking*) Hey! Anybody minding this door? Open up, someone, and call Lovey out here!

LOVEY (*from inside*)   Who wants me?

MENAECHMUS OF EPIDAMNUS   Someone who'd sooner see his own self hurt than hurt you.

LOVEY (*opening the door*)   Menaechmus! Darling! What are you standing outside for? Come on in. (*Turns to go inside.*)

MENAECHMUS OF EPIDAMNUS (*seriously*)　No, wait. You don't know what I've come for.

LOVEY (*walking up to him and stroking his cheek*)　Sure I do. So you can have your fun with me.

MENAECHMUS OF EPIDAMNUS (*as before*)　Damn it all, it's not that. Would you please do me a big favor and give me back that dress I just gave you? My wife's found out everything, she knows exactly what happened. I'll buy you another that costs twice as much, anyone you like.

LOVEY (*staring at him blankly*)　But I just gave it to you a few minutes ago to take to the dressmaker! Along with that bracelet you were to take to the jeweler so he could make it over.

MENAECHMUS OF EPIDAMNUS (*staring at her blankly*)　What's that? You gave *me* the dress and a bracelet? Oh, no. You never did. Figure it out. Right after I gave it to you, I went downtown, I came back from there just a few minutes ago, and this is the first I've seen of you since.

LOVEY (*stepping back and eying him frigidly*)　*I* see what your game is. I trusted you with the dress, and now you're looking for a way to do me out of it.

MENAECHMUS OF EPIDAMNUS (*earnestly*)　I swear I'm not asking for it to do you out of it. I tell you my wife knows everything!

LOVEY (*building up a head of feminine steam*)　*I* didn't ask you to give it to me. *You* brought it to me of your own free will. You gave it as a gift, and now you want it back. Well, *I* don't mind. Take it. Keep it. Let your wife wear it, wear it yourself, lock it up in a closet, for all I care. But don't you fool yourself: you're not setting foot inside this door from now on. After all I've done for you, you'll treat me like dirt under your feet, will you? Unless you come with cash in your hands, you're wasting your time, you'll get nothing out of me. Find some other girl to treat like—like a fool under your feet!

MENAECHMUS OF EPIDAMNUS　Don't carry on so, please! (*As*

she turns her back on him and flounces inside) Hey, wait,
I tell you! Come on back! Stop, won't you? Please, do me
a favor, and come back! (*She slams the door behind her.
Menaechmus turns despondently to the audience*) She's
gone in and shut the door. I'm the shuttest-out man there
is: my wife, my mistress—nobody believes a thing I say.
Well, I'll go and talk things over with my friends and see
what they think I ought to do.

(*Menaechmus leaves, stage left. The stage is now empty.*)

ACT V

(*Menaechmus of Syracuse enters, stage right, back from his search for Messenio along the waterfront. At the same moment, the door of Menaechmus of Epidamnus' house opens, and the wife comes out.*)

MENAECHMUS OF SYRACUSE (*to himself, disgustedly*) That was a stupid stunt I pulled a little while ago, to trust the wallet with all our money to Messenio. If you ask me, he's made himself at home in some dive somewhere.

WIFE (*to herself*) I'll keep an eye out for that husband of mine. See how soon he comes back. (*Noticing Menaechmus of Syracuse*) Well! There he is! And the day's saved—he's bringing back my dress.

MENAECHMUS OF SYRACUSE (*to himself, testily*) I wonder where that Messenio would be wandering about now?

WIFE (*to herself*) I'll go up to him and give him the welcome he deserves. (*Striding up to Menaechmus*) Aren't you ashamed to show yourself in front of me with that dress, you criminal!

MENAECHMUS OF SYRACUSE (*startled*) What's the matter, madam? What's all the agitation about?

WIFE (*shrieking*) The nerve of him! How dare you talk to me! How dare you utter a single solitary word in my presence!

MENAECHMUS OF SYRACUSE (*in astonishment*) Will you please tell me what I did that I'm not allowed to utter a word?

WIFE (*as before*) What a question! The unmitigated gall of this man!

MENAECHMUS OF SYRACUSE (*tartly*) Madam, do you happen to know why the Greeks called Hecuba a bitch?

WIFE (*huffily*) No, I don't.

MENAECHMUS OF SYRACUSE (*as before*) Because she used

to do exactly what you're doing now. Everyone she laid
eyes on, she loaded with insults. And so they began to call
her The Bitch—and she deserved it.

WIFE (*after staring at him blankly for a few seconds, unable
to believe her ears*)   I *will* not put up with this criminal
behavior! I'd sooner spend the rest of my days a divorcée
than put up with this absolutely criminal behavior of yours!

MENAECHMUS OF SYRACUSE (*shrugging*)   What difference
does it make to me whether you put up with your marriage or walk out on your husband? Is it the custom around
here for people to talk nonsense to every stranger who
comes to town?

WIFE (*as before*)   Talk nonsense? Well! I tell you I can't
stand this one second longer. I'll die a divorcée rather than
put up with the likes of you.

MENAECHMUS OF SYRACUSE (*as before*)   Die a divorcée or
live till doomsday. Believe me, it makes no difference to
me.

WIFE   A minute ago you were insisting you hadn't stolen it
and now you're holding it right in front of my eyes. Aren't
you ashamed of yourself?

MENAECHMUS OF SYRACUSE (*finally needled into an angry
retort*)   Good god, woman, you certainly have a nerve!
You're a bad one, you are! How dare you say I stole from
you what another woman gave me to have trimmed and
altered for her?

WIFE (*throwing up her hands*)   So help me, you know what
I'm going to do? I'm going to call my father right here and
now and tell him about every one of your crimes. (*Calling*) Decio! (*A scared houseboy scurries out and listens
breathlessly.*) Go get my father and bring him right here;
tell him he must come. (*Decio dashes off, stage left.*) In
a few minutes the whole world will know all about these
crimes of yours.

MENAECHMUS OF SYRACUSE   Are you in your right mind?
What crimes of mine?

WIFE   That you stole dresses and jewelry from your own wife and carried them off to your lady friend. Is it the truth or isn't it?

MENAECHMUS OF SYRACUSE (*helplessly*)   Please, lady, if you know of any tranquilizer I can take to help me put up with your tantrums, for god's sake, lead me to it! I haven't the vaguest idea of who you think I am. I know you about as well as I know the man in the moon.

WIFE (*pointing toward the wings, stage left*)   You can make fun of me, all right, but, believe me, you're not going to make fun of *him*. There's my father coming this way. Turn around and look. I suppose you don't know him.

MENAECHMUS OF SYRACUSE (*his gaze following her finger*)   About as well as I know the old man of the mountain. You know when I saw him before? The same day I saw you.

WIFE   You deny that you know me? You deny that you know my father?

MENAECHMUS OF SYRACUSE (*airily*)   And the same goes for your grandfather, if you want to add him.

WIFE (*disgustedly*)   Ugh! Just what I'd expect from you!

(*Menaechmus moves away, stage right, and stands moodily, looking off into the wings trying to catch the first glimpse of Messenio. A wizened graybeard emerges from the wings, stage left, leaning heavily on a stick; he makes his way at a snail's pace across the stage.*)

SONG

FATHER (*stopping to address the audience*)
        As fast as these old legs can go—
        When duty calls I can't say no—
        I'll step, I'll stride, I'll speed, I'll run.
        I'm well aware this is no fun:
        The spryness has gone out of me,
        I'm buried deep in senility,
        My body's hard to haul along,
        I've lost the strength I had when young.

In getting old you don't do well;
It's bad stuff, age. Do well? It's hell!
Its coming brings a load of grief—
But, to tell it all, I can't be brief.

(*Totters on a few more steps, then stops abruptly and shakes his head worriedly*)

Now here's the thing that's on my mind
And worries me to the core:
What brought my daughter so suddenly
To call me to her door?
What does she want? She doesn't say!
What is it she's called me for?

(*Goes on for a few more steps, then halts again*)

I'm sure I know what it's all about:
A fight with her husband has broken out.
It's bound to happen to every shrew
Who feels her dowry entitles her to
A husband whose sole aim in life
Is to fetch and carry for his wife.

(*A few more steps, then another stop and more worried headshakings*)

Yet the men are not exactly pure.
And there's just so much a wife can endure.
A daughter doesn't call her dad
Unless the insult's pretty bad,
Or else the squabbling got too rough.
Whatever it is, I'll know soon enough.

(*Turns and catches sight, finally, of his daughter and Menaechmus*)

There she is before the door.
There's her husband, looking sore.
Just what I thought—a brawl once more.

FATHER (*to himself*)   I'll have a word with her.

WIFE (*to herself*)   I'll go up to him. (*Walking up to her father*) Papa! I'm *so* glad to see you!

FATHER   Glad to see you too. Well, here I am; any glad tidings? Were things glad around here when you sent for me? What are you looking so black for? (*Pointing to Menaechmus still watching out moodily for Messenio*) And what's he standing off over there in a huff for? You two have had a skirmish about something, all right. Well, speak up. Who's to blame? And make it short—no long lectures.

WIFE   *I* haven't done a thing wrong. Let me put your mind at ease about that first, Papa. It's simply that I can't go on living here, it's impossible, I can't stand it. So please take me away from here.

FATHER   (*wearily*)   What's the trouble this time?

WIFE   Papa, he's making a fool of me.

FATHER   Who is?

WIFE   That man you trusted me to. That husband of mine.

FATHER   (*throwing up his hands*)   I knew it! Another squabble. (*Peevishly*) How many times have I expressly warned you to watch out about coming to me with your complaints. Both of you.

WIFE   (*plaintively*)   Watch out about *that*? How can I, Papa!

FATHER   (*snappishly*)   What a question! You can if you want to. How many times have I pointed out to you that you *must* give in to your husband and not keep checking on what he does and where he goes and how he spends his time.

WIFE   (*expostulating*)   But, Papa, he's passionately in love with that prostitute who lives next door!

FATHER   Very sensible of him. And, believe me, all this effort of yours will simply make him more passionate.

WIFE   (*sulking*)   He goes there for drinks too.

FATHER   (*angrily*)   If he likes to have a drink there—or anywhere—what's he supposed to do? Not go just to please you? You do have a devil of a nerve! By the same token

you ought to stop him from accepting invitations to eat out
or from bringing dinner guests to the house. If you think
husbands are such slaves, why don't you hand him some
wool, sit him down with the maids, and have him do a
daily stint of spinning.

WIFE (*with heavy sarcasm*) Naturally, it wasn't *me* I
brought you here to defend, but my husband. You take
the stand for *me*—and plead *his* case!

FATHER (*sharply*) If he's done anything wrong, I'll go after
him lots harder than I've gone after you. Since he keeps
you in money and clothes, gives you maids, and pays for
the household, the best thing you can do, my lady, is to
start getting some sense.

WIFE (*in desperation*) But he steals my jewelry and dresses
right out of my closets, he robs me, he carries off my things
behind my back and brings them to those whores of his!

FATHER If he does that, he's to be blamed. But if he doesn't,
you're to be blamed for blaming a blameless man.

WIFE Papa, he's got the dress and bracelet that he gave her
with him right now. I found out all about it, so he's bringing them back.

FATHER (*shaking his head perplexedly, to himself*) I'll find
out all about this right now. I'll go up and have a word
with him. (*Tottering over to Menaechmus, who is still
looking impatiently, stage right, for Messenio*) Tell me,
Menaechmus, what have you two been—er—discussing?
What are you looking so black about? What are you
standing off here in a huff for?

MENAECHMUS OF SYRACUSE My dear sir, I don't know who
you are or what your name is, but I swear to you by god
almighty and—

FATHER (*interrupting in astonishment*) Swear? What in the
world about?

MENAECHMUS OF SYRACUSE (*holding up the dress*) This
woman claims I stole this out of her house and made off
with it. She's crazy. I swear I never did a thing wrong to

her. (*Solemnly*) So help me, may I become more miserable than the most miserable specimen of humanity alive if I ever set foot in the house where she lives.

FATHER Listen, you madman, if you take an oath like that, if you say you never set foot in your own house, you're stark-raving mad.

MENAECHMUS OF SYRACUSE (*pointing to Menaechmus of Epidamnus' house*) My dear sir, are you telling me that I live in that house?

FATHER Do you deny it?

MENAECHMUS OF SYRACUSE I most certainly do deny it.

FATHER No, you most certainly can't deny it. (*Suddenly struck by a thought*) Unless you moved out last night. (*Turning to the wife*) Daughter, come over here. What's this? You two haven't moved out of here?

WIFE Now, just where or why would we be moving?

FATHER Good god, *I* don't know.

WIFE (*disgustedly*) It's so obvious. He's pulling your leg. Don't you get it?

FATHER (*turning back to Menaechmus, sharply*) All right, Menaechmus, enough jokes. Now get to the point.

MENAECHMUS OF SYRACUSE (*finally losing his patience*) Please, what do you want with me? Where do you come from? Who are you? What have I got to do with you or this woman here who's pestering the life out of me?

WIFE (*fearfully, to her father*) Look! His eyes are green! He's turning green around his temples and his forehead! Look at the glitter in his eyes!

MENAECHMUS OF SYRACUSE (*to the audience*) They say I'm insane. Well, in that case, the best thing for me to do is act the part and scare them away.

(*Menaechmus proceeds forthwith to put on a garish performance.*)

WIFE (*as before*) Look at the way he's throwing his arms

around! Look at the faces he's making! Papa! What should
I do!

FATHER (*taking her by the arm and tottering off with her*)
Come over here, daughter. As far away from him as we
can get.

MENAECHMUS OF SYRACUSE (*pretending to be calling to the
God of Wine*) Yoho! Yoho! Bacchus! Where away in
what wood do you call me for the hunt? I hear you—but
I can't leave these parts. They've got their eyes on me—on
my left that mad bitch and, behind, that old stink-goat
who's perjured himself plenty of times in his day to the
ruination of innocent men.

FATHER You go to hell!

MENAECHMUS OF SYRACUSE (*listening attentively as if to an
unseen voice, and nodding briskly*) Ah! Orders from the
Oracle of Apollo for me to burn her eyes out with blazing
brands.

WIFE Papa! This will be the end of me! He says he's going
to burn my eyes out!

MENAECHMUS OF SYRACUSE (*aside, chuckling*) They say *I'm*
crazy. Damn it all, they're the ones who're crazy.

FATHER Psst! Daughter!

WIFE What is it? What are we going to do?

FATHER Why don't I call the servants out here? I'll go get
some to carry him in the house and tie him up before he
causes any more commotion.

MENAECHMUS OF SYRACUSE (*aside*) Stuck! If I don't come
up with some scheme first, they're going to haul me into
the house. (*Resumes his elaborate listening and nodding
to celestial commands.*) Yes, Apollo: I'm not to spare the
socks on the jaw unless she gets the hell out of my sight.
I will carry out your orders, Apollo. (*Advances menacingly toward the wife.*)

FATHER (*frantically*) Run home as fast as you can or he'll
beat you to a pulp!

WIFE (*making for the door*)   I am! Papa dear, please, please keep an eye on him and don't let him get away. (*To herself*) Oh, this is terrible! The things I have to listen to! (*Rushes into the house and slams the door behind her.*)

MENAECHMUS OF SYRACUSE (*aside*)   Not bad at all, the way I got rid of her. Now for this Titan here—a Titan with the shakes, a bearded, benighted one begat by the Holy Swan. (*Starts listening and nodding again.*) So your orders are to grab that stick he's holding and make pulp of his arms, legs, bones, and joints?

FATHER (*raising his stick*)   You lay a hand on me or come any closer, and you're in for trouble!

MENAECHMUS OF SYRACUSE (*as before*)   I will carry out your orders, Apollo: I'm to take an ax and chip off every scrap of flesh this old boy has until I'm down to the bone.

FATHER (*aside*)   I've got to watch out and take care of myself now. These threats of his have me worried: he might hurt me.

(*Menaechmus advances, brandishing an imaginary ax, but the old man, instead of running, whirls his stick menacingly, and Menaechmus stops short before that formidable instrument. Forced to take another tack, he resumes his listening and nodding act.*)

MENAECHMUS OF SYRACUSE   That's a big order, Apollo. Now I'm to get a team of fierce wild horses, harness them to a chariot, and mount it so I can trample down this stinking, toothless, broken-down lion, eh? (*Launches into an elaborate dumb show.*) Now I'm in the chariot, I'm holding the reins, the whip's in my hand. (*Mimicking the manner of grand opera*) Come, my steeds! Let the clatter of your hoofs ring out! Bend the nimble knee in headlong haste!

FATHER (*grimly*)   Threatening me with a team of horses, eh?

(*Menaechmus gallops madly about, then, full tilt, makes for the old man, who holds his ground gamely, swinging his stick. Just before getting within range, Menaechmus pru-*)

dently swerves aside, pulls up, and readies himself for another try.)

MENAECHMUS OF SYRACUSE   Ah, Apollo, the orders are to make a second charge and wipe out this one who insists on standing his ground, eh? (*Charges down on the old man but the stick, whistling through the air, brings Menaechmus to an abrupt halt. He throws his head back and staggers backward as if irresistibly dragged against his will.*) What's this? Someone has me by the hair and is hauling me from my car! Who is it? Apollo! He's changing your direct orders!

FATHER (*shaking his head dolefully, to the audience*)   Dear, oh dear! These fits are such terrible things! Heaven help us! This fellow, for instance, was perfectly sane a minute ago and now he's completely out of his mind. And it came on him so suddenly and with such force! I'll go get a doctor as quick as I can. (*Rushes out, stage left.*)

MENAECHMUS OF SYRACUSE (*to himself, in surprise*)   Have they really gone? That pair who made a sane man insane? What am I waiting for? I should be off for the ship while the coast is clear. (*Walking downstage and addressing the audience*) Please, all of you, if the old fellow comes back, don't show him which street I took to get out of here.

(*Menaechmus of Syracuse dashes off, stage right. A second later the father re-enters, stage left, followed by a self-important little man who struts along majestically.*)

FATHER (*to the audience, grumbling*)   My seat hurts from sitting and my eyes from watching while I waited for the doctor to finish his rounds. Finally the pain-in-the-neck tore himself away from his patients and came back. "Aesculapius fractured a leg and Apollo an arm, and I was mending the breaks," he tells me. I wonder what I'm bringing, a doctor or a repairman? Look at that walk! (*Under his breath*) Shake a leg, you ant!

DOCTOR (*in his professional manner*)   What did you say his trouble is? Please describe it to me. Is it hallucinations or delirium? I'd like to know. Is he in a coma? Does he have water on the brain?

FATHER (*testily*) Listen, that's just the reason I brought you here. To give *me* the answers—and to cure him.

DOCTOR (*airily*) Nothing easier. He'll be a well man, I give you my word.

FATHER I want you to be careful to take good care of him.

DOCTOR Listen, I'll heave sixty sighs an hour for him. That's how careful I'll be to take good care of him.

FATHER (*pointing toward the wings, stage left*) Look, there's your patient. Let's watch what he does.

(*The two back off to an unobtrusive spot. As they do, Menaechmus of Epidamnus trudges in despondently. Without noticing them, he walks downstage and addresses the audience.*)

MENAECHMUS OF EPIDAMNUS God! What a day this one's been! Everything's gone against me. I thought I had kept what I did a secret—and my parasite spills the whole story, leaving me scared to death and in disgrace. That Ulysses of mine! The trouble he stirred up for his lord and master! (*Shaking his fist so hard his mantle slips from his shoulder*) As sure as I'm alive, I'll see to it he and his life part company. (*Snorting*) Now that's stupid of me, to call it *his* life. It's *mine:* he's stayed alive eating my food and at my expense. All right then, I'll make him part company with his soul. And that whore was every bit as bad. What else can you expect from a whore? Because I ask for the dress, so I can bring it back to my wife, she tells me she's already given it to me! Lord, oh lord, what a miserable life I lead!

FATHER (*sotto voce to the doctor*) You hear what he's saying?

DOCTOR (*sotto voce, with a knowing air*) Claims he's miserable.

FATHER (*sotto voce*) I wish you'd talk with him.

DOCTOR (*walking up to Menaechmus*) Good afternoon, Menaechmus. Will you please tell me why you have to leave your arm bare? Don't you realize the harm this can do to a man in your condition?

MENAECHMUS OF EPIDAMNUS (*glaring*) Oh, go hang yourself.

FATHER (*sotto voce to the doctor, anxiously*) Notice anything?

DOCTOR (*sotto voce to the father*) Lord, yes! (*Shaking his head*) Even an acre of hellebore[1] couldn't cure this case. (*Turning back to Menaechmus*) I say, Menaechmus—

MENAECHMUS OF EPIDAMNUS (*impatiently*) What do you want?

DOCTOR (*assuming his professional manner*) Answer my questions, please. Do you·drink white or red wine?

MENAECHMUS OF EPIDAMNUS Why don't you go straight to hell?

DOCTOR (*sotto voce to the father, clucking mournfully*) Beginning to show the initial symptoms of a seizure.

MENAECHMUS OF EPIDAMNUS (*disgustedly*) Why don't you ask me whether my diet includes purple or red or yellow bread? Or birds with scales? Or fish with feathers?

FATHER (*sotto voce to the doctor, urgently*) Good god! You hear him talk? He's delirious! What are you waiting for? Quick, give him some medicine before he goes completely insane!

DOCTOR (*sotto voce, pontifically*) Not yet. I still have some questions to ask.

FATHER (*to himself, between his teeth*) Your nonsense will be the death of me!

DOCTOR (*to Menaechmus*) Tell me this: do your eyes at times become fixed and staring?

MENAECHMUS OF EPIDAMNUS What's that? You damned fool! What do you think I am, a lobster?

[1] The standard ancient remedy for insanity.

DOCTOR (*ignoring the outburst and nodding knowingly*) Now tell me this: does your stomach ever growl, so far as you've noticed?

MENAECHMUS OF EPIDAMNUS   After meals, no; when I'm hungry, yes.

DOCTOR (*sotto voce to the father, puzzled*) So help me, there's nothing insane about that answer! (*Turning back to Menaechmus*) Do you sleep through the night? Do you have trouble falling asleep when you go to bed?

MENAECHMUS OF EPIDAMNUS   When my bills are paid, I sleep through. (*Suddenly losing his patience*) You and your questions! God damn you to hell!

DOCTOR (*sotto voce to the father, nodding knowingly*) The start of a fit of insanity. Did you hear what he said? Watch out for him!

FATHER (*sotto voce to the doctor*) Oh no. To hear him talk now, he's Nestor himself compared with what he was before. After all, just a few minutes ago he was calling his wife a mad bitch.

MENAECHMUS OF EPIDAMNUS (*overhearing this, roaring*) *What* did I call her?

FATHER   I was saying that, in a fit of insanity—

MENAECHMUS OF EPIDAMNUS (*interrupting, as before*) Insanity? Me?

FATHER (*angrily*) Yes, you. And you threatened to trample me down with a four-horse chariot. I saw you do it with my own eyes. I can prove you did it.

MENAECHMUS OF EPIDAMNUS (*snorting*) Oh sure. And I can prove you stole the holy halo from god almighty. And that you were packed off to prison for it. And that after they let you out, you were tarred and feathered. And what's more, I can prove you killed your father and sold your mother. What do you say? Don't I swap insult for insult just like some one who's sane?

FATHER (*to the doctor, pleading*) For god's sake, please, doctor, hurry and do whatever you're going to do! Don't you see the man's losing his mind?

DOCTOR Do you know the best thing to do? Have him brought to my clinic.

FATHER (*doubtfully*) You really think so?

DOCTOR (*heartily*) Of course. I'll be able to treat him there just the way I want.

FATHER Well, as you wish.

DOCTOR (*to Menaechmus, cheerily*) I'll dose you with helle-bore for about three weeks.

MENAECHMUS OF EPIDAMNUS And I'll string you up and dose you with a whip for four. (*Stomps away angrily out of earshot.*)

DOCTOR (*to the father*) Go get some men to carry him.

FATHER How many will we need?

DOCTOR Considering the symptoms I've observed, four would be the minimum.

FATHER I'll have them here right away. Doctor, you keep an eye on him.

DOCTOR (*hastily*) Oh no. I've got to get back to make ready whatever—er—has to be made ready. (*Airily, as he prudently hustles off, stage left*) You just have your servants bring him to me.

FATHER I'll see to it. He'll be there.

DOCTOR (*as he disappears into the wings*) I'm off now.

FATHER (*as he limps off resignedly at his top speed after the doctor*) Good-by.

MENAECHMUS OF EPIDAMNUS (*to the audience*) My father-in-law's left; the doctor's left; I'm alone. God almighty, what's going on? What are these men saying I'm crazy for? Why, I haven't had a sick day since the day I was born. Me insane? I don't even start fights or get into arguments! And I'm sane enough to think everyone else is sane and to recognize people and talk with them. If they can make the mistake of saying I'm crazy, maybe they're the ones who are crazy!

(*Paces up and down a moment in silence. Then, shaking his head despondently*) Now what do I do? I want to go home but my wife won't let me. (*Gesturing toward Lovey's house*) And no one's going to let me in *there*. Oh, the whole thing's a mess! I'll stay right where I am. I suppose when it gets dark I'll be allowed to go inside. (*Sits down gloomily in front of the door of his house.*)

(*Enter Messenio, stage right. He walks downstage and addresses the audience.*)

SONG

You know what marks the servant who's good,
The kind that'll watch, take care, arrange,
And plan for a master's livelihood?
It's taking as good—or better—care
When the master is out as when he's there.

If a slave's more concerned for his belly than back,
And his gullet than shins, then his brain's out of whack.

He must not forget that masters pay
The good-for-nothings in just one way:
With shackles, whip, and mill,
Hunger, fatigue, and chill;
The wage of no work and all play.

So to hell with bad acting, I'll be good, I've decided,
Since I hellishly hate to get hurt or get hided.
I can stomach the curses and cries—
It's the beatings and blows I despise.
And I'm many times happier having for lunch
The bread that's been browned
From what others have ground
Than grinding myself for all others to munch.

So I see that orders get obeyed
 With speed and skill and no fuss made.
The system works out well for me:
        Others are free to test
        What seems for them the best,
    But *I'll* be as I have to be.

Be a Johnny-on-the-spot when the master commands—
If I only can keep this one worry in mind,
Not a fault will he ever be able to find.

But the day's soon to come when my worrying's done,
When he'll pay me the freedom I've worked for and won.
        So till then I'll behave
        Like a dutiful slave,
        And I'll practice my knack
        Of being kind to my back!

(*He turns and walks briskly toward Lovey's door.*)

   Well, I settled the bags and the servants in the hotel as
he ordered, and now I've come to get him. I'll knock on the
door so he knows I'm here. Let's see if I can spring him safe
and sound from this sink of iniquity. I'm afraid, though, I
may be too late; the battle may be all over.

   (*Enter, stage left, the father with four husky slaves at his
heels.*)

FATHER (*to the slaves*)   I'm warning you: in the name of all
   that's holy, make sure you use your head when you carry
   out my orders, the ones I gave you before and am giving
   you now. Unless you don't give a damn for your shins and
   ribs, you'll pick up that man there (*pointing to Menaechmus of Epidamnus*) and carry him to the clinic. And none
   of you are to pay the slightest attention to any threats he
   makes. Well, why are you standing there? What are you
   waiting for? You should have had him up on your shoulders and on his way by now! I'm off to the doctor's; I'll be
   waiting when you get there.

(*The old man hurries off, stage left. The four huskies make for Menaechmus, who looks up as they gallop toward him.*)

MENAECHMUS OF EPIDAMNUS (*to himself*) This looks bad! What's going on here? God knows why, but these men are running toward me! (*To the men as they draw near*) What do you want? What are you after? (*Frantically*) Why are you surrounding me? (*With a rush they grab him and swing him on to their shoulders.*) Where are you taking me? Where am I going? Help! Murder! Save me, citizens of Epidamnus! (*To his abductors*) Let go of me!

MESSENIO (*whirling about at the commotion*) Good god in heaven, what's this I see? Some strangers carrying off my master! This is an outrage!

MENAECHMUS OF EPIDAMNUS (*despairingly*) Doesn't anyone have the heart to help me?

MESSENIO (*calling*) I do, master, the heart of a hero! (*Orating at the top of his lungs, as he races to the rescue*) People of Epidamnus! This is a foul, a criminal act! In a city street, in broad daylight, in peacetime, to kidnap my poor master, a gentleman on a visit to your town! (*Tearing into the abductors*) Let go of him!

MENAECHMUS OF EPIDAMNUS Whoever you are, for god's sake, stand by me! Don't let them get away with this flagrant miscarriage of justice!

MESSENIO (*shouting, as he flails away*) They won't. I'll stand by you. I'll help you. I'll defend you to the death. I won't let them kill you—better I get killed myself! Master, for god's sake, the one there that's got you by the shoulder —gouge his eye out! These three here, why I'll plow their jaws and plant my fists there. (*To his opponents*) Kidnap him, will you? You'll pay for it and pay plenty! Let go of him!

MENAECHMUS OF EPIDAMNUS (*triumphantly*) I got him by the eye!

MESSENIO   Tear it out of the socket! (*To his adversaries*) Criminals! Kidnapers! Bandits!

THE SLAVES (*shouting*)   Don't kill us! Please!

MESSENIO (*snarling*)   Then let go!

MENAECHMUS OF EPIDAMNUS (*to his abductors*)   What do you mean by laying hands on me! (*To Messenio*) Sock 'em on the jaw!

MESSENIO (*as his three opponents break and run*)   On your way! Go to hell, the bunch of you! (*Rushes over and lands a haymaker on Menaechmus' opponent*) And here's this from me! A bonus for being the last one out of here. (*To Menaechmus, smugly, as the four scamper off, stage left*) Well, I rearranged the geography of their faces to suit my taste. Believe me, master, I came to the rescue just in time.

MENAECHMUS OF EPIDAMNUS (*fervently*)   I don't know who you are, mister, but god's blessings on you forever. If it hadn't been for you, I wouldn't have lived to see the sun go down today.

MESSENIO (*promptly*)   Then if you want to do right by me, damn it all, you'll set me free.

MENAECHMUS OF EPIDAMNUS   Set you free? Me?

MESSENIO   Sure, master. I just saved your life, didn't I?

MENAECHMUS OF EPIDAMNUS   What are you talking about? Mister, you're making a mistake.

MESSENIO   Me making a mistake? What do you mean?

MENAECHMUS OF EPIDAMNUS   I give you my solemn oath, I'm not your master.

MESSENIO (*taking this as a cruel joke, bitterly*)   Don't give me that!

MENAECHMUS OF EPIDAMNUS (*earnestly*)   I'm not lying to you. (*Ruefully*) No servant of mine ever did as much for me as you have.

MESSENIO (*as before*)   All right. If you say I'm not your slave, why don't you let me go free?

MENAECHMUS OF EPIDAMNUS (*smiling*) If it's up to me, by all means. Be a free man. Go where you like.

MESSENIO (*unable to believe his ears*) You mean it? It's official?

MENAECHMUS OF EPIDAMNUS (*as before*) If I have any official rights over you, it certainly is.

MESSENIO (*ecstatically*) Hail, my patron! (*Menaechmus winces at the title, remembering the experience in that capacity that cost him his lunch. Messenio launches into an imaginary dialogue with his fellow slaves*) "Well, well, Messenio, so you're a free man. Congratulations!" "Thank you, thank you all." (*Turning back to Menaechmus, earnestly*) Patron, I want you to keep ordering me around the same as when I was your servant. I'll live with you, and, when you go back home, I'll go with you.

MENAECHMUS OF EPIDAMNUS (*aside, wincing again*) Not a chance!

MESSENIO I'll go back to the hotel now and get the bags and the money for you. The wallet with our cash is safe under lock and key in my satchel. I'll bring it to you right now.

MENAECHMUS OF EPIDAMNUS (*promptly*) You do that. And hurry.

MESSENIO (*over his shoulder as he rushes off, stage right*) You'll get it back just as it was when you gave it to me. Wait for me here.

MENAECHMUS OF EPIDAMNUS (*to the audience, shaking his head in bewilderment*) Amazing, the amazing things that have happened to me! People tell me I'm not me and lock me out of the house. Then this fellow, (*grinning*) the one I just now emancipated, comes along, claims he's my slave, and tells me he's going to bring me a wallet full of cash. If he actually does, I'll tell him he's a free man and he's to leave me and go wherever he likes; I don't want him asking for the money back when he gets his sanity back. My father-in-law and the doctor say *I'm* mad. It's all a mystery to me. I must be dreaming the whole business.

Well, I'll pay a call on this whore here, even if she is sore at me. Maybe I can get her to give back the dress so I can bring it home.

(*He enters Lovey's house. A second later Menaechmus of Syracuse and Messenio enter, stage right, deep in conversation.*)

MENAECHMUS OF SYRACUSE (*angrily*) I sent you off with orders to come back here for me. Where do you get the nerve to tell me I saw you anywhere since?

MESSENIO (*frantically*) Just a minute ago I rescued you, right in front of this house, from four men who were carrying you off on their shoulders. You were hollering to heaven and earth for help, and I ran up and by fighting hard made them let you go. And, because I saved your life that way, you set me free. (*Bitterly*) And then, when I said I was going for the money and the bags, you ran ahead and got there first just so you could deny everything you did!

MENAECHMUS OF SYRACUSE (*incredulously*) I set you free?

MESSENIO You certainly did.

MENAECHMUS OF SYRACUSE (*grimly*) I'll tell you what I certainly did: made up my mind to be a slave myself before I ever set you free. (*Starts stalking off, stage right.*)

(*The door of Lovey's house opens, and Menaechmus of Epidamnus stomps out. He turns and talks to Lovey and her maid inside.*)

MENAECHMUS OF EPIDAMNUS (*through the doorway, excittedly*) Listen, you bitches, you can cross your heart and swear all you want but, damn it all, that's not going to change things: I did *not* walk off with that bracelet and dress.

(*Messenio glances over his shoulder at the sound of the voice—and does a double take.*)

MESSENIO Good god in heaven! What's this I see?

MENAECHMUS OF SYRACUSE (*sourly, and without stopping*) What?

MESSENIO Your reflection!

MENAECHMUS OF SYRACUSE (*stopping*) What are you talking about?

MESSENIO (*excitedly*) He's your image! He couldn't be more like you.

MENAECHMUS OF SYRACUSE (*following Messenio's gaze*) By god, you know, when I think about what I look like, he *does* resemble me.

MENAECHMUS OF EPIDAMNUS (*turning from the door and noticing Messenio*) Hello there, my savior, whoever you are.

MESSENIO (*to Menaechmus of Epidamnus, tensely*) Mister, would you please do me a favor and tell me your name, if you don't mind?

MENAECHMUS OF EPIDAMNUS (*earnestly*) I mind any favors you ask for? I should say not. That isn't the treatment you deserve from me! The name's Menaechmus—

MENAECHMUS OF SYRACUSE (*interrupting*) Hell, no! That's my name!

MENAECHMUS OF EPIDAMNUS (*ignoring him*) —and I was born at Syracuse in Sicily.

MENAECHMUS OF SYRACUSE (*resentfully*) That's *my* city and country.

MENAECHMUS OF EPIDAMNUS (*looking at him for the first time*) What's that you say?

MENAECHMUS OF SYRACUSE (*glowering*) Nothing but the truth.

MESSENIO (*stares at the two in utter puzzlement. Then, to himself, uncertainly, pointing to Menaechmus of Epidamnus*) This must be the one I know; *he's* my master. I thought I was (*pointing to Menaechmus of Syracuse*) his servant, but I'm really (*pointing to Menaechmus of Epidamnus*) his. (*Addressing Menaechmus of Epidamnus*) I thought he was you; (*guiltily*) matter of fact, I gave him quite a bit of trouble. (*To Menaechmus of Syracuse*) Please forgive me if I said anything to you that sounded stupid. I didn't mean to.

MENAECHMUS OF SYRACUSE (*in astonishment*) Are you crazy? You sound it. You and I came off the ship together today. Don't you remember?

MESSENIO (*astonished in his turn*) You're absolutely right. *You're* my master. (*To Menaechmus of Epidamnus, apologetically*) You'd better find yourself another servant. (*To Menaechmus of Syracuse*) Hello. (*To Menaechmus of Epidamnus*) Good-by. Take my word— (*pointing to Menaechmus of Syracuse*) this man is Menaechmus.

MENAECHMUS OF EPIDAMNUS No. *I* am.

MENAECHMUS OF SYRACUSE (*to Menaechmus of Epidamnus*) What sort of nonsense is this? You're Menaechmus?

MENAECHMUS OF EPIDAMNUS That's what I said. Son of Moschus.

MENAECHMUS OF SYRACUSE (*bewildered*) The son of my father? You?

MENAECHMUS OF EPIDAMNUS (*smiling*) No, mister, of *mine*. I have no intention of adopting your father or stealing him from you.

MESSENIO (*to the audience, in great excitement*) Something just dawned on me! A hope that no one could have hoped for! God in heaven, make it come true! I tell you, unless my mind is going back on me, these two are the twin brothers! After all, they both give the same names for father and fatherland. I've got to have a word with my master in private. (*Calling out*) Menaechmus!

MENAECHMUS OF EPIDAMNUS ⎫
                              ⎬ What do you want?
MENAECHMUS OF SYRACUSE   ⎭

MESSENIO I don't want you both! Which one of you was on the ship with me?

MENAECHMUS OF EPIDAMNUS Not I.

MENAECHMUS OF SYRACUSE I.

MESSENIO Then you're the one I want. Step over here, will you?

(*Messenio walks a few steps off to the side, and Menaechmus of Syracuse joins him.*)

MENAECHMUS OF SYRACUSE Here I am. What's up?

MESSENIO (*sotto voce, excitedly*) That man there is either a swindler or your twin brother! I've never seen two people more alike. Believe me, you two are more like each other than one drop of water or one drop of milk to another. Besides, he gives the same names as you for father and fatherland. We'd better go up to him and ask him some questions.

MENAECHMUS OF SYRACUSE (*catching Messenio's excitement*) That's a darned good idea! Thanks very much. But, please, do me a favor: you do it. (*As they walk back toward Menaechmus of Epidamnus*) Messenio, you're a free man if you can find out he's my brother.

MESSENIO (*fervently*) I hope I can.

MENAECHMUS OF SYRACUSE I hope so too.

MESSENIO (*to Menaechmus of Epidamnus, drawing himself up self-importantly, like a judge questioning a party to a case*) Harrumph! (*As Menaechmus of Epidamnus looks at him inquiringly*) You stated, as I remember, that your name was Menaechmus.

MENAECHMUS OF EPIDAMNUS That's right.

MESSENIO (*gesturing toward Menaechmus of Syracuse*) This man's name is Menaechmus too. You stated you were born at Syracuse in Sicily; he was born there. You stated your father's name was Moschus; so was his. Now you can both help me—and yourselves at the same time.

MENAECHMUS OF EPIDAMNUS Anything you want from me, the answer's yes; you've earned it. I'm a free man, but I'm at your service just as if you'd bought and paid for me.

MESSENIO (*solemnly*) My hope is that the two of you will discover you are twin brothers, born the same day to the same mother and the same father.

MENAECHMUS OF EPIDAMNUS (*wistfully*)   What you're talking about is a miracle. Ah, if you could only do what you hope to!

MESSENIO (*determinedly*)   I can. But now let's start. Answer my questions, both of you.

MENAECHMUS OF EPIDAMNUS (*promptly*)   Ask away. I'll tell you everything I know.

MESSENIO   Is your name Menaechmus?

MENAECHMUS OF EPIDAMNUS   It is.

MESSENIO (*to Menaechmus of Syracuse*)   And yours too?

MENAECHMUS OF SYRACUSE   Yes.

MESSENIO (*to Menaechmus of Epidamnus*)   And you say your father's name was Moschus?

MENAECHMUS OF EPIDAMNUS   I do.

MENAECHMUS OF SYRACUSE   So do I. (*Receives a lordly look of disapproval from Messenio for anticipating the question.*)

MESSENIO (*to Menaechmus of Epidamnus*)   And you were born at Syracuse?

MENAECHMUS OF EPIDAMNUS   Absolutely.

MESSENIO (*to Menaechmus of Syracuse*)   What about you?

MENAECHMUS OF SYRACUSE   You know I was.

MESSENIO   So far everything agrees perfectly. We'll go on; your attention please. (*To Menaechmus of Epidamnus*) Tell me, what is your earliest recollection of your homeland?

MENAECHMUS OF EPIDAMNUS (*holding his forehead and closing his eyes as he struggles to remember*)   Going off to Tarentum with my father on a business trip. Then wandering off in the crowd and being carried away.

MENAECHMUS OF SYRACUSE (*exclaiming involuntarily*)   God in heaven! Help me now!

MESSENIO (*with the voice of authority*)   What's the meaning of this shouting? Can't you keep quiet! (*To Menaech-*

mus of Epidamnus) How old were you when your father took you from your fatherland?

MENAECHMUS OF EPIDAMNUS Seven. I remember because I was just beginning to lose my baby teeth. (*Sadly*) I never saw my father again.

MESSENIO Answer this: how many sons were there in your family?

MENAECHMUS OF EPIDAMNUS As best as I can remember, two.

MESSENIO Which was the older, you or your brother?

MENAECHMUS OF EPIDAMNUS We were the same age.

MESSENIO How is that possible?

MENAECHMUS OF EPIDAMNUS We were twins.

MENAECHMUS OF SYRACUSE (*exclaiming fervently*) Heaven has come to my rescue!

MESSENIO (*icily*) If you're going to interrupt, I'm not going to say another word!

MENAECHMUS OF SYRACUSE (*meekly*) No, no—I won't say another word.

MESSENIO (*to Menaechmus of Epidamnus*) Tell me: did you both have the same name?

MENAECHMUS OF EPIDAMNUS Oh, no. You see, I was called Menaechmus, as now, but his name was Sosicles.

MENAECHMUS OF SYRACUSE (*to himself, wildly excited*) For me the case is proved. I can't hold back, I've got to take him in my arms. (*Taking his hands*) Welcome, my brother, my twin brother! I'm Sosicles!

MENAECHMUS OF EPIDAMNUS (*gently disengaging his hands; uncertainly*) If that's so, how come you got the name Menaechmus?

MENAECHMUS OF SYRACUSE When the news came about you and about father's death, grandfather changed it: he gave me yours instead.

MENAECHMUS OF EPIDAMNUS I guess it could have happened that way. But answer this question.

MENAECHMUS OF SYRACUSE (*eagerly*)   What is it?

MENAECHMUS OF EPIDAMNUS (*intently*)   What was our mother's name?

MENAECHMUS OF SYRACUSE   Teuximarcha.

MENAECHMUS OF EPIDAMNUS (*rushing to embrace him*) Right! Welcome to you, my brother! I never expected to see you again, and now, after so many years, I have you before me.

MENAECHMUS OF SYRACUSE   And welcome to you, my brother. I searched and searched for you right up to this moment, and now, after so many trials and tribulations, I have the joy of having found you.

MESSENIO (*to Menaechmus of Syracuse, a light dawning*) That explains it! That girl called you by your brother's name. I'm sure she thought it was he she was inviting in to lunch, not you.

MENAECHMUS OF EPIDAMNUS (*smiling broadly*)   As a matter of fact, I had told her to prepare lunch for me today. My wife wasn't to know a thing about it. I sneaked a dress of hers out of the house and gave it to the girl.

MENAECHMUS OF SYRACUSE (*holding up the dress*)   You mean the one I have here?

MENAECHMUS OF EPIDAMNUS (*astonished*)   That's it! How did it ever get to you?

MENAECHMUS OF SYRACUSE (*laughing*)   That girl who carried me off to give me lunch insisted I had given it to her. The wench wined me and dined me in style and then went to bed with me. I made off with the dress and this bracelet (*holding it up*).

MENAECHMUS OF EPIDAMNUS   Believe me, I'm delighted to hear something nice happened to you because of me. When she invited you in, she thought it was me, you know.

MESSENIO (*breaking in, anxiously*)   There's nothing to stop you now, is there, from giving me my freedom the way you promised?

MENAECHMUS OF EPIDAMNUS A perfectly proper and fair request, my brother. Do it for my sake.

MENAECHMUS OF SYRACUSE Messenio, you're a free man.

MENAECHMUS OF EPIDAMNUS (*his eyes twinkling, mimicking the exact tone of voice Messenio had used a few moments ago*) Well, well, Messenio, so you're a free man. Congratulations!

MESSENIO (*meaningfully, holding out his hand, palm upward*) But I could use a better beginning to make sure I stay free.

MENAECHMUS OF SYRACUSE (*pointedly ignoring the hand and the remark*) Now that things have turned out just the way we wanted, my brother, let's both of us go back to our homeland.

MENAECHMUS OF EPIDAMNUS Brother, I'll do whatever you wish. I can hold an auction and sell whatever I own around here. (*Leading him toward the door of his house*) But let's go inside for now.

MENAECHMUS OF SYRACUSE Yes, let's.

MESSENIO (*who had been listening avidly to the last exchange*) Do you know what favor I'd like to ask?

MENAECHMUS OF EPIDAMNUS What?

MESSENIO (*eagerly*) Let me run the auction.

MENAECHMUS OF EPIDAMNUS It's all yours.

MESSENIO (*rubbing his hands delightedly*) Then how about my announcing right now that an auction will take place?

MENAECHMUS OF EPIDAMNUS All right. Make it a week from today. (*The two brothers enter the house.*)

MESSENIO (*to the audience, in an auctioneer's chant*): Hear ye, hear ye! Selling at auction, one week from today, rain or shine, the property of Menaechmus. For sale: slaves, household effects, farm land, and buildings. All items to go for whatever they'll bring, and all payments strictly cash. Sale includes one wife—if anyone will bid. (*Leaning for-*

ward, in a confidential tone) If you ask me, the whole auction won't net fifty cents.

(*Straightening up, in ringing tones*) And now, ladies and gentlemen, good-by. Your loudest applause, please!

PSEUDOLUS

DRAMATIS PERSONAE

PSEUDOLUS, *servant of Simo* (*slave*)

CALIDORUS, *a young man about town, son of Simo*

BALLIO, *a pimp*

SIMO, *an elderly gentleman, father of Calidorus*

CALLIPHO, *an elderly gentleman, neighbor of Simo*

HARPAX, *orderly of an officer in the Macedonian army* (*slave*)

CHARINUS, *friend of Calidorus*

A SLAVE BOY OF BALLIO

A COOK

MONKEY (SIMIA), *servant belonging to Charinus' family* (*slave*)

SERVANTS AND COURTESANS

SCENE

A street in Athens. Three houses front on it: stage left Simo's, center Callipho's, right Ballio's. The exit on stage left leads downtown, that on stage right to the country.

PROLOGUE

You'd better get up and stretch your legs. There's a play by Plautus coming on, and it's a long one.[1]

ACT I

(*The door of Calidorus' house opens, and Calidorus and Pseudolus walk out.*

Calidorus, "beauty's gift," is ancient comedy's traditional rich man's son: handsome, well-dressed, empty-headed, and unemployable. At the moment he is in a ludicrously blank state of despair, staring wordlessly at a set of waxed wooden tablets bound with cord (the ancient equivalent of folded sheets of paper) which he clutches with both hands.

If Calidorus has no brains, Pseudolus, "tricky," the family servant, has enough for both. These are encased in an enormous head, which, along with a bulging belly and a pair of oversize feet, give Pseudolus a most deceptively clownlike appearance.)

PSEUDOLUS If I could figure out from this silence of yours what's the misery that's making you miserable, I'd have the pleasure of saving two men trouble: me of asking you questions and you of answering them. But I can't, so I've got to put the question. Tell me, what's the matter? For days now you've been going around more dead than alive, holding that letter in your hands, washing it down with tears, and not confiding in anyone. Talk, will you! I'm in the dark; share the light with me.

CALIDORUS (*dully*) I'm miserable. Miserably miserable.

PSEUDOLUS God forbid!

[1] The original prologue has been lost.

CALIDORUS   God has no jurisdiction in my case. I'm serving a sentence from Love, not God.

PSEUDOLUS   Am I allowed to know what it's all about? After all, up to now I was Accessory-in-Chief to all your projects.

CALIDORUS   I haven't changed.

PSEUDOLUS   Then let me in on what's ailing you. (*Importantly*) Resources, services, or good advice at your disposal.

CALIDORUS   (*handing him the tablets*)   Take this letter. Then you can recite yourself the story of the worry and woe that's wasting me away.

PSEUDOLUS   (*taking the tablets*)   Anything to make you happy. (*Turning them every which way and holding them at various distances from his eyes*) Hey, what's this?

CALIDORUS   What's what?

PSEUDOLUS   If you ask me, the letters here want to have babies: each one's mounting the other.

CALIDORUS   (*bitterly*)   Got to have your joke, don't you?

PSEUDOLUS   (*still turning and twisting the tablets*)   Maybe our Lady of the Riddles can read them, but I swear nobody else can.

CALIDORUS   (*choking up*)   Why are you so cruel to the lovely letters of this lovely letter written in such a lovely hand?

PSEUDOLUS   Damn it all, I ask you now: do hens have hands? Because, believe me, some hen scribbled these letters.

CALIDORUS   (*exasperated*)   You make me sick! (*Reaching for the tablets*) Either read it or hand it back.

PSEUDOLUS   (*holding them out of reach*)   Oh no. I'll read it to the bitter end. Listen, and keep your mind on what I say.

CALIDORUS   (*dumbly*)   I can't—it left me.

PSEUDOLUS   Call it back.

CALIDORUS   No, I'll keep quiet. *You* call it back. From that letter there. Because that's where my mind is now; it's not inside me.

PSEUDOLUS (*slyly*)   I see your girl friend, Calidorus.

CALIDORUS (*coming out of his apathy with a start*)   Pseudolus, please, I beg you! Tell me where she is!

PSEUDOLUS (*holding up the tablets and pointing to the signature*)   Here. Stretched out in this letter here. Lying on the lines.

CALIDORUS (*throwing a punch at him*)   I swear by all that's holy, I hope you go straight—

PSEUDOLUS (*ducking nimbly and grinning*)   —to heaven.

CALIDORUS (*tragically*)   I was like grass in summer, a minute ago: suddenly sprang up, and just as suddenly died down.

PSEUDOLUS   Quiet now while I read the letter. (*Clears his throat, adjusts the tablets, and makes other elaborate preparations.*)

CALIDORUS (*impatiently*)   Get going, will you!

PSEUDOLUS (*reading aloud*)   "Dear sweetheart Calidorus. With tears in my eyes and tremors in my mind and heart and soul, through these waxed boards and piece of line and lines of communication, I send you my best wishes for *your* well-being—and my prayers for your help with *mine*."

CALIDORUS (*frenzied*)   Pseudolus! I'm lost! I'll never get what I need to help with hers!

PSEUDOLUS   What do you need?

CALIDORUS (*dolefully*)   Gold.

PSEUDOLUS (*sticking the tablets in front of Calidorus' nose*)   She sends best wishes in wood, and you want to answer in gold? Watch what you're doing, will you!

CALIDORUS (*dully*)   Just go on reading. You'll find out soon enough how urgent it is that I get my hands on some gold.

PSEUDOLUS (*resuming his reading*)   "The pimp has sold me for five thousand dollars to a foreigner, a major from Macedon. He's already left for home, after putting up a deposit of four thousand; all that's holding matters up is a mere one thousand dollars. To arrange payment of this, the major left behind as means of identification his own picture

stamped by his seal ring on a wax seal; the pimp is to hand
me over to whoever arrives with an identical seal. And the
date fixed for my departure is this coming Dionysus Day."

CALIDORUS (*miserably*)   That's tomorrow. My end is practically upon me—unless you can help.

PSEUDOLUS (*impatiently*)   Let me finish reading.

CALIDORUS   Go ahead. (*Starry-eyed*) It makes me feel I'm
talking with her. Read on; now you'll mix in some sweet
for me along with the bitter.

PSEUDOLUS (*reading*)   "Now our love, our life, the things
we shared, our jokes and play and talks and soft-sweet
kisses, the tight embrace of impassioned bodies in love,
the soft pressure of parted lips meeting tenderly, the bur-
geoning of my breasts under the sweet caress of your hand
—all these joys will be taken away, torn away, trampled
away—for you as well as for me—if you do not come to my
rescue and I to yours. I have done my share: now you know
all that I know. I shall soon find out whether your love
is real or pretended. Your loving Rosy."

CALIDORUS (*sobbing*)   A piece of writing to make a man
miserable, Pseudolus.

PSEUDOLUS (*glancing at the handwriting again*)   Oh yes.
Absolutely miserable.

CALIDORUS (*reproachfully*)   Then why aren't you crying?

PSEUDOLUS   My eyes are made out of sand. I can't get them
to squirt a single tear.

CALIDORUS   How come?

PSEUDOLUS (*dryly*)   Chronic dryness of the eyes. Runs
through the whole family.

CALIDORUS (*dismayed*)   You don't have the heart to help me?

PSEUDOLUS (*shrugging disinterestedly*)   What do you expect
from me?

CALIDORUS (*groaning*)   Ai!

PSEUDOLUS   Ai's? Good god, don't spare *them*. I'll be your
supplier.

CALIDORUS (*dolefully*) I'm in a bad way. I can't borrow a sou from a soul—

PSEUDOLUS (*grinning*) Ai!

CALIDORUS —and I don't have a cent of my own—

PSEUDOLUS (*as before*) Ai!

CALIDORUS —and tomorrow that man's going to take my girl away.

PSEUDOLUS Ai!

CALIDORUS (*bitterly*) Is this the way you help me?

PSEUDOLUS I'm giving you what I've got to give. (*Shaking his head ruefully*) It's the one item I have a vast accumulation of in our house.

CALIDORUS (*resigned*) Then it's all over with me today. Could you please lend me two dollars? I'll pay you back tomorrow.

PSEUDOLUS I couldn't raise that much even if I put my own self in hock. What are you going to do with two dollars, anyway?

CALIDORUS Buy myself a rope.

PSEUDOLUS What for?

CALIDORUS To turn myself into a pendulum. I've decided to darken my eyes before dark today.

PSEUDOLUS Then who'll pay me back my two dollars if I lend it to you? (*Suspiciously*) Are you deliberately planning to hang yourself just to do me out of two dollars if I lend it to you?

CALIDORUS (*starting to sob again*) I simply can't go on living if she's taken away from me and carried far, far away.

PSEUDOLUS Stop crying, you dumb cluck! You'll live.

CALIDORUS Why shouldn't I cry? I don't have a penny in my pocket and not the slightest prospect of borrowing anything from anybody.

PSEUDOLUS (*impatiently*) As I gather from this letter, unless you can cry some cash for her, all this shedding of tears to demonstrate your affections does about as much good as using a sieve for a cistern. (*As Calidorus starts wailing louder than ever*) But stop worrying, fond lover: I won't desert you. I'm a good operator; I have high hopes of finding salvation for you somewhere—financial salvation. Where am I going to get it? I can't tell you where; I don't know where. But I'll get it all right: I have a hunch today's my lucky day.

CALIDORUS (*hopelessly*)   You say you can do it—if only you can do what you say!

PSEUDOLUS (*hurt*)   Why, you know darn well the kind of ruckus I can raise once I start my hocus-pocus.

CALIDORUS (*desperately*)   My life depends on you! You're my only hope!

PSEUDOLUS (*airily*)   I'll arrange either to get you the girl or the five thousand. Will that satisfy you?

CALIDORUS (*doubtfully*)   Yes—if you'll do it.

PSEUDOLUS (*in the best lawyerlike fashion*)   Now put in a formal request for five thousand so I can prove I perform what I promise. (*Calidorus stares at him blankly*) For god's sake, ask, will you! I'm dying to make you a promise.

CALIDORUS (*his heart not in it*)   Do you hereby agree to give me five thousand in cash today?

PSEUDOLUS   I hereby agree. And now stop bothering me. And, just so you won't tell me later that I didn't tell you, I'm telling you in advance: if I can't get it from anyone else, I'll hit your father up for it.

CALIDORUS (*fervently*)   God bless you! (*Becoming very grave*) But I want to be a dutiful son, so, if possible, put the touch on my mother too.

PSEUDOLUS (*confidently*)   You're all set. Go to bed. Close your little ears.

CALIDORUS   Ears? Don't you mean eyes?

PSEUDOLUS   Less hackneyed the way I said it. (*Turning to the audience; in the tones of a town crier*) And now, so no one will say I didn't warn him, I hereby give public notice

to everybody, voters, citizens, all my friends and acquaint-
ances: watch out for me all day long! Don't trust me!

CALIDORUS   Shh! Keep quiet! Please!

PSEUDOLUS (*surprised*)   What's up?

CALIDORUS   The pimp's door handle just twisted.

PSEUDOLUS   I wish to god it was his neck.

CALIDORUS   And there he is, the dirty double-crosser. He's
coming out.

(*The two move to an unobtrusive spot off to the side. The
door swings open, and Ballio, "tosser around," the pimp, steps
out, hefting a mean-looking whip.*

*Ballio is a businessman in a thoroughly unpleasant business:
he owns a bevy of slave girls whom he supplies to those with
the wherewithal to hire them or buy them outright. A strag-
gly beard on his chin, a permanent snarl on his lips, an
avaricious glint in his eye, and a filthy miserly get-up make
him as unappetizing in appearance as in métier.*)

SONG

BALLIO (*turning and shouting through the open door*)
Come out of the house, good-for-nothings, come out!
What a mistake to have bought you and kept you about!

(*Six terrified slave boys—miserable, underfed specimens in
rags—scamper out of the door and huddle in front of it; one
holds a shopping basket and a purse, another a jug, another
an ax. Ballio eyes them distastefully, then turns to the audience.*)

Not a one in the lot ever got the idea
To do anything good.
(*Brandishing the whip*)
                    Without using this here,
They're all useless. To put them to use takes abuse.
And i've never seen hides more like donkeys', I swear:
They've been drubbed so, they've even grown calluses
there;

Why, to thrash them takes less out of them than of you.
To be wear-the-whip-outers comes natural to
   The whole breed. The one thought in their heads
      Is to snatch, steal,
      Grab, make hay,
      Gorge, swill,
      And run away.
It's their one, single purpose in life. Why, I say
I'd as soon let a wolf guard my sheep any day,
As let these watch my house any time I'm away.

(*Ballio glares at them. They summon up sickly smiles. He turns back to the audience.*)

Oh, their faces look fine; you can't go by their looks.
It's at work that they pull every trick in the books.

(*He swings around abruptly and starts flailing with the whip.*)

Get the sleep from your eyes! Get the sloth from your
   brain!

(*Lowers the whip. Importantly*)

Pay attention. I'll shortly begin to explain
   The orders of the day.
Listen hard or I'll batter your butts till they turn
   Every color, as gay
As a highly embroidered Neapolitan shawl
Or a Persian brocade with its beasties and all.

(*Shifts to a deadly menacing tone*)

I issued orders yesterday assigning each of you
A station and official list of things he had to do.
You're such a bunch of loafers, though, such inborn stink-
   ers that

(*Shaking the whip*)

You've forced me to remind you of your duties with this
   cat!

(*Wearily lowering the whip*)

My whip and I admit defeat; the victory's yours instead.
And it's all because of the way you're made—so hard in
   hide and head!

(*As the slaves visibly relax, he suddenly flails about madly
with the whip, and they all make a wild scramble for safety.
He addresses the audience with mock exasperation, gesturing
toward the cowering slaves who are paying far more attention
to the arc described by the whip than to him.*)

Now look at that, if you please! You see the way their
   minds will stray?

(*Turning back to the slaves*)

You mind me now, you hear! You tune those ears to what
   I say.

You stinkers, born and bred with special whip-proof back
   and side,

Remember that my rawhide's always harder than your hide.

(*Lunges suddenly and lands a blow on the nearest one,
who lets out a howl.*)

What's up? It hurts? It's what I give a slave who's snotty
   to

His master. Now come here; face me, and hear what you're
   to do.

(*The slaves line up, keeping a wary eye on the whip. Ballio
addresses the one who is carrying a jug.*)

First you who's got the jug. Get water and fill the cooking
   pot.

(*He turns to the one carrying an ax.*)

And you with the ax I appoint my Chief of Fuel Supply.

SLAVE (*timidly showing the ax*)

                                        But it's not

Got an edge, it's too dull to use!

BALLIO (*grinning like a hyena*)

                     So what?

(*Gesturing toward the whole cowering group*)

                     The whip's dulled your edge too.

Doesn't make the slightest difference to me—I keep using
   all of you.

(*Ballio turns to the third.*)

You make that whole house shine. You've got your job, now
   hop, you lout!

(*To the fourth*)

And you're Official Chair-Man.

(*To the fifth*)

                        And you clean silver and lay it out.

(*To all of them*)

Once I'm back from shopping, mind I find that everything's
   done—

Sweeping, setting, cleaning, shining—no chore undone, not
   one!

(*Switching to a tone of bloodcurdling enthusiasm*)

   It's my birthday today. You must help celebrate.
   Put the pig in the pot, from the trotters to pate.
   Is that clear? I'm inviting big names; a big splash
   Is the thing—make them think that I squander the cash.
   Now go in and get going so there'll be no delay
   When the chef makes it here. Because *I'm* on my way
   To the market; I'm off on a fish-buying jag.

(*To the slave carrying a basket under one arm and a purse
over one shoulder*)

   Go in front. I'm back here to keep thieves from that bag.

(*They start walking off, while the others race inside. Ballio
suddenly stops short.*)

   Wait a second. I almost forgot. I'm not through.

(*Goes to the doorway and calls through it*)

   Can you hear me, you girls? I've an announcement for
     you.

(*Four flashily dressed, heavily made-up girls step out and
line up sullenly in front of him. He gives them his hyena grin,
and then addresses them.*)

You're all living in clover, my sweet little sprites.
You're all girls with a name, and the town's leading
    lights
Are your clients. Today I'll find out what you're at.
Do you work to get free? Or to gorge and get fat?
To acquire a nest egg? Or sleep until three?
Yes, today I'll work out who I think will get free
Or I think will wind up being sold for a whore.

(*Rubbing his hands, his eyes gleaming*)

Have your clients bring in birthday presents galore!
For today we lay in one year's bread, drink, and meat,
Or tomorrow I'll have you out walking the street.
Now, you know it's my birthday. Well, have them kick
    in,
All the boy friends for whom you've been "Doll," "Bunny-
    kin,"
"Cutie-pie," "Honeybunch," "Sweetheart," and "Pet,"
"Snookle-puss," "Babykins," "Ducky," et cet.
Make their slaves, bearing gifties, come by in brigades!

(*Glaring at them*)

All the jewelry, money, the clothes and brocades
That I've had to provide—what's it got me, I say?
Not a dime, only woe, from you bitches today!
All your passion's for drink, to tank up, whereas I
Have to live my whole life with a gullet bone dry!

(*He paces up and down a few seconds in a rage. Then, in
calmer tones*)

And now I'll call you up by name and give you each the
    word.
This plan's the best since no one then can claim she hadn't
    heard.
                    So, all of you,
                    Here's what you do.
I'll start with Sweetsie, darling of the men who market
    grain.

Since each one stocks a good-sized hill, you're please to
    make them rain
Enough on me to give our house a year's supply to eat,
A flood so big my name will change from "Pimp" to "King
    of Wheat."

PSEUDOLUS (*sotto voce, to Calidorus*)
    Do you hear the rat talk? Like a pretty big dealer,
    Don't you think?

CALIDORUS (*sotto voce, to Pseudolus*)
                Good god, yes! And a pretty big stealer.
Now shut up. Pay attention to what he says next.

BALLIO (*turning to the second girl*)
    Now listen, Golddig. You're the girl the butchers all adore.
    (They're like us pimps: they take their cut—their pound
        of flesh and more!)
    You bring me in three meathooks loaded down with beef
        today
    Or tomorrow you play Dirce—and her story goes this way:
    Her stepsons squared accounts with her by hitching her to
        a bull.
    Well, you I'll stretch on a meathook, see—and *that's* a bull
        with pull!

PSEUDOLUS (*aside, raging*)
    You hear him talk? I'm burning up—he's got me hopping
        mad!
    How *can* you, Youth of Athens, patronize a man this bad?
    Come out here, all you youngsters who've been buying love
        from pimps,
    Let's gather altogether, boys, and everyone take part
    To rid the citizen body of this canker at its heart!

(*Shakes his head gloomily, all his excitement suddenly
drained from him.*)

        Pseudolus, you've got to learn,
        Pseudolus, you've got no brains.

> Why, sex makes youngsters all behave
> Toward any pimp just like his slave
> And rush to do his every whim.
> And *you* want them to be so brave
> They'll up and do away with *him!*

CALIDORUS (*sotto voce, wildly*)

Oh, shut your trap! You give me a pain—you're drowning out what he's saying!

PSEUDOLUS (*meekly, deflated by his horrendous discovery*)

All right, I will.

CALIDORUS (*sotto voce, urgently*)

> Well, don't just say so. Do it! Stop your braying.

BALLIO (*turning to the third girl*)

Your turn. Now listen, Olive, sweetheart of the oil-trade crew.

When it comes to ready stock on hand, your lovers keep beaucoup.

I want a load of jugs of oil, and you'll produce tout' suite,

Or tomorrow *you'll* get boiled in oil and dumped out on the street;

I'll set a bed for you out there, where *you* won't get much rest

Though you'll be plenty tired—why say more? By now you've guessed.

You've got a mob of boy friends who just roll in oil, but you

Couldn't give your fellow slaves today a drop for their shampoo

Or give your lord and master some for juicing up his stew.

> I know the reason too:
> You don't have very much use for oil—
> Your anointing's done with alcohol!

(*Glaring at all of them*)

All right! You carry out the orders that I've given you today,

(*Shaking the whip*)

Or, gad, I'll let you have it, all at once and in one way!
*(He turns to the last girl, by far the best looking of the four.
It is* Phoenicium, *"Rosy," Calidorus' inamorata.)*

> And now the girl always just about to buy her freedom
> and dash.
> You're good at promising payment—but no good at raising
> cash.
> Now, heartthrob of the upper crust, to you I've this to say.
> Your boy friends, Rosy, own big farms; so you produce
> today
> A load of all the stuff they raise or tomorrow *you* will pay:
>> I'll have you walking streets, my dame,
>> Your hide tanned brighter than your name.

*(Ballio and his marketing attendant remain where they are.
The girls, shuffling despondently, start filing into the house
under Ballio's baleful gaze. He does not hear the following
conversation which Calidorus and Pseudolus hold sotto voce.)*

CALIDORUS *(agonized)*
> Pseudolus! Hear what he says?

PSEUDOLUS *(mimicking his tone)*
>> Calidorus! I heard.

(Thoughtfully)
> And I'm thinking it out.

CALIDORUS *(as before)*
>> What ideas have you got
> Of a gift I can send so he'll weaken and not
> Make a whore of my girl.

PSEUDOLUS *(patting his back encouragingly)*
>> Don't you worry. Don't be blue.

(Tapping his breast importantly)
> Because *I'll* do the worrying for me and for you.

(Smiling cannily)
> We've been swapping good wishes for years, he and I;
> We're old friends. Since today is his birthday, let's try

To prepare as a gift, which we'll send very soon,
A whole potful of trouble, one big as the moon!

CALIDORUS (*hopelessly*)
What's the use?

PSEUDOLUS (*taking him by the arm and starting to haul him off*)
                    Won't you please run along? You just go
And get thinking about something else.

CALIDORUS (*stubbornly resisting the pulling*)
                                        Whoa there, whoa!

PSEUDOLUS (*tugging harder*)
No there, no!

CALIDORUS (*almost in tears*)
            But I'm heartbroken!

PSEUDOLUS (*still hauling, though without much effect*)
                            Harden your heart.

CALIDORUS (*piteously*)
No, impossible.

PSEUDOLUS (*as before*)
            Do the impossible. Start.

CALIDORUS (*dumbly*)
I'm to start the impossible? How?

PSEUDOLUS (*as before*)
                            Fight your heart.
Turn your mind to what's good. Heart's in tears? Close
your ears!

CALIDORUS (*sadly and thoughtfully*)
Oh, that's nonsense. A lover must act like a fool.
Otherwise it's no fun.

PSEUDOLUS (*giving up the hauling and throwing up his hands in disgust*)
                    Since you won't stop this drool—

CALIDORUS (*taking him by the arm, piteously*)
My dear Pseudolus, please! Let me stay just a fool!

PSEUDOLUS (*pulling himself free, icily*)
Will you *please* let me go?

CALIDORUS (*dumbly*)

Let me be, let me be—

PSEUDOLUS (*ostentatiously turning on his heel and stalking off*)
All right, *I'll* let you be. In return you let *me*
Go on home.

CALIDORUS (*frantically*)
No, no, wait!

(*As Pseudolus stops, unenthusiastically*)

I'll be just as you wish.

PSEUDOLUS (*swiveling about and clapping him on the back*)
Now you're using your head!

(*At this moment the last of the girls shuffles inside, and Ballio turns around.*)

BALLIO (*to his marketing attendant*)

We should go for that fish.
Time's awasting. Lead on.

CALIDORUS (*catching sight of them going off, frantically*)
Hey, he's off! Call him back!

(*He wheels about to go after Ballio. Pseudolus grabs him.*)

PSEUDOLUS (*calmly*)
Easy, boy! What's the hurry?

CALIDORUS (*frantically*)

Because, if we're slack
He'll be gone!

BALLIO (*to his slave boy, kicking him brutally*)
So you're taking it easy, boy, eh?

PSEUDOLUS (*calling in dulcet tones*)
May I speak with you, birthday boy? Birthday boy! Hey!
Turn around and look back, will you please? Yes, we know
That you're rushed but we *must* hold you up, even so.

(*As Ballio keeps walking*)

Hey there, stop, will you! Look, there's some people here
  who
Are most anxious to talk over matters with you.

BALLIO (*stopping—but not turning; exasperated*)
  It's just when I'm rushed that these goddam yahoos
  Hold me up! What's the matter? Who is it?

PSEUDOLUS (*dramatically*)
                                      One who's
  Spent his life making sure that you prosper and thrive!

BALLIO (*as if to himself, muttering*)
  Spent his life? Then he's dead. I prefer one who's alive.

PSEUDOLUS
  Don't be snooty, there, you!

BALLIO
                         Don't annoy me, there, you!
  (*Ballio, still without turning around, starts walking again.*)

CALIDORUS (*to Pseudolus, frantically*)
  Hurry up! Hold him back!

BALLIO (*over his shoulder to his slave who is standing goggle-
eyed*)
                      Get a move on, you, too!

PSEUDOLUS (*to Calidorus*)
            Hey, come this way! Don't let him through!
  (*The two race around and stand blocking Ballio's way.*)

BALLIO (*to Pseudolus*)
           Whoever you are, I'll see you in hell!

PSEUDOLUS (*his voice carefully maintaining the ambiguity*)
  I'd like to see you.

BALLIO (*to Calidorus*)
                  And you as well.
  (*Over his shoulder to his slave as he charges off on a different tack.*)
        This way!

PSEUDOLUS (*nimbly barring the way again*)
        There's some things I'd like to clear.

BALLIO

But *I* wouldn't.

PSEUDOLUS (*wheedling*)

Things you'll like to hear.

BALLIO (*beginning to lose his temper*)

Will you let me go or not?

PSEUDOLUS (*grabbing his arm*)

At ease!

BALLIO (*thundering*)

Hands off!

CALIDORUS (*grabbing the other arm, desperately*)

But, Ballio, listen, please!

BALLIO (*contemptuously*)

I'm deaf to boys who talk hot air.

CALIDORUS (*humbly*)

I gave while I had.

BALLIO (*grinning evilly*)

And I took. That's fair.

CALIDORUS (*as before*)

When I get, I'll give.

BALLIO (*as before*)

When you do, I'll give too.

CALIDORUS (*tearing his hair*)

Oh my god! All the money and gifts that I gave!
And to think how I lost it! All gone to the grave!

BALLIO (*airily*)

With your cash dead and buried, you're just talking for
fun.
You're a fool if you try to go over what's done.

PSEUDOLUS (*to Ballio, trying bluster and pointing importantly
to Calidorus*)

Let me tell you, at least, who he happens to be—

BALLIO (*contemptuously*)

Oh, I've known all along who he was. And now he
Can just know who he is by himself, without me.

(He wheels about and starts to stomp off, calling over his shoulder to his slave.)

Shake a leg, will you!

PSEUDOLUS (*slyly*)

Ballio, turn around, please;
Turn around just this once, and you'll pocket some fees!

(Ballio stops in his tracks and swivels about.)

BALLIO (*to the audience*)   For that price I'll turn around. I could be praying to god almighty, I could have the holy offerings in my hand ready to give to him, and if a chance to make a buck came along, I'd forget all about religion. No matter what, the almighty dollar's one religion there's no resisting.

PSEUDOLUS (*to the audience*)   We bend the knees to heaven —and he snaps his finger at it.

BALLIO (*to the audience, rubbing his hands*)   I'll have a talk with them. (*To Pseudolus*) Greetings, stinkingest slave in Athens!

PSEUDOLUS (*with radiant benevolence*)   Heaven put its blessing upon you and give you what (*winking to Calidorus*) this boy and I wish for you. (*Switching to moral sternness*) But, if you deserve otherwise, may it put its curse upon you!

BALLIO (*blandly*)   How're you doing, Calidorus?

CALIDORUS   I'm dying. Perishing for love—and dead broke.

BALLIO   I'd have some pity—if I could feed my household on pity.

PSEUDOLUS (*breaking in impatiently*)   Look, we know what you're like, so you can skip the speeches. Do you know what we're here for?

BALLIO (*grinning*)   Just about. To see me in hell.

PSEUDOLUS   That plus what we just called you back for. Now listen carefully.

BALLIO (*brusquely*)   I'm listening. But whatever it is you're after, make it short. I'm busy now.

PSEUDOLUS (*gravely*) This boy here promised you five thousand for his girl, he promised it for a certain day, he hasn't
paid it yet, and he feels terribly sorry about it all.

BALLIO (*snarling*) Feeling sorry is a lot easier for a fellow
than feeling sore. He feels sorry because he didn't pay; I
feel sore because I didn't get paid.

PSEUDOLUS (*earnestly*) He'll pay; he'll find a way. Just hold
everything these next few days. You see, he's afraid you'll
sell his girl because you have it in for him.

BALLIO (*sullenly*) He had the chance to give me my money
a long time ago—*if* he had really wanted to.

CALIDORUS (*helplessly*) What if I didn't have it?

BALLIO (*to Calidorus, contemptuously*) If you were really in
love you'd have negotiated a loan—gone to a moneylender,
given him his few pennies interest, and then stolen it all
back from your father.

PSEUDOLUS (*with histrionic rage*) He steal from his father?
You have a nerve! No chance of *your* ever giving lessons in
honesty.

BALLIO (*grinning*) I'm a pimp. That's not my job.

CALIDORUS (*bitterly*) How could I steal anything from my
father? He's always so careful! (*Suddenly remembering
himself, in ringing tones*) What's more, even if I could, I
wouldn't. Filial duty, you know.

BALLIO (*disgustedly*) I hear you. Then snuggle up to that
filial duty of yours at night instead of Rosy. So filial duty
is more important to you than your love life, is it? All right,
then: is every man in the world your father? Isn't there
anyone you can hit up for a loan?

CALIDORUS (*miserably*) Loan? There's no such word any
more.

PSEUDOLUS (*to Ballio, confidentially*) Listen, ever since that
gang of fakers finished tanking up at the till—the ones who
always guard their own pockets but take from others' and
never pay back—all the moneylenders have been playing it
safe, they're not trusting anyone.

CALIDORUS (*to Ballio, nodding dumbly*)   I'm in a bad way.
I can't scrape up a cent anywhere. I'm so bad off I'm dying
twice, from love and insufficient funds.

BALLIO (*helpfully*)   Why don't you buy olive oil on credit
and sell for cash? Believe me, you could end up fifty thousand to the good in no time.

CALIDORUS (*brightening visibly—then wilting again*)   Damn!
I'm damned by that damned law against minors. Everyone's scared to give me credit.

BALLIO (*grinning*)   I come under the same law, you know.
I'm scared to give you credit too.

PSEUDOLUS (*exploding*)   Scared to give him credit? After all
you've taken him for? Are you still not satisfied?

BALLIO (*loftily*)   All decent, upright lovers never let their
largess lapse. Clients should give and keep on giving. When
there's nothing left to give, they should quit being in love.

CALIDORUS (*dumbly*)   So you won't take pity on me?

BALLIO   Money talks—and you're here with empty pockets.
(*Assuming a funereal expression and shaking his head
mournfully*) Yet I'd have liked to see you alive and well.

PSEUDOLUS   Hey! He's not dead yet!

BALLIO   Whatever he is, when he talks the way he's been
talking, believe me, to me he's dead. The minute a lover
begins to plead with a pimp, life's over for him. (*To Calidorus*) When you come running to me, come with tears
that clink. For example, this sob story of yours about not
having any money. You're weeping on a stepmother's shoulder, boy!

PSEUDOLUS   Well! And just when did *you* marry his father?

BALLIO (*irascibly*)   God forbid!

PSEUDOLUS (*earnestly, in a last stab at persuasion*)   Do what
we're asking, Ballio, please! If you're afraid to give *him*
credit, trust me. Somewhere, on land or sea, I'll excavate
the cash for you.

BALLIO (*in astonishment*)   *I* trust *you?*

PSEUDOLUS (*stoutly*)   Why not?

BALLIO   Good god, I'd sooner tie up a runaway dog with a string of sausages than trust you.

CALIDORUS (*bitterly*)   Is this the thanks I deserve from you? I act nice and you act nasty?

BALLIO (*savagely*)   What do you want now, anyway?

CALIDORUS   Just hold everything for the next six days or so. Don't sell her. (*Tragically*) Don't destroy the man who loves her!

BALLIO (*suddenly effusively affable*)   Don't worry. I'll even hold off for the next six months.

CALIDORUS (*in a transport of delight*)   That's wonderful! Ballio, you're terrific!

BALLIO (*expansively*)   Now that you're so happy, would you like me to make you even happier?

CALIDORUS   What do you mean?

BALLIO (*beaming*)   Rosy's not even for sale now.

CALIDORUS (*his jaw dropping*)   She's not?

BALLIO   Nosirree!

CALIDORUS (*deliriously*)   Pseudolus! Quick! Get fatted calves and lambs! Get slaughterers! I want to make an offering to God Almighty. (*Pointing to Ballio*) Because this god here is lots more almighty in my book than God Almighty.

BALLIO (*haughtily*)   No fatted calves. I want the sacramental meats of the sacrificial lamb!

CALIDORUS (*to Pseudolus, as before*)   Hurry! What are you standing there for? Go get lambs! Didn't you hear what God Almighty said?

PSEUDOLUS (*to Calidorus*)   Be back in a flash. (*Gesturing in the direction of the city gate, beyond which lie the public execution grounds*) But first I'll have to run down past the city gate.

CALIDORUS   Why there?

PSEUDOLUS (*to Calidorus—but eying Ballio*)   To bring back slaughterers from *there*. Two of them. With bells for the victim—the kind that clank. And I'll drive back two whole herds—of birch rods. (*Grimly*) Then we'll have plenty for a successful sacrifice today to God Almighty here.

BALLIO (*to Pseudolus*)   You go to hell.

PSEUDOLUS (*genially*)   That's where our Patron God of Pimps is going.

BALLIO (*gravely*)   Do you know it's to your advantage if I die?

PSEUDOLUS   How's that?

BALLIO   I'll tell you. Because you'll never be an honest man as long as I live. (*Roars at his joke, recovers, and resumes his gravity.*) Do you know it's to your advantage if I stay alive?

PSEUDOLUS   How's that?

BALLIO   Because, if *I* die, *you'll* be the worst stinker in Athens. (*Second roar.*)

CALIDORUS (*to Ballio, deadly serious*)   Listen, I've got a question to ask you, and I want a serious answer. Do I understand that Rosy is not for sale?

BALLIO   She most certainly is not. (*Flashing his hyena grin*) You see, I've already sold her.

CALIDORUS (*stunned*)   How?

BALLIO (*deadpan*)   Garments excluded; just the carcass, guts and all.

CALIDORUS (*as before*)   You sold *my* girl?

BALLIO (*cheerfully*)   That's right. For five thousand dollars.

CALIDORUS (*gulping*)   Five thousand?

BALLIO (*as before*)   Let's say five times one thousand, if you prefer. To a major from Macedon. And I've already collected four thousand.

CALIDORUS (*still unable to believe his ears*)   What's this you're telling me?

BALLIO   That your girl friend's had a transformation. Into cash.

CALIDORUS (*as before*)   And you dared do a thing like that?

BALLIO (*shrugging*)   I felt like it. She was my property.

CALIDORUS (*to Pseudolus, roaring*)   Pseudolus! Get my sword!

PSEUDOLUS   What do you need a sword for?

CALIDORUS   To kill him. (*Tragically*) And myself.

PSEUDOLUS (*brightly*)   Why don't you just kill yourself? After all, starvation's going to take care of him before long.

CALIDORUS (*to Ballio*)   Listen here, you dirtiest double-crosser that ever walked the face of the earth, didn't you give me your solemn word you'd sell her to nobody but me?

BALLIO (*blandly*)   I admit it.

CALIDORUS   Didn't you even cross your heart?

BALLIO (*as before*)   I crossed my fingers *too*.

CALIDORUS (*thundering*)   You filthy liar, you went back on your word!

BALLIO (*as before*)   But I came into my money. (*Contemptuously*) I'm a filthy liar, but now I've got money to burn tucked away. You're a model son, you come from the right family—and you don't have a dime.

CALIDORUS   Pseudolus! Stand on the other side of him and cuss him out!

PSEUDOLUS (*racing around*)   Right! I'm covering ground faster than I would en route to City Hall for my emancipation proclamation.

(*The two take up positions on either side of Ballio. Calidorus, breathing fire, and Pseudolus, champing at the bit, face each other; Ballio, standing unconcerned between them, faces the audience.*)

CALIDORUS (*to Pseudolus*)   Give it to him! Pile it on!

PSEUDOLUS (*to Ballio*)   Now I'm going to tear you to tatters. With my tongue. (*At the top of his lungs*) Good-for-nothing!

BALLIO (*nodding agreeably*)   That's right.

PSEUDOLUS (*as before*)   Dirty rat!

BALLIO (*as before*)   It's the truth.

PSEUDOLUS   Jailbait!

BALLIO   Naturally.

PSEUDOLUS   Grave robber!

BALLIO   Of course.

PSEUDOLUS   Skunk!

BALLIO (*admiringly*)   Very good!

PSEUDOLUS   You'd rob your best friend!

BALLIO   Yes, I'd do that.

PSEUDOLUS   And kill your father!

BALLIO (*to Calidorus, enthusiastically*)   Now you take a turn.

CALIDORUS   Church-robber!

BALLIO   I admit it.

CALIDORUS   Dirty double-crosser!

BALLIO (*reproachfully*)   Old hat. You sang that song before.

CALIDORUS   Criminal!

BALLIO   Absolutely.

PSEUDOLUS   Corrupter of the young!

BALLIO   That's the stuff!

CALIDORUS   Housebreaker!

BALLIO   Voilà!

PSEUDOLUS   Jailbreaker!

BALLIO   Voici!

CALIDORUS   Lawbreaker!

BALLIO   Obviously.

PSEUDOLUS   Crook!

CALIDORUS   Lousy—

PSEUDOLUS   —pimp!

CALIDORUS   Scum!

BALLIO (*bursting into a round of applause*) In fine voice, both of you!

CALIDORUS (*losing steam*) You beat your father and mother.

BALLIO (*imperturbably*) What's more, I killed them sooner than pay for their upkeep. Nothing wrong in that, was there?

PSEUDOLUS (*to Calidorus, disgusted*) We're pouring into a punctured pot. We're wasting our breath.

BALLIO (*making preparations to move on*) Any further comments you two would like to make?

CALIDORUS (*weakly*) Aren't you ashamed of anything?

BALLIO (*angrily*) Aren't *you* ashamed of turning out to be a lover as broke as a nutshell? (*Starts to leave, then suddenly turns around.*) In spite of all the nasty names you've called me, I'll do this for you. Today's the last day for payment; if before tonight that major hasn't handed over the thousand he owes, I think I'll be in a position to do my duty.

CALIDORUS What's that?

BALLIO If you pay me first, I'll break my promise to him. (*With his hyena grin*) That's doing my duty. Well, if there was anything in it for me, I'd go on with this chat, but, without any cash, you're just kidding yourself if you think I'll have any pity on you. That's my considered opinion, so you can start figuring out what you're going to do next.

(*Ballio turns and stalks off, stage left, his attendant at his heels.*)

CALIDORUS (*in alarm*) Leaving already?

BALLIO (*over his shoulder*) I'm busy every minute right now.

PSEUDOLUS (*shaking his fist at the retreating back*) You'll be even busier a little later! (*To himself*) That fellow's my meat, unless god and man both desert me. I'll fillet him just the way a cook fillets an eel. (*To Calidorus*) Calidorus, I want your help now.

CALIDORUS (*promptly*)   At your orders, sir!

PSEUDOLUS (*gesturing toward Ballio's house, thoughtfully*)
I want this town besieged and taken by storm before tonight. For this we need a cagey, clever, careful, competent
man capable of carrying out orders, who won't go to sleep
on his feet.

CALIDORUS   Tell me—what are you up to?

PSEUDOLUS   I'll let you know when the time comes. I don't
want to go over it twice. (*Grinning at the audience*) Plays
are long enough as is.

CALIDORUS (*nodding vigorously*)   Absolutely and perfectly
right.

PSEUDOLUS   Get going! Bring your man back here fast.

CALIDORUS (*doubtfully*)   Out of a whole group of friends,
there are very few you can really rely on.

PSEUDOLUS   I know that. So do it in two steps: first make a
rough selection; then pick the one man you're sure of.

CALIDORUS (*enthusiastically*)   I'll have him here right away.

PSEUDOLUS (*pushing him off*)   Can't you get going? All this
talk is holding you up.

(*Calidorus dashes off, stage left. Pseudolus stands where
he is, meditating.*)

PSEUDOLUS (*to himself, despondently*)   Well, Pseudolus, he's
gone off, and you're here on your own. What are you going
to do now after all the big talk you handed him? What's
going to happen to those promises of yours? You haven't
even the shred of a plot in mind. You'd like to weave one,
but you don't have a beginning to start from or an end to
finish at. It's like being a playwright: once he's picked up
his pen, he's on the hunt for something that exists nowhere
on the face of the earth; yet he finds it anyway, he makes
fiction sound like fact. I'll play playwright: that five thousand exists nowhere on the face of the earth, yet I'll find it
anyway. I told the boy a long time ago that I'd come up
with the money for him. I wanted to get it out of the old

man but somehow or other he always caught wise first. (*Looking toward the wings, stage left*) But I've got to turn off the talk and shut up! Look who I see coming—our Simo and his neighbor, Callipho. (*Gesturing derisively toward Simo*) This is the grave I'm going to rob today for the five thousand I need for his son. (*Going over to an unobtrusive spot off to one side*) I'll just move over here where I can listen in on what they say.

(*Two graybeards, deep in conversation, totter in, leaning heavily on their sticks.*

Simo, Calidorus' father and Pseudolus' owner, has the face you would expect on a man who all his life has been a canny, tightfisted businessman; a card shark would look benevolent in comparison. Callipho is the exact opposite; his round, innocent countenance exudes goodness and implicit faith in his fellow man.

From the waggling of the head and other gesticulating, it is clear that Simo is in a foul mood.)

SIMO (*angrily*)   If we decided to pick a spendthrift or a rake for Governor of Athens, no one, I swear, would be any competition for that son of mine. He's the one topic of conversation in the whole town, how he's got his heart set on freeing his girl friend and is hunting for the money to do it. I've been getting reports from all sides. But I had smelled something fishy and knew all about it a long time ago; I just pretended I didn't.

PSEUDOLUS (*aside, dismayed*)   So his son smelled fishy! The campaign's collapsed, the offensive's stuck in a rut. There's a tight roadblock across the route I wanted to take to the cash depot. He found out! No looting any loot there.

CALLIPHO (*indignantly*)   If I had my way, people who babble gossip or listen to it would all hang—babblers by the tongue and listeners by the ears. Why, these reports that you're getting, that your son has a love affair and wants to steal from you, may be all just talk, a pack of lies. But even if every word is true, the way people behave these days, what's he done that's so out of the ordinary? What's so odd about a young fellow falling in love and setting his girl friend free?

PSEUDOLUS (*aside*)   What a nice old man!

SIMO (*snarling*)   Well, I'm an old fellow, and I don't want it!

CALLIPHO (*smiling indulgently*)   It won't do you the slightest good not to want it. It *might* have, if you hadn't behaved the same way when you were young. Only a parent who was a paragon can expect his son to be better than he was. And you—the money you threw away and the affairs you had could have taken care of every single solitary male in the city, barring none! Is it any wonder that the son takes after the father?

PSEUDOLUS (*to himself—but good and loud*)   *Mon dieu!* How few of you decent people there are in this world. Now, *there's* the kind of father a father should be to a son!

SIMO (*whirling around*)   Who's that talking? (*To Callipho, disgusted*) It's my servant Pseudolus. He's the archcriminal who's corrupted my son; he's his guide and mentor. I'd like to see him at the end of a rope!

CALLIPHO (*sotto voce*)   Now that's very silly of you, to show how angry you are. You'll get much further by being nice to him and finding out whether those reports you're getting are true. (*Wagging his head sagely*) "Trouble's double for the hasty heart."

SIMO (*sotto voce*)   All right. I'll take your advice.

(*The two oldsters start walking toward Pseudolus.*)

PSEUDOLUS (*to himself*)   The offensive's under way, Pseudolus! Have some fast talk ready for the old man. (*As they draw near, beaming*) Greetings to you first, master, as is only right and proper. And, if any are left over, (*with a respectful bow to Callipho*) greetings to the neighbors.

SIMO   Greetings. (*All affability*) Well, now, how are we doing?

PSEUDOLUS (*leaning back negligently and grinning*) Oh, we're just standing here this way.

SIMO (*reverting immediately to type, to Callipho*) Look at that pose, will you? His lordship!

CALLIPHO I think his pose is very nice. (*Nodding approvingly*) Self-confident.

PSEUDOLUS (*virtuously*) If a servant is honest and his conscience is clear, he *should* hold his head high, especially in front of his master.

CALLIPHO (*beaming on Pseudolus*) We have a few things we'd like to ask you about. Some rumors we've been hearing that we're a bit vague about.

SIMO (*to Callipho, disgusted*) He'll talk you to death. You'll think it's Socrates· and not Pseudolus you're talking to.

PSEUDOLUS (*to Simo, pathetically*) Yes, you haven't thought very well of me for quite some time now, I can see it. I know—you don't have very much faith in me. (*Squaring his jaw*) You'd like to see me bad and wicked, but, in spite of you, I'm going to be honest and decent!

SIMO (*resignedly*) Pseudolus, will you kindly vacate the rooms in your ears so some things I have to say can move in?

PSEUDOLUS (*gravely*) Even though I'm very annoyed with you, you go right ahead, say whatever you like.

SIMO (*staring at him*) You annoyed with me? The servant annoyed with the master?

PSEUDOLUS (*haughtily*) And does that seem so strange to you?

SIMO My god, the way you talk, I'd better watch out you don't get angry with me. (*Eying him narrowly*) You're thinking of giving me a beating, aren't you? And *not* the kind I'm accustomed to give you! (*To Callipho*) What's your idea?

CALLIPHO (*vehemently*) I really think he has every right to be angry. After all, you *don't* have much faith in him.

SIMO (*sneering*) Well, let him be angry. I'll see to it he does me no damage. (*To Pseudolus, brusquely*) Listen, you. What about the things I want to find out?

PSEUDOLUS (*all co-operation*) Anything you want to know, just ask. And consider whatever you hear from me an oracle from heaven.

SIMO (*curtly*) Then pay attention and don't forget your promise. Listen, are you aware that my son is having an affair with a certain chorus girl?

PSEUDOLUS (*like an oracle from heaven*) Yea, verily.

SIMO And that he wants to set her free?

PSEUDOLUS Yea, verily to that too.

SIMO And that you're getting your stunts and smart schemes set to steal a certain five thousand dollars from me?

PSEUDOLUS (*wide-eyed*) *I* steal from *you*?

SIMO (*grimly*) That's right. To give to my son so he can set the girl free. (*Impatiently, as Pseudolus hesitates*) Admit it, just say "Yea, verily to that too."

PSEUDOLUS (*meekly*) Yea, verily to that too.

CALLIPHO (*in shocked surprise*) He admits it!

SIMO (*to Callipho, smugly*) I told you so, all along.

CALLIPHO (*sadly*) Yes, I remember.

SIMO (*to Pseudolus, angrily*) Why didn't you tell me the minute you heard instead of hiding it from me? Why didn't *I* hear about it?

PSEUDOLUS (*readily*) I'll tell you why. I didn't want to be the one to start a bad precedent—this business of a servant carrying tales about one master to another.

SIMO (*to Callipho, snarling*) He should have been hauled off by the heels to the mill wheel!

CALLIPHO (*anxiously*) He didn't do anything wrong, did he?

SIMO Anything? Everything!

PSEUDOLUS (*to Callipho*) Don't, Callipho. I know how to handle my own affairs. I deserve the blame. (*To Simo*) Now listen carefully. Why did I keep you in the dark about your son's love affair? Because he had the mill wheel all set for me if I talked.

SIMO And you didn't know *I'd* have it all set for you if you kept quiet?

PSEUDOLUS I knew that.

SIMO (*menacingly*) Then why wasn't I told?

PSEUDOLUS (*glibly*) Because one evil was in front of me and the other a little farther on. His was right there; with yours I had a teensy breathing spell.

(*Simo glares at him. Pseudolus looks him in the eye serenely.*)

SIMO (*deciding to accept the explanation*) What are you two going to do now? After all, you can't get any money out of me; I know everything. And I'm going to pass the word right now to everyone in town not to lend you a dime.

PSEUDOLUS (*blandly*) Believe me, I'm not going to go begging. Not as long as *you're* alive. Because, by god, *you're* going to give me the money. I'm going to get it from you.

SIMO (*superciliously*) So you're going to get it from me, eh?

PSEUDOLUS And how!

SIMO Well, by god, you can poke my eyes out if I ever give you that money!

PSEUDOLUS (*airily*) You will. I'm telling you about it right now so you'll be on your guard.

SIMO One thing I'm sure of: if you do pull it off, you deserve a citation for the sensation of the century.

PSEUDOLUS (*casually*) I will.

SIMO (*ghoulishly*) Suppose you don't?

PSEUDOLUS (*promptly*) Whip me to shreds. But suppose I do?

SIMO (*promptly*) As god's my witness, I won't lay a finger on you and you can keep the money all your life.

PSEUDOLUS (*pointing a warning finger at him*) Don't you forget that.

SIMO (*taken aback by Pseudolus' cocksureness, uneasily*) How can you possibly catch me off guard, now that I've been forewarned?

PSEUDOLUS I gave you fair warning to be on your guard. And I'm telling you now, in so many words: be on your guard. BE ON YOUR GUARD! (*Pointing to Simo's hands*) Watch out—today, with those two hands, you're going to give me the money.

CALLIPHO (*goggle-eyed*) The man's a virtuoso, a maestro, if he keeps his word!

PSEUDOLUS (*to Callipho, in ringing tones*) Carry me off and make me your slave if I don't!

SIMO Very nice and friendly of you—but don't you happen to be *my* slave at the moment?

PSEUDOLUS (*ignoring the last remark*) Would you like to hear something that'll amaze the both of you even more?

CALLIPHO (*enthusiastically*) Oh yes! I'm dying to hear it. I love listening to you.

PSEUDOLUS (*turning to Simo*) Before I conduct my campaign against you, I'm going to fight still another glorious and memorable campaign.

SIMO What campaign?

PSEUDOLUS (*gesturing toward Ballio's house*) Against the pimp who lives next door. You watch—with my stunts and smart schemes I'm going to pluck that chorus girl your son's pining for plunk from under his pimpish nose.

SIMO What's that you say?

PSEUDOLUS (*triumphantly*) And I'll have both jobs done by tonight!

SIMO (*dubiously*) Well, if you make good on all this big talk, you're a better man than Alexander the Great. (*Sternly*) But, if you don't, is there any reason why I shouldn't have you shut up in the mill, pronto?

PSEUDOLUS (*promptly*) And not just for one day. For every day of my life as long as I live. But, if I do, will you, of your own free will, give me money for the pimp, pronto?

CALLIPHO (*as Simo hesitates*) That's a fair proposition. Tell him you will.

SIMO (*clutching Callipho's arm*) You know what I just thought of? Supposing those two have a deal on! Suppose they're in cahoots and have a scheme cooked up to do me out of the money?

PSEUDOLUS (*laughing off the suggestion*) Even I wouldn't have the nerve to pull a stunt like that! No, Simo, it's not that way at all. (*Earnestly*) If he and I have any deal on, or if we ever had a single meeting or discussion about any deal, you can take a rawhide pen and scribble over my whole hide just as if you were filling up a page with writing.

SIMO (*shrugging in acquiescence*) You can announce your act now, whenever you want.

PSEUDOLUS (*to Callipho*) Callipho, would you please help me and not get tied up in any other business? It's just for today.

CALLIPHO (*hesitating*) But I've had everything set up since yesterday to go off to the country . . .

PSEUDOLUS Well, please dismantle the set-up, will you?

CALLIPHO (*suddenly making up his mind*) All right, I've decided to stay, for your sake. (*His eyes glistening*) I'm dying to watch your act, Pseudolus. And, if I hear that (*gesturing toward Simo*) he won't pay you the money he promised, I'll pay it myself rather than see you lose out.

SIMO (*muttering*) I won't go back on my word.

PSEUDOLUS (*to Simo, promptly*) Darned right—because, if you don't come across, I'll dun you, and the din will be long and loud. Now out of here, both of you; get inside and leave the field clear for my hocus-pocus.

CALLIPHO (*moving off toward his house*) Right. Anything you say.

PSEUDOLUS (*calling to him*)   Now I don't want you to leave the house, you hear?

CALLIPHO   Of course. Glad to oblige.

SIMO (*to Pseudolus*)   But I have to go downtown. I'll be back right away.

PSEUDOLUS (*warningly*)   Then hurry.

(*Callipho goes into his house, and Simo leaves, stage left. Pseudolus walks downstage and addresses the audience.*)

PSEUDOLUS   I suspect that you suspect that I've made all these big promises just to keep you entertained until I get through this play, and that I'm not going to do the things I said I'd do. (*Mimicking Simo's tones*) "I won't go back on my word." (*Gaily*) So far as I can see, I can't see how I'm going to do it—but, if there's one thing I *can* see, it's that I *will* do it. After all, when a character comes on stage, he ought to bring something fresh and new in a fresh and new way. And, if he can't, let him make way for someone who can. (*Moving off toward Simo's house*) And now I'd like to step inside here for a minute while I carry out a mental mobilization of my underhand forces. I won't keep you long; I'm coming right out. Our flutist will entertain you with a selection in the meantime.

(*Pseudolus races into Simo's house, leaving the stage empty. A second later the flutist comes on to play an entr'-acte.*)

ACT II

(The door of Simo's house flies open. Pseudolus bursts out and races downstage to address the audience.)

SONG

PSEUDOLUS *(excitedly)*
> Holy mackerel! It's marvelous! Everything I try
> > Works out just like a charm.

(Tapping his brow)
> Up in here is a scheme I can certify
> > Is guaranteed free of harm.

(Importantly)
> When your eye's on the big things, it's madness, I say,
> To proceed in a timid or half-hearted way.

> > The way that things work out
> > Is completely up to you.
> > You want to do big things?
> > Then think and act big too!

> You take *me*. Why, up here in this head,
> > Standing by for the fray,
> Are my armies—plus ambush, intrigue,
> > Dirty deals, and foul play.

> With the courage inherited from a long line of heroes,
> > With the double-cross serving as shining shield,
> The enemy's mine wherever I'll meet him—
> > I'll phony my foemen from the field!

> > Just watch me now. I'm set to go,
> > To fight the man who's our common foe,
> > To rally-oh,
> > And sally-oh
> > > 'Gainst Ballio!

(*Pointing to Ballio's house*)

Here's the fortress I want to lay siege to today.
So I'll draw up my forces in battle array,
And I'll take it by storm—to the joy of the nation—
And then quickly re-form for the next operation,

(*Pointing to Simo's house*)

To lay siege to the doddering fort over here.
Here I'll load my allies and myself with such plunder
I'll be hailed as the scourge of my foes, as a wonder.

(*Puffing out his chest*)

>I was born to be great;
>It's a family trait—
>To fight battles victorious,
>Memorable, glorious.

(*Suddenly looking toward the wings, stage right*)

Someone's coming this way. Who's this man that I spy?
Who's this stranger so suddenly in the way of my eye?
What's he want with that cutlass there, *I'd* like to know.
What's his business here? Pseudolus! Ambush the foe!

(*Pseudolus moves to an unobtrusive spot off to the side, and, a second later, Harpax, "snatcher," enters. Harpax has a sort of primitive cunning and suspicion in his make-up but, aside from that, is not very bright. He is an officer's orderly; he wears a uniform and carries a sword. In one hand he clutches a purse, obviously well-filled.*

The hesitant way in which he walks along, stopping to peer at the doorways, reveals immediately that he is a stranger in town.)

HARPAX (*to himself*)

The report of my eyes confirms, I can see,
The report my commander imparted to me,
>Here's the district and quarter he meant.
Seven blocks from the entrance to town I should spot
The pimp's house, where the master said leave the whole
>lot,
>Both this cash and the seal that he sent.

But I'd like to see someone come by who'd make clear
If a pimp, name of Ballio, lives around here.

PSEUDOLUS (*to himself*)

Not a sound! Not a word! Unless heaven and men
    All desert me, this man is my meat!
But I need a new gambit since all of a sudden
    A new path has appeared at my feet.
All the plans I worked out must be jettisoned now;
    In my new start I'll concentrate here (*pointing to
    Harpax*).
So you've come as an errand boy, *mon général?*
    Watch me soon stand you up on your ear!

(*Harpax walks up to Ballio's house and raises his hand to knock.*)

HARPAX (*to himself*)   I'll knock on the door and get someone to come out.

PSEUDOLUS (*calling*)   Hey, whoever you are, I wish you'd cut out that knocking. You see, I'm patron protecter of portals. Popped out here for a precautionary peep.

HARPAX (*dubiously*)   Are you Ballio?

PSEUDOLUS (*importantly*)   Not exactly. I'm Vice-Ballio.

HARPAX   What's that mean?

PSEUDOLUS (*as before*)   Chief layer-outer and layer-inner. Lord of the larder.

HARPAX (*impressed*)   You mean to say you're the major-domo?

PSEUDOLUS   Me? I give orders to the major-domo!

HARPAX (*puzzled, unable to square Pseudolus' tones with his slave's get-up*)   Are you a slave or aren't you?

PSEUDOLUS (*deflated*)   Well, for the moment, still a slave.

HARPAX (*inflated*)   You look it. You don't look the type to be anything but.

PSEUDOLUS (*promptly*)   Ever take a look at yourself before making cracks about others?

HARPAX (*to the audience, gesturing toward Pseudolus*) Must be a bad egg, this one here.

PSEUDOLUS (*to the audience, gesturing toward Harpax*) Well, look what heaven sent me! A nest all my own—I'll hatch plenty of schemes in it today!

HARPAX (*to himself, suspiciously*) What's he talking to himself about?

PSEUDOLUS (*calling*) Hey, mister!

HARPAX What?

PSEUDOLUS Are you from that Macedonian major? Servant of the fellow who bought a girl from us and paid my master four thousand and still owes him a thousand?

HARPAX (*surprised*) That's right. But where in the world do you know me from? Where did you ever see me or talk to me, anyway? I never set foot in Athens before and never laid eyes on you till this minute.

PSEUDOLUS (*studiedly offhand*) You looked as if you came from him. After all, when he left he agreed on today as the last day for payment, and he hasn't yet made good.

HARPAX (*hefting the purse*) Oh, no. It's here.

PSEUDOLUS (*affecting surprise*) You brought it?

HARPAX (*importantly*) I certainly did.

PSEUDOLUS (*reaching for the purse, as if in a considerable hurry*) What are you waiting for? Hand it over.

HARPAX (*jerking the purse out of his reach*) Hand it over to who? You?

PSEUDOLUS Certainly to me. I'm in charge of Ballio's books. I handle the cash—receive all receivables, pay all payables.

HARPAX (*grimly*) Certainly *not* to you. You could be cashier for god almighty and all the treasures of heaven, but I'm not trusting you with a cent.

PSEUDOLUS (*ignoring the last remark, all business*) Why, in two shakes of a lamb's tail, we could have the whole thing done.

HARPAX (*as before, showing the tightly bound purse*)   I'd rather keep it *undone*.

PSEUDOLUS   You go to the devil! So you've come here to blacken my good name, eh? As if people don't trust me personally with a thousand times that much money!

HARPAX (*stubbornly*)   Others can think that way. Doesn't mean *I* have to trust you.

PSEUDOLUS (*working himself up*)   You mean to say I'm trying to do you out of your money?

HARPAX   Oh, no. *You* mean to say it. I mean to say I have my suspicions. What's your name, anyway?

PSEUDOLUS (*to the audience*)   The pimp has a servant named Syrus. That's who I'll say I am. (*To Harpax*) Syrus.

HARPAX   Syrus, eh?

PSEUDOLUS   That's my name.

HARPAX (*impatiently*)   Enough talk. Listen, whatever your name is, if your master's home, call him out so I can do what I was sent here to do.

PSEUDOLUS (*apologetically*)   If he *were* here, I'd call him out. (*Earnestly*) But don't you want to give it to me? (*Innocently*) You'll be relieved of the whole business— more so than if you gave it to him in person.

HARPAX (*contemptuously*)   You don't get the point. The commander gave it to me to pay with, not play with. Oh, I can see you're practically running a fever because you can't dig your claws into it. I don't hand over a cent to a soul except to Ballio in person.

PSEUDOLUS   He's tied up right now. In court on a case.

HARPAX   Well, I hope he wins. I'll come back when I figure he'll be at home. (*Pulling out a letter and handing it to Pseudolus*) Here, take this letter and give it to him. It's got the identification seal my master agreed on with yours in this deal for the girl.

PSEUDOLUS (*taking it, studiedly casual*)   Yes, I know. The major told us what he wanted: we're to send the girl off with a fellow who'd bring the money and a seal with his picture. He left a duplicate with us, you know.

HARPAX (*impressed in spite of himself*)   You know everything, don't you?

PSEUDOLUS (*with a shrug, carelessly*)   Why shouldn't I?

HARPAX (*pointing to the letter*)   So you give him that identification.

PSEUDOLUS   Right. What's your name, anyway?

HARPAX   Snatcher.

PSEUDOLUS (*pretending fright*)   On your way, Snatcher boy, I don't like you. You're not coming inside this house, believe me; I want none of your snatching there.

HARPAX (*puffing out his chest*)   I take my enemies alive, right out of the front line. That's how I got the name.

PSEUDOLUS   If you ask me, you take the silverware right out of the front rooms.

HARPAX (*loftily*)   No, sir! (*Struck by a thought*) Say, Syrus, you know what I'd like to ask you to do?

PSEUDOLUS   Tell me and I'll know.

HARPAX   I'm staying at the third inn outside the city gate. The one run by that old buttertub, Chrysis, the lame dame.

PSEUDOLUS   What do you want?

HARPAX   Come and pick me up there when your master gets back.

PSEUDOLUS   Sure. Anything you say.

HARPAX   I'm tired from the trip. Want to get some rest.

PSEUDOLUS (*nodding vigorously*)   Very smart. Good idea. But don't make me go looking all over the place when I come to get you.

HARPAX   Oh, no. After a bite to eat, a nap is all I'm interested in.

PSEUDOLUS (*as before*)   I'll bet.

HARPAX (*preparing to leave*)   Well, anything I can do for you?

PSEUDOLUS   You go take that nap.

HARPAX   I'm going. (*Starts walking off, stage right.*)

PSEUDOLUS (*calling after him, solicitously*)   Snatcher! Listen! Use plenty of blankets. You get a good sweat up, and you'll feel tiptop.

(*Harpax leaves. The minute he is out of earshot, Pseudolus races downstage and addresses the audience.*)

PSEUDOLUS (*exultantly*)

Ye gods! That fellow saved my life by turning up, I swear!
I was heading wrong, he set me right—and *he's* to pay the fare!
Lady Luck herself could never have come at a luckier time, you see,
Than when I had this lucky letter luckily left with me.

(*Brandishing the letter*)

He's handed me a horn of plenty, in here's what I want and more:
Embezzlement, swindle, double-cross, dirty tricks, shady deals galore,
The cash we're after plus that girl the boy is crazy for.
And now I'll show my generous soul; my name and fame shall soar!

(*Shaking his head wonderingly*)

My army of plans had been mobilized, was at stations, was all set—
The way I'd go about the job, approach the pimp and get
The girl away from him. It all was in my head, but it seems
Lady Luck by herself can overturn a hundred wise men's schemes.
The fact is that, when we're doing well, and people say we're smart,
We owe it all to just how much Lady Luck has taken our part.
We hear that someone's plans have worked out; "He's a genius!" all of us chime.

We hear that someone's plans went wrong; "What a fool!"
we chime this time.

Why, we're the fools—we're unaware how wasted is our
whole

Benighted, greedy struggle toward any particular goal,

As if the right path's ever known to any human soul!

The bird in hand we always leave to go for those in the
bush;

And then 'mid all our sweat and strain, enter Death to give
his push!

(*Suddenly snapping his fingers*) But enough of this
philosophizing. I've been talking too much and too long.
(*Gleefully*) Ye gods! That brain storm I suddenly got a
little while ago, to bluff and say I belonged to the pimp, is
worth a fortune! Now, with this letter, I'll double-cross
the three of them, master, pimp, and letter giver. (*His
attention suddenly caught, looks toward the wings, stage
left.*) Well, look at that! Something else I wanted is happening, just as good as this. Here comes Calidorus, and he's got
somebody with him.

(*Calidorus and his friend Charinus [pronounced ka-RYE-
nus], "charitable," enter, so deep in conversation they don't
notice Pseudolus.*)

CALIDORUS So I've told you everything, the sweet and the
bitter. You know my toils, my troubles, my financial tribulations.

CHARINUS (*nodding*) I have everything in mind. Now just
tell me what you want me to do.

CALIDORUS Pseudolus gave me orders to bring someone who
can get things done and who'd be willing to do me a good
turn.

CHARINUS You carry out orders to the letter: you're bringing
a good friend ready to do you a good turn. But who's this
Pseudolus? He's new to me.

CALIDORUS (*enthusiastically*) The greatest virtuoso alive,

my maestro of miracles. He's the one who told me he was
going to do all the things I told you about.

PSEUDOLUS (*to himself, importantly*)   I'll go up and greet
him in the grand manner.

CALIDORUS (*his attention caught*)   Whose voice is that?

PSEUDOLUS (*adopting the tones and gestures of a character in
grand opera*)

> 'Tis thee I seek, Your Majesty, yea thee
> Whom thy servant Pseudolus serves. 'Tis thee I seek
> To give thee thrice, in triplewise, in form
> Threefold, three thrice-deserved delights derived
> From dumbbells three and by devices three:
> Deceit, deception, and double-cross.

(*Waving the letter*)

> Delights that I bring thee signed and sealed
> In this here paltry piece of paper.

CALIDORUS (*to Charinus, excitedly*)   That's the fellow!

CHARINUS (*admiringly*)   The devil's better than an opera
star!

PSEUDOLUS (*walking toward them, as before*)

> Advance thy step as I do mine and boldly
> Extend to me thy hand and welcome words.

CALIDORUS

> To welcome rescue true—or welcome *words?*

PSEUDOLUS (*dropping the act and grinning*)   Both!

CALIDORUS (*with great relief*)   Welcome, words and rescue!
(*Tensely*) What happened?

PSEUDOLUS (*amused*)   What are you so nervous about?

CALIDORUS (*pointing to Charinus, proudly*)   I've produced
your man.

PSEUDOLUS   What's this "produced" business?

CALIDORUS (*meekly*)   I mean I've brought him here.

PSEUDOLUS (*looking Charinus over*)   Who is he?

CALIDORUS   Charinus.

PSEUDOLUS   Bravo!

> No man named Charinus
> Will ever malign us.

CHARINUS (*energetically*)   What do you need done? Step up and give me my orders.

PSEUDOLUS (*playing disinterested to test his man's interest*) Thanks just the same and all the best to you, Charinus, but we really don't want to put you to any trouble.

CHARINUS (*promptly*)   You won't put me to any trouble. Not a bit.

PSEUDOLUS (*promptly*)   Then stick around. (*Ostentatiously examines the letter.*)

CALIDORUS   What's that?

PSEUDOLUS (*triumphantly*)   I've just intercepted this letter and this identification!

CALIDORUS   Identification? What identification?

PSEUDOLUS   The one the major just sent. His servant, the fellow who came to take your girl away, brought it along with the one thousand dollars—(*grinning*) and did I make a monkey out of him just now!

CALIDORUS   How?

PSEUDOLUS (*gesturing toward the audience*)   Look, this play's being given for the benefit of these people. And they were here, they know all about it. I'll tell you two later.

CALIDORUS   What do we do now?

PSEUDOLUS (*in ringing tones*)   By tonight you'll have your girl friend in your arms—and she'll be a free woman!

CALIDORUS (*dumfounded*)   I?

PSEUDOLUS   Yes, you, I say—if I manage to stay alive. Provided, however, you two find me a man in a hurry.

CHARINUS   What kind of man?

PSEUDOLUS   A good-for-nothing. But one who's slick and smart enough, once he's been given a start, to figure out what to do next on his own. And it mustn't be anyone too well known around here.

CHARINUS Does it matter if he's a slave?

PSEUDOLUS (*in a what-a-silly-question tone of voice*) On the contrary, I prefer a slave.

CHARINUS I think I have the man for you. He's a good-for-nothing, he's smart, and my father just sent him here from overseas. He came to Athens only yesterday, and he hasn't been out of the house yet.

PSEUDOLUS (*to Charinus, nodding*) That'll be a great help. (*Frowning in thought*) Now I've got to borrow a thousand dollars which I'll need just till tonight. (*Gesturing toward Calidorus, grinning*) His father owes me money.

CHARINUS (*expansively*) Oh, I'll give it to you. Don't bother going to anyone else.

PSEUDOLUS My lifesaver! (*Thoughtful again*) But I also need a uniform and a sword.

CHARINUS I've got some to spare.

PSEUDOLUS (*exultantly*) Ye gods! This Charinus is all plus and no minus! Now, about that servant of yours who's just arrived—is he strong in the head?

CHARINUS No, just under the armpits.

PSEUDOLUS He ought to wear long sleeves. Is he tough? Does he have the old vinegar in the veins?

CHARINUS As sour as it comes.

PSEUDOLUS Suppose he has to give out with the old sweetness, instead? Has he got it in him?

CHARINUS Has he! Honey, sugar, syrup—he once tried to run a grocery in his guts.

PSEUDOLUS (*grinning*) Touché, Charinus: beat me at my own game. But what's this servant of yours called?

CHARINUS Monkey.

PSEUDOLUS Can he do a good turn?

CHARINUS Like a top.

PSEUDOLUS Does he grasp things easily?

CHARINUS   All the time—other people's things.

PSEUDOLUS   Suppose he's caught in the act?

CHARINUS   He slips out. He's an eel.

PSEUDOLUS   Has he got any sense?

CHARINUS   More sense than the Board of Censors.

PSEUDOLUS   Well, from what you say he sounds like a good man.

CHARINUS   You have no idea how good! Why, the minute he sees you he'll tell *you* what you want him for. What have you got in mind, anyway?

PSEUDOLUS   I'll tell you. When I'm done dressing your man up, I want him to impersonate the major's orderly. He'll take this identification along with a thousand dollars to the pimp and make off with the girl. There, now you know the whole plot. The mechanics of how to do it I'll save for our impersonator.

CALIDORUS   (*impatiently*)   Well, what are we standing around for?

PSEUDOLUS   I'm off to the Aeschinus Loan Company. You two dress your man in dress uniform and bring him to me there. But hurry!

CHARINUS   We'll be there before you will.

PSEUDOLUS   Then you'd better shake a leg! (*As Calidorus and Charinus dash off, stage left, he turns and addresses the audience.*)

It's left my mind, it's gone away, the last shred of doubt and fear

I'd had before. My mind's been scoured, the road ahead is clear.

With flying flags I'm leading out the troops in my command;

The sky is blue, all dark clouds gone, and everything goes as planned;

Morale is high: I can—I know it!—wipe out the enemy band.

But first downtown to hand a load of sage advice to Monk:

Tell him what to do so he plays it smart and doesn't go kerplunk.

And then to storm Castle Pimp itself—and the enemy's cause is sunk!

(Pseudolus dashes off triumphantly, stage left, and the stage is empty.)

ACT III

(*The door of Ballio's house opens, and Ballio's catamite steps out, a repulsive little boy with an ugly face as heavily made up as any whore's. He minces downstage and addresses the audience.*)

BOY When Fate makes a boy a slave in a pimp's home and, on top of that, makes him homely, believe me, as I can tell from my feelings right now, she's made him plenty of toil and trouble. Take me—that's the kind of slavery that came my way; I'm the sole support of all sorts of sorrows, small and large. (*Whimpering*) And I can't find any lover boy to love me and care for me so that for once in my life things would be a teeny bit brighter.

(*Whimpers a second or so longer, then continues worriedly*) Today is this pimp's birthday, and he's laid down the law to everyone in the house from the lowest to the highest: whoever doesn't get him a gift today gets the life tortured out of him tomorrow. In the position I'm in, what in heaven's name can I do? *I* can't give what people who can give usually give. And, if I don't give the pimp a gift today, tomorrow he'll empty the chamber pots down my throat. (*Blubbering*) I'm still too small for things like that!

(*Getting his blubbering under control*) Golly, poor me, I'm so scared of swilling slops, (*leering*) if someone slipped something into my palm to give it a little weight, (*archly*) I think I could somehow grit my teeth and bear it even though it makes a person cry hard—(*innocently*) so they tell me.

(*His attention caught, looks toward the wings, stage left*) But right now I have to shut my mouth and bear it —there's Ballio coming back bringing a cook with him.

(*The boy hurries into the house. A second later Ballio enters, at his heels his slave boy, and at his side an enormously fat cook behind whom trails a long line of young assistants.*)

BALLIO (*to the world at large*) And people, the damn fools, say the market is where you hire cooks! It's where you hire crooks, not cooks! I tell you, if I had actually taken an oath to find a worse cook than the one I've got here, I couldn't have done it. Useless, brainless, a blowhard and a blabbermouth! I know why he never died and went below: so he could be on hand here to cater funeral feasts: he's the only one who can cook what a corpse would eat.

COOK (*unabashed*) If you really think I'm the type you tell me I am, why did you hire me?

BALLIO Shortage. There was no one else. If you're such a great cook, why were all the others already gone from the square and you were still sitting there all by yourself?

COOK (*with a great air of candor*) I'll tell you. I'm considered a poorer cook. Not through any fault of my own, mind you. Through human greed.

BALLIO How's that?

COOK (*as before*) I'll tell you. It's because, when people come to hire a cook, they never go after the best who'll cost the most; they'd rather hire the cook who costs the least. That's why I was sitting in sole possession of the square today. (*Contemptuously*) Let those other poor devils cook their five-buck feeds. (*Pounding his chest*) Nobody gets me off my seat for less than ten. I don't do a dinner like other cooks. They pile up plates with potted pasture, that's what they do. They make cattle out of the guests—feed 'em fodder! And even the fodder they season with still more fodder. Inside they put coriander, fennel, garlic, celery. Outside they put cabbage, beets, sorrel, spinach. On top of it all, they throw in a pound of asafetida. Then they'll grate in that damned mustard, which has the graters' eyes going at a great rate before they're done grating. When these cooks cook a meal and it comes to the seasoning, they don't season with seasonings, they season with vultures—gives 'em a chance to get at the easy livers around the table while still alive. That's why people hereabouts don't live very long: they bloat their bellies with all this fodder that's horrible to mention let alone eat. Fodder a cow wouldn't eat, a person will.

BALLIO (*snarling*)   What about yourself? If you sneer at these seasonings, what do you use? Seasonings from heaven to make people live longer?

COOK (*promptly*)   You can say that again. If people ate regularly the meals I prepare, they could live to even two hundred. Once I drop some clovidoopus in a pan, or some dillipoopus, or a dash of fathead or cutathroat, right away the pan starts sizzling on its own. (*Becoming the maître d'hôtel*) Now, these seasonings are for your dishes made from the finny tribe. For your dishes made from the earthy tribes I season with nutmegoopus. Or tenus tenerus or even muvius fluvius.

BALLIO (*exploding*)   You and your seasoning can go plumb to hell! And take all your damned lies with you!

COOK (*unruffled*)   Will you kindly allow me to continue?

BALLIO   Continue—and then go to hell!

COOK   When every pot is hot, I uncover every one, and (*closing his eyes in rapture*) the aroma flies to heaven with feet outspread.

BALLIO   The aroma with feet outspread, eh?

COOK (*apologetically*)   Made a slip. Didn't realize it.

BALLIO   How's that?

COOK (*straight-faced*)   With arms outspread, I meant to say. (*Resuming his rapture*) The lord in heaven sups nightly on this aroma.

BALLIO (*sarcastically*)   And if you don't happen to be cooking anywhere, what in the world does the lord in heaven sup on?

COOK (*promptly*)   He goes to bed unsupped.

BALLIO (*roaring*)   And you go to hell! (*Indicating by a contempestuous wave of the hand all the cook's big talk*) So for all this I'm supposed to pay you ten dollars today, am I?

COOK (*smugly*)   Oh, I admit I'm a very expensive cook. But I make sure the people get their money's worth in any house I go to cook in.

BALLIO   To rob in, you mean.

COOK (*shrugging*)   You think you can find a cook who doesn't have a pair of claws like a vulture?

BALLIO   And you think you can go just anywhere to cook and not pull those claws in while you're cooking? (*Turning to his slave boy*) Now listen, you, you're on my side, so I'm giving you orders right now to get everything that belongs to us out of sight in a hurry. And after that you keep your eyes on (*gesturing toward the cook*) his. Wherever he looks, you look too. If he takes a step in any direction, you take a step in the same direction. If he reaches a hand in any direction, you reach a hand in the same direction. If he takes hold of anything that's his, you let him. If he takes hold of anything that's ours, you take hold of the other end. If he moves, you move. If he stands, you stand. If he squats, you squat. (*Looking down the line of the cook's assistants*) And I'm appointing personal watchmen for these assistants of his too.

COOK (*soothingly*)   Now you just stop worrying.

BALLIO   I ask you, just show me how I can stop worrying when I'm bringing *you* into my house?

COOK (*heartily*)   Because I'll make a concoction for you to-day that'll do for you what Medea did for Pelias when she cooked the old fellow up. They say that by using her poisonous potions she turned the old fellow back into a young one. Well, I'll do the same for you.

BALLIO   So you poison people, do you?

COOK   No sir. On the contrary, I cure them.

BALLIO   Look here, how much will you charge to teach me that one recipe?

COOK   Which?

BALLIO   The one that'll cure me from your stealing.

COOK (*promptly*) If you trust me, ten dollars; if you don't, even five hundred's not enough. (*Thinking for a moment*) This dinner you're giving, is it for friends or enemies?

BALLIO My god! For my friends, of course.

COOK (*enthusiastically*) Why don't you invite your enemies instead? I'll do your diners such a dinner, make such deliciously delicious dishes, that, as soon as they pick up something and taste it, they'll chomp off their fingers in the process.

BALLIO Please do me a favor, will you? Before you serve anything to any of my guests, you first take a taste and let your assistants taste too—so all of you can chomp off those thieving hands of yours.

COOK (*innocently*) Maybe you don't believe what I'm telling you?

BALLIO (*impatiently*) Now don't be a nuisance, please! I've had enough of your cackling. Shut up! (*Gesturing toward his house*) Look, there's where I live. Go on in and cook dinner. And get a move on!

(*The cook stalks in, Ballio's slave boy scampers in in his wake, and the line of assistants follows. The last boy in line turns and calls out to Ballio.*)

ASSISTANT (*like a butler making an announcement*) Kindly take your place at the table and call your guests. Dinner's now being—spoiled! (*Disappears into the house.*)

BALLIO (*to the audience*) Look at that, will you! What a breed! (*Gesturing toward the boy who has just gone in*) That Chief Dishlicker there is already a full-fledged good-for-nothing. (*Shaking his head*) I honestly don't know which to keep an eye on first: I've got thieves inside my house and (*gesturing toward Pseudolus' house*) a bandit next door. You see, just a few minutes ago while downtown, my neighbor here, Calidorus' father, warned me over and over to watch out for his servant Pseudolus, not to trust him. Says Pseudolus is out to pull a fast one and get the girl away from me if he can. Claims Pseudolus swore up and down that he was going to sneak Rosy away from me. I'll go in now and warn the household that none of them is to trust that Pseudolus one bit.

(Ballio enters his house, and the stage is now empty.)

ACT IV

(*Enter Pseudolus, stage left, walking on air.*)

SONG

PSEUDOLUS (*as if to Monkey who he assumes is at his heels*)
If Fate has ever felt an urge to help a mortal out,
She feels it now for the boy and me, of that I have no
doubt:
If she's produced an assistant like you, with brains and
education,
Then she wants to see the saving of us, and the pimp's
extermination.

(*Turns to face Monkey—and discovers there is no Monkey
to face.*)
Where is he? I'm talking to myself
Like someone not all there!
By god, he's put one over on me
And left me flat, I'll swear.
For one crook dealing with another,
I've been caught off guard for fair.
If Monk's made off, my goose is cooked. The job I wanted
done
I'll never be able to do today. But wait, I see someone—
There he is. He's coming now, our answer to a hangman's
prayer.
And look at the way he steps along. Quite a strut our boy
has there!

(*Enter Monkey, resplendent in a uniform somewhat like
Harpax's, and swaggering along as magnificently as a major
general.*)

PSEUDOLUS (*calling to him, petulantly*)
Hey, I've been looking all over for you,
Damned scared you'd run out on me.

MONKEY (*haughtily*)

> And if I'd been acting the way that I should
> I damned well would, I agree.

PSEUDOLUS (*as before*)

> Well, where did you stop?

MONKEY (*coolly*)

>   Where I wanted to be.

PSEUDOLUS (*peevishly*)

> I know that.

MONKEY (*shrugging*)

>   You do? Then why ask me?

PSEUDOLUS (*hastily changing the subject*)

> I wanted to give you this warning to—

MONKEY (*interrupting*)

> Don't you warn me, I'm warning *you!*

PSEUDOLUS (*resentfully*)

> Now you look here. You're treating me
> Like dirt, and I don't like it, see?

MONKEY (*ostentatiously adjusting his hat and sword, distastefully*)

> A holder of the *croix de guerre*
> Be nice to you? I wouldn't dare!

PSEUDOLUS (*throwing a worried look at Ballio's door*)

> We've started something, and now I'd like
> To do the job.

MONKEY (*drawing his sword and trying a few practice thrusts*)

>   For the love of Mike,
> Just what do you think I'm doing, eh?

PSEUDOLUS (*as before*)

> Then shake a leg. Don't take all day!

MONKEY (*ambling along with maddening slowness*)

> I do things in a leisurely way.

PSEUDOLUS (*urgently, gesturing toward Ballio's house*)

> Here's our chance! While our soldier boy snores,
> I want *you* to be first through those doors.

MONKEY (*lazily*)

> What's your hurry?
> Take it easy, don't worry.
> The good lord can let
> That soldier be set
> On *this* same spot, right here with me.
> Whatever's the name
> Of this fellow who came,
> I'll make a better Snatcher than he!
> So don't worry, I'll see
> That it's done, one two three.
> I'll bamboozle him so,
> With my lying, I'll throw
> Such a scare in our foe
> He'll deny that he really is he
> And declare that he really is me!

PSEUDOLUS (*doubtfully*)

> Yes, but how?

MONKEY (*working himself up*)

> > All these questions I get!
> Oh, you *will* be the death of me yet!

PSEUDOLUS (*sweetly*)

> You're so gracious and charming, my pet.

MONKEY (*snarling*)

> Now there's something I'd like you to know:
> I admit you're my boss in this show,
> But in cheating and double-cross you
> Can't come close to the things I can do.

PSEUDOLUS (*all innocent gratitude*)

> Oh, god bless you! For my sake.

MONKEY (*with gracious condescension*)

> > No, *mine*.

(*Squaring his shoulders and straightening his uniform*)

> Look me over now, please. Does the line
> Of this uniform suit me this way?

PSEUDOLUS (*enthusiastically*)

    Oh, it's perfect, it's great!

MONKEY (*condescendingly*)

                Then okay.

PSEUDOLUS (*humbly*)

    May god in heaven hear your prayers and grant them all,
my hero—

    For if he listens to mine instead, he'll grant your worth,
and that's zero.

    (*To the audience, gesturing toward Monkey*)

    The lowest, sneakiest good-for-nothing I ever laid eyes
upon.

MONKEY (*menacingly*)

    You'd say a thing like that to me?

PSEUDOLUS (*swiftly switching back to humility*)

                My lips are sealed from now on.

    (*Clamps his lips shut—and manages to stay that way for
five full seconds at least; then, bursting out—*)

    You do a careful job for me and what gifts you'll get!

MONKEY (*snarling*)

                    Shut up!

    Remind a man who remembers things, and you'll make the
man forget

    The things he has to remember. I've got it all by heart, it's
set

    (*Tapping his head*)

    In here. My tricks are all worked out—and worked out
trickily.

PSEUDOLUS (*to the audience, admiringly*)

    This man is good.

MONKEY (*to the audience, gesturing toward Pseudolus*)

        And this one's not—and the same is true for me.

PSEUDOLUS (*worriedly*)

    Now watch your step.

MONKEY

          Oh, shut your mouth.

PSEUDOLUS

          I swear, so help me god—

MONKEY (*interrupting witheringly*)

  Help you? Not he! You're set to spout the lies and spout
    them hard!

PSEUDOLUS (*unruffled*)

  —by my love and fear and vast respect for your consum-
    mate treachery—

MONKEY (*as before*)

  I teach that sort of thing to others. *You* can't soft-soap *me*.

PSEUDOLUS (*as before*)

  —you pull this job successfully, and I'll see you have things
    nice—

MONKEY

  Some joke!

PSEUDOLUS (*gathering momentum*)

    —nice wine, hors d'oeuvres and food, a regular paradise,
  Plus a nice little girl to make things nice with kiss upon
    kiss upon kiss.

MONKEY (*acidly*)

  You're too nice to me.

PSEUDOLUS (*rising to a climax*)

        You pull this job, and the word you'll use is bliss!

  (*Monkey stares at him for a full ten seconds, deadpan and
without batting an eyelash. Suddenly he breaks into a broad
grin and slaps him resoundingly on the back.*)

MONKEY (*enthusiastically*)

        If *I* don't do
        This job for you,
        Tell the torturer to
        Give me rack and screw!

  (*Monkey sets his hat firmly on his head, adjusts his sword
and, girded for action, turns to Pseudolus.*)

MONKEY (*all business*) All right, hurry and show me where I enter the jaws of the pimp's house.

PSEUDOLUS (*pointing*) The third this way.

(*The "jaws" suddenly open, and Ballio appears on the threshold.*)

MONKEY Shh! They've opened wide.

PSEUDOLUS If you ask me, the house has a bellyache.

MONKEY Why?

PSEUDOLUS It's throwing up the pimp.

MONKEY Is that the fellow?

PSEUDOLUS That's the fellow.

MONKEY (*distastefully*) Rotten piece of merchandise, that.

PSEUDOLUS (*as Ballio sidles out the door*) Look, will you? He walks sideways, not frontwards. Like a crab!

(*Pseudolus and Monkey move off to the side where they can overhear without being seen. Ballio sidles downstage and addresses the audience.*)

BALLIO He wasn't as bad as I thought, that cook I hired. All he's made off with so far is a cup and a jug.

PSEUDOLUS (*to Monkey, sotto voce*) Hey! Now's our chance!

MONKEY (*to Pseudolus, sotto voce*) My feelings exactly.

PSEUDOLUS (*to Monkey, sotto voce*) On your way and play it smart. I'll stay here in ambush.

(*Monkey steps into the street while Ballio's back is turned, and walks slowly along, acting as if he is looking for some house.*)

MONKEY (*to himself—but good and loud*) I kept count carefully: this is the sixth street from the town gate, and this is where he told me to turn in. But how many houses he said, I can't for the life of me remember.

BALLIO (*swiveling about at the sound of a voice, to himself*) Who's this fellow in uniform? Where does he come from?

Who's he looking for? Looks like a stranger; I don't recognize the face.

MONKEY (*turning and assuming an expression of pleased surprise at seeing Ballio; to the world at large*) Well, here's someone who certainly can relieve my uncertainty.

BALLIO (*to himself*) He's heading straight for me. Now where in the world could he be from?

MONKEY (*like a top sergeant*) Hey, you standing there, you with the beard like a billy goat, I have a question for you.

BALLIO (*snappishly*) Just like that, eh, without even a "Good afternoon"?

MONKEY Anything good I don't give away.

BALLIO (*snarling*) Then, damn it all, the same goes for me!

PSEUDOLUS (*aside, shaking his head despairingly*) Doing just great, right from the start!

MONKEY Know anybody who lives in this street? (*As Ballio remains stubbornly silent*) How about it, you?

BALLIO (*sullenly*) Me? Sure, myself.

MONKEY Aren't many who can say that. Downtown there isn't one in ten who really knows himself.

PSEUDOLUS (*aside, sarcastically*) I'm safe—now he's become a philosopher!

MONKEY I'm looking for someone around here—a nasty, filthy, low-down, lawbreaking liar.

BALLIO (*aside, promptly*) He's looking for me. Those are all my titles. Now, if he'd only mention the name—(*To Monkey*) What's the fellow's name?

MONKEY Ballio. A pimp.

BALLIO (*aside*) I knew it! (*To Monkey, tapping himself on the chest*) Mister, the man you're looking for is right here.

MONKEY (*incredulously*) You're Ballio?

BALLIO Sure I'm Ballio.

MONKEY (*eying the unappetizing get-up*) From the clothes I'd say you're a pickpocket.

BALLIO (*promptly*) So when *you* hold me up some dark night, you won't bother to put your thieving hands on them.

MONKEY (*getting down to business*) My master wants me to give you his best regards. (*Taking out the letter*) Here, take this letter; I have orders to give it to you.

BALLIO Orders from whom?

PSEUDOLUS (*aside, clutching his hair*) I'm a goner! My man's in a jam—he doesn't know the name! We're stuck!

BALLIO (*noticing Monkey hesitate, sharply*) Who do you say sent this to me?

MONKEY (*in his best top sergeant's manner, pointing to the seal*) Identify that picture, and then *you* tell me his name. I want to make sure you're really Ballio.

BALLIO Give me the letter.

MONKEY (*handing it over*) Here. Now identify the seal.

BALLIO (*taking a quick look, to himself*) Major I. Kutall Hedzoff to the life. I recognize him. (*To Monkey*) Hey, his name is I. Kutall Hedzoff.

MONKEY (*dryly*) Well, now that you've told me his name is I. Kutall Hedzoff, I know I gave the letter to the right man.

BALLIO What's he doing these days, anyway?

MONKEY (*striking a military pose*) What any brave, honest soldier does, by god! (*Relaxing*) Now get a move on and read the letter through—that's first on the docket—then take the money and deliver the girl, and make it snappy. Because if I'm not in Sicyon by today, I'm in my coffin by tomorrow. That's the way the major operates.

BALLIO (*nodding understandingly*) Don't I know! You're talking to someone who knows him.

MONKEY (*curtly*) Then get a move on and read the letter.

BALLIO Just keep quiet and I will. (*Opens the letter and starts reading*) "Letter of Major I. Kutall Hedzoff to Pimp Ballio sealed with picture as provided by previous mutual agreement."

MONKEY (*pointing*)   It's the seal on the letter.

BALLIO   I see it, I recognize it. But does he always write letters this way? With no salutation?

MONKEY (*sternly*)   Standard military procedure, Ballio. They send greetings to friends (*saluting*) with the hand—and (*going through the motions of a saber cut*) destruction to enemies with ditto. But keep on with the reading. Go ahead, find out what the letter says.

BALLIO   Then listen. (*Reading*) "This is my orderly Harpax who has come to you—" (*Looking up*) Are you Harpax?

MONKEY   That's me—the Snatcher in the flesh.

BALLIO (*resuming his reading*)   "—and who is delivering this letter. I want you to accept payment of the money from him and at the same time send the girl off with him. Deserving people deserve a letter with a salutation. If I thought you were deserving, I'd have sent one."

MONKEY (*as Ballio looks up*)   What do we do now?

BALLIO (*promptly*)   You hand over the money and take the girl.

MONKEY (*impatiently*)   Well, who's holding up who?

BALLIO (*going toward his door*)   Follow me in, then.

MONKEY   I'm following.

(*The two go into Ballio's house. The minute the door closes behind them, Pseudolus bursts out of his hiding place.*)

PSEUDOLUS (*to the audience, excitedly*)   I swear to god, never in all my life have I seen a dirty rat as fiendishly clever as that fellow! I'm afraid of him. I'm really scared of him. He might pull the same sort of dirty trick on me he pulled (*gesturing toward Ballio's house*) on him. With things going so well, he might lower his horns and charge *me*, if he ever gets the chance to do me dirt. And that's something I would not like—because (*smiling*) I like the guy!

(*Shaking his head despairingly*) Right now I've got three good reasons to be scared stiff. First of all, I'm scared that

that colleague of mine will desert me and defect to the enemy. Next, I'm scared that Simo will be back any minute from downtown: we'll capture the loot, and *he'll* capture the looters. And, along with all these scares, I'm scared (*gesturing in the direction of the town gate*) that *that* Harpax will get here before *this* Harpax gets out of here with the girl.

(*Staring intently at the door*) This is killing me! They're taking so long to come out! My heart's all ready with its bags packed: if he doesn't come out of there with the girl, it's saying good-by to my chest and taking off for good. (*The door opens and Monkey and Rosy step out.*) I win! My guards were all on their guard, and I beat them all!

(*Monkey walks from the door dragging a reluctant Rosy who is dissolved in tears.*)

MONKEY (*earnestly*) Please don't cry, Rosy. You don't understand what's happening. I promise you, you'll find out very soon, at the party. I'm not taking you to that snaggle-toothed monster of a major from Macedon, who's making you cry this way. I'm taking you to the one man you want to belong to most of all. I promise you, in a little while you'll be giving Calidorus a big hug.

PSEUDOLUS (*frantically*) What were you hanging around inside there for? My heart's been pounding in my chest so long, it's all bruised!

MONKEY (*angrily*) Damn you, a fine time you pick to cross-examine me, in the middle of an enemy ambush! Out of here on the double!

PSEUDOLUS (*swiveling about*) You're a good-for-nothing but, so help me, you have good ideas. (*Shouting*) Hip, hip, hooray! Forward march! Straight for that jug, men!

(*They dash off, stage left, dragging the bewildered Rosy after them. A second later the door of Ballio's house opens, and Ballio sidles out. He looks positively gay for a change.*)

BALLIO (*to the audience*)   Whew! My mind's finally at rest, now that that fellow's gone and taken the girl away. Now let that dirty rat of a Pseudolus come and try to sneak her away from me! There's one thing I know for sure: I'd sooner commit perjury under oath a thousand times than have him pull a fast one and get the laugh on me. Now I'll have the laugh on him, if I ever meet him. You ask me, though, the only thing he'll be meeting is his deserts—on a mill wheel. I wish Simo would come along so he could enjoy some of my joy.

(*At this point Simo conveniently enters, stage left.*)

SIMO (*to himself*)   I've come to see what that Ulysses of mine has accomplished. Whether he's stolen the statue from Fort Ballio yet.[2]

BALLIO (*heartily*)   Hey, lucky fellow, let me shake that lucky hand.

SIMO (*taken aback by the strange phenomenon of a genial Ballio*)   What's the matter?

BALLIO (*deliberately*)   There is no longer—

SIMO (*impatiently*)   No longer what?

BALLIO   —anything for you to be afraid of.

SIMO   What's happened? Has he been to your house?

BALLIO (*smiling beatifically*)   Nope.

SIMO (*sourly*)   Then what's happened that's so good?

BALLIO (*as before*)   That five thousand Pseudolus solemnly swore he'd get out of you today is safe and sound.

SIMO (*fervently*)   God, do I wish it!

BALLIO (*cockily*)   If he gets his hands on that girl today or gives her to your son today, the way he said he would, you get the five thousand from *me*. Do me a favor: let's make it official. I'm dying to do it that way just to prove that

2 Ulysses in the *Iliad* stole the sacred statue of Athena from the citadel of Troy.

there's absolutely no chance for a slip-up anywhere. I'll even throw in the girl as a gift, too.

SIMO (*shrugging*) I can't see a thing I've got to lose by taking you up. All right—do you hereby agree to give me five thousand dollars on those terms?

BALLIO (*airily*) I hereby agree.

SIMO (*finally convinced, rubbing his hands delightedly*) Well, this isn't a bad turn of affairs at all. Did you run into him?

BALLIO Into the both of them, as a matter of fact.

SIMO (*eagerly*) What did he say? What did he tell you? What kind of story did he give you?

BALLIO (*shrugging*) The nonsense you hear on the stage. The stuff they always say about pimps in comedies, stuff any schoolboy knows by heart. He told me I was a dirty, filthy double-crosser.

SIMO Believe me, he wasn't lying.

BALLIO (*grinning*) I wasn't the least bit sore. What difference do insults make to a fellow who doesn't give a damn or bother to deny them?

SIMO But why don't I have to be afraid of him? That's what I want to hear.

BALLIO (*gleefully*) Because he'll never get the girl away from me. He can't! Remember I told you a little while ago that I had sold her to a major from Macedon?

SIMO Yes.

BALLIO (*deliberately drawing his story out*) Well, his orderly brought me the money plus a sealed letter with identification—

SIMO (*impatiently*) Yes, yes.

BALLIO (*not to be hurried*) —which he and I had agreed on between us. (*Triumphantly*) Well, just a few minutes ago, the orderly took the girl away with him!

SIMO (*excitedly*) Is this the truth you're telling me? On your honor?

BALLIO (*grinning*)   Where would *I* get any honor?

SIMO (*doubtfully*)   Just watch out that he hasn't pulled some fancy stunt on you.

BALLIO (*cockily*)   The letter and the picture make me absolutely certain. I tell you, he just left the city with her. He's headed for Sicyon.

SIMO (*jubilantly*)   Well done, by god! Why don't I have Pseudolus put his name down for immigration to Treadmill Town this minute? (*His attention caught, looks toward the wings, stage right.*) Who's this fellow in uniform?

BALLIO (*following Simo's gaze*)   I don't know. Let's watch where he goes and what he does.

(*Enter Harpax looking a bit worried. He walks downstage and addresses the audience.*)

SONG

HARPAX

The servant who doesn't give a damn for the orders a master's issued

> Is a dirty good-for-nothing, that's a fact.

And *I* don't give a damn for the kind whose memory's so short

> They need a second warning before they'll act.

> > And those who think they're emancipated
> > The minute they find themselves located
> > Out of the master's sight, and drink and whore
> > And go through every cent they've saved and more,
> > Will bear the name of slave
> > To the grave.
> > There's nothing good in them—unless you add
> > The knack to stay alive by being bad.

Now *I* won't mix or be seen with this ilk; I cut them dead on the spot.

When *I* get orders, and the master's away, I act as if he's not.

It's when he's gone I start to fear—
In order not to when he's near.

(Holds up the purse and continues more agitatedly.)

Here's a job that I'd better begin.
Up till now I've been out at the inn,
Where that Syrus—the fellow that I
Gave the documents to—let me lie.
There I stayed, since he told me to stay:
He'd come back and he'd fetch me away,
So he said, when the pimp had come home.
When he didn't show up, on my own
I came here to find out what the matter could be,
And not give him a chance to get funny with me!

(Walking up to the pimp's door)

The best I can do is knock right here and find someone
who's free;
I want the pimp to take this cash, and send the girl with me.

BALLIO *(to Simo sotto voce, his eyes glistening)*
Hey, Simo!

SIMO *(sotto voce)*
What?

BALLIO *(as before)*
He's mine!

SIMO
How's that?

BALLIO *(smacking his lips)*
Because this man's my meat.
He wants a wench, he's got the cash—I'm dying to start to
eat!

SIMO *(incredulously)*
You'll eat him up this minute?

BALLIO *(as before)*
Fresh and hot and nicely brown
And served you on a platter thus, that's the time to gulp
them down.

(*Flashing his hyena grin*)

All decent people let me starve, but the sinners don't, you
see;

The solid citizen slaves for the state—and the sinner slaves
for me!

SIMO (*disgusted*)

You're such a rat, when the good lord acts, what tortures
he'll decree!

HARPAX (*to himself*)   I'm wasting time. I'll knock on the
door this minute and find out whether Ballio's in or not.

BALLIO (*to Simo, sotto voce, gleefully*)   These blessings come
to me from Lady Love. She brings them here, these people
who run away from profit to chase after loss by spending
their lives having a good time. They eat, they drink, they
whore, (*eying Simo distastefully*) they have different ideas
from the likes of you, who won't let yourself have a good
time and begrudge those who do.

HARPAX (*banging on the door and shouting*)   Hey, where is
everybody?

BALLIO (*to Simo, sotto voce, rubbing his hands*)   The fellow's coming straight at me by the straightest route.

HARPAX (*shouting even louder*)   Hey, where are you people?

BALLIO (*calling to Harpax*)   Hey, mister, someone in there
owe you money? (*To Simo, sotto voce*) I'll get a good haul
out of him. I can tell: this is my lucky day.

HARPAX (*not hearing, despairingly*)   Isn't anyone going to
open this door?

BALLIO (*calling louder*)   Hey, soldier, someone in there owe
you money?

HARPAX (*finally looking up and seeing the two of them*)   I'm
looking for the master of the house. Ballio, the pimp.

BALLIO   Mister, you can cut your looking short, whoever you
are.

HARPAX   Why?

BALLIO Because you are personally in the flesh looking at him personally in the flesh.

HARPAX (*pointing to Simo*) You're Ballio?

SIMO (*visibly shuddering and shaking his stick*) Soldier, you watch your step or you'll be in trouble from this stick. Point that finger at *him;* he's your pimp.

BALLIO (*to Harpax, with a contemptuous gesture in Simo's direction*) Oh yes, *he's* an honest man. (*To Simo, sneering*) And you, my honest man, every time you go downtown you get plenty of dunning from your creditors since you don't have a cent outside of what said pimp helps you out with.

HARPAX (*impatiently*) Would you mind talking to *me?*

BALLIO (*leaving Simo's side and walking up to Harpax*) I am. What's on your mind?

HARPAX (*holding out the purse*) Take this money.

BALLIO (*whipping his hand out*) I've had my hand out for hours ready for you to hand over.

HARPAX (*handing it over*) Take it: exactly one thousand dollars, every coin full weight. Major I. Kutall Hedzoff, my master, gave me orders to deliver it—it's the balance he owes—and take Rosy away with me.

BALLIO (*studying him closely*) Your master?

HARPAX That's right.

BALLIO A major?

HARPAX That's correct.

BALLIO From Macedon maybe?

HARPAX Exactly.

BALLIO I. Kutall Hedzoff sent you to me, eh?

HARPAX Precisely.

BALLIO To give me this money?

HARPAX If you're Ballio the pimp.

BALLIO And to take the girl away with you?

HARPAX Right.

BALLIO   Rosy he said her name was?

HARPAX   You've got a good memory.

BALLIO   Wait a second. I'll be right back. (*Turns and rushes over to Simo.*)

HARPAX   (*calling after him*)   But hurry, because *I'm* in a hurry. You can see for yourself how late it is.

BALLIO   (*calling back*)   I see, all right. I want to consult with this man here. You just wait there. I'll be right with you. (*To Simo, sotto voce, gleefully*) What's next, Simo? What do we do now? This fellow who's brought the money—I've caught him in the act!

SIMO   (*sotto voce, blankly*)   What do you mean?

BALLIO   (*sotto voce, chuckling*)   Don't you know what this is all about?

SIMO   (*as before*)   I haven't the slightest idea.

BALLIO   (*sotto voce, triumphantly*)   That Pseudolus of yours has sent this fellow to make believe he's from the major!

(*Ballio grins delightedly. An answering grin gradually spreads over Simo's face as the import sinks in. They continue talking, sotto voce.*)

SIMO   (*his eyes gleaming*)   Did you get the money from him?

BALLIO   (*hefting the purse*)   Do you have to ask? Can't you see?

SIMO   (*quickly*)   Just remember to hand over half of that loot to me. It's only right we share it.

BALLIO   (*his grin widening*)   Why the hell not? It all comes from you!

HARPAX   (*calling impatiently*)   When are you going to take care of me?

BALLIO   (*calling back, meaningfully*)   I am right now! (*To Simo*) What do you suggest I do now?

SIMO   (*excitedly*)   Let's have some fun with our spy, the faker! And let's keep it up till he catches on we're making fun of him.

BALLIO   Let's go. (*The two walk up together to Harpax.*) So you're the major's orderly, eh?

HARPAX   Of course.

BALLIO (*sneering*)   How much did you cost him?

HARPAX (*drawing himself up*)   Every ounce of strength he had, to win me in battle. I'll have you know I was commander in chief of the armed forces back in my homeland.

BALLIO (*as before*)   Your homeland? When did the major ever capture a jail?

HARPAX (*sharply*)   You pass any nasty cracks and you'll hear some yourself.

BALLIO   How long did it take you to get here from Sicyon?

HARPAX   Day and a half.

BALLIO   Pretty fast traveling, that.

SIMO (*To Ballio*)   Oh this fellow's quick, all right. One look at those legs and you can see they're just the kind for—carrying shackles, extra-heavy shackles.

BALLIO (*to Harpax*)   Tell me, when you were a boy, did you used to (*leering*) play around with girls?

SIMO (*to Ballio, eying Harpax distastefully*)   Of course he did.

BALLIO (*to Harpax*)   And did you used to—(*leering*) you know what I'm going to say?

SIMO (*to Ballio, with alacrity*)   Of course he did.

HARPAX (*looking from one to the other blankly*)   Are you two in your right mind?

BALLIO   Answer me this. When the major stood watch at night and you used to go along with him, (*making an obscene gesture*) did his sword fit in your scabbard?

HARPAX (*losing his temper*)   You go to the devil!

BALLIO (*unruffled*)   You can go there yourself. Today. Very soon today.

HARPAX (*grimly*)   Are you going to give me the girl? If not, hand back the money. (*Reaches for the purse.*)

BALLIO (*quickly putting it behind his back*)   Wait a second.

HARPAX   Why should I?

BALLIO (*mockingly*)   Tell me, how much did it cost to hire that uniform?

HARPAX   What are you talking about?

SIMO (*to Harpax*)   And how much for the sword?

HARPAX (*to himself*)   These fellows need a dose of helle-bore![3]

BALLIO (*to Harpax, reaching for his cap*)   Hey—

HARPAX (*pulling back*)   Hands off!

BALLIO (*to Harpax*)   —how much is that headpiece earning for its owner?

HARPAX (*bewildered*)   What do you mean, owner? What are you two dreaming about? Everything I'm wearing belongs to me, bought with my own money.

BALLIO (*leering*)   Sure—earned by the sweat of your thighs.

HARPAX (*to himself, grimly, as he girds for action*)   This pair has had the steam bath. Now what they're asking for is a good old-fashioned massage.

BALLIO (*promptly backing away, and changing his tune*)   In all seriousness now, I ask you: how much are you getting out of this? What's the pittance Pseudolus is paying you?

HARPAX (*blankly*)   Pseudolus? Who's Pseudolus?

BALLIO   Your trainer, the fellow who coached you in this swindle so you could swindle the girl away from me.

HARPAX (*as before*)   What Pseudolus? What's this swindle you're talking about? I don't know the man, never saw hide nor hair of him.

BALLIO (*wearily*)   Why don't you just be on your way. There's no pickings for any crooks around here today. You tell Pseudolus that someone else made off with the loot, that Harpax beat him to it.

HARPAX (*angrily*)   God damn it, *I'm* Harpax!

---

[3] The standard ancient remedy for mental illness.

BALLIO (*sneering*) God damn it, you mean you wish you were! (*To Simo*) This man's a crook, plain as the nose on your face.

HARPAX (*heatedly*) Listen, I just now gave you the money and a little while ago, the minute I arrived, right in front of this door I handed your servant the identification, the letter sealed with the major's picture.

BALLIO (*taken aback*) You handed a letter to my servant? What servant?

HARPAX Syrus.

BALLIO (*to Simo, nervously*) He lacks confidence. Not very good at being a crook, this fellow here: hasn't even thought up a good story. Damn that good-for-nothing Pseudolus! He sure figured out a smart stunt: he gave this fellow the exact amount of money the major owed and dressed him all up so he could do me out of the girl. (*With great assurance—as if to convince himself*) As a matter of fact, this letter he's talking about was delivered to me by the real Harpax himself.

HARPAX (*frantically*) I'm Harpax! I'm the major's orderly! I'm not trying any tricks or pulling any swindles! I haven't the faintest idea who that Pseudolus of yours is, I never heard of him in my life!

(*There is a dead silence as Ballio and Simo stare at each other.*)

SIMO (*slowly and emphatically*) Pimp, unless I am very much mistaken, you are out one girl.

BALLIO (*nodding gloomily*) Damn it all, the more I hear, the more I'm afraid of just that. Damn it all, I got cold shivers a second ago from that there Syrus who took this fellow's identification. I wouldn't be at all surprised if it was Pseudolus. (*To Harpax*) Listen, that fellow you gave the identification to before, what did he look like?

HARPAX Red hair, pot belly, piano legs, big head, pointy eyes, darkish skin, red face, and whopping big feet.

BALLIO (*groaning*) The minute you mentioned those feet,

you did for me! It was Pseudolus, all right. (*To Simo*)
Simo, it's all over with me. I'm a dead man!

HARPAX (*promptly*)　I'm not letting you do any dying until
I get my money back—five thousand dollars.

SIMO (*blandly*)　And another five thousand for me.

BALLIO (*reproachfully*)　You mean you'd actually take a
bonus like that from me when I promised it just for a joke?

SIMO (*archly*)　It's a man's duty to take bonuses—or booty—
from crooks.

BALLIO (*between his teeth*)　At least hand Pseudolus over
to me.

SIMO (*shrugging*)　I hand Pseudolus over to you? What
crime did he commit? Didn't I tell you a thousand times to
watch out for him?

BALLIO (*desperately*)　He's killed me!

SIMO　And hit me for a forfeit of a measly five thousand.

BALLIO (*as before*)　What do I do now?

HARPAX　Pay me back my money, and you can go hang
yourself.

BALLIO (*to Harpax*)　Damn your hide! (*Turns and starts
walking off, stage left.*) All right, follow me downtown and
I'll settle up.

HARPAX (*falling in behind with alacrity*)　I'm following.

SIMO (*calling after him*)　What about me?

BALLIO (*stopping*)　Aliens today, citizens tomorrow. (*To the
audience*) Pseudolus practically held a session of the Su-
preme Court and got a death sentence against me when he
sent that fellow today to sneak off my girl. (*To Harpax*)
Follow me, you. (*To the audience, gesturing toward the
street*) Don't think I'm coming back by this street here.
The way things have worked out, I've decided to use the
back alleys.

HARPAX (*impatiently*)　If you did as much walking as talking, you'd be downtown by now.

BALLIO (*starting to trudge off, forlornly*)　I've decided to change today from my birthday to my deathday. (*He exits, stage left, with Harpax at his heels.*)

SIMO (*to the audience*)   I made a monkey out of him for fair—and my servant made a monkey out of his worst enemy for fair.

(*After a moment's thought*) I've decided not to spring on Pseudolus what they always do in comedies. No whips, no canes. I'm going in now to get the five thousand I promised him if he pulled off this stunt. I'll hand it over to him without waiting to be dunned. (*Shaking his head admiringly*) There's a fellow who's really smart, really tricky, a real scoundrel. He did better than Ulysses and the Trojan Horse, that Pseudolus. I'll go in now, bring out the money, and spring my surprise on him.

(*Simo enters his house, and the stage is now empty.*)

ACT V

(*Enter Pseudolus, stage left. He has just left a wild party at Charinus' house—and looks it: he has a chaplet askew on his head, is grinning drunkenly from ear to ear, and is staggering along, combating, with not too much success, a certain rubberiness in shanks and feet.*)

SONG

PSEUDOLUS

What's goin' on? What a way to act!
Hey, feet, will *you* stand up or not?
You want to leave me lying here
Till someone heaves me from the spot?
If *I* go into a somersault,
Believe you me, it's all your fault!

(*Makes a wild lurch*)

Insist on keeping at it, eh?
I'll have to tell you off today!

(*Finally makes the center of the stage and stands there weaving*)

'At's the trouble with wine. Always wrestles unfair;
First thing in the ring, has your feet in the air.

(*Grins blissfully*)

I'm as drunk as a lord, I'm loaded, I'm high!
What with elegance fit for the gods in the sky,
  And the choicest of foods for us all,
And a spot just as gala as a room for a ball,
  Boy, oh boy, did *we* have a ball!

(*With drunken gravity*)

Now, why should I beat about the bush?
  This is why we stay alive,
  This is where all pleasure lies,
  This is where all joys derive—
  And *my* view is—it's paradise!

(*Rapturously*)

>When a man takes a girl in his arms,
>When he presses his mouth against hers,
>When the two, without trying to hide,
>Hold on fast, tongue on tongue—neither stirs,
>When her bosom is pressed to his breast,
>Or their bodies, if they choose, become one—
>Ah, that's when the time is the best
>To take from a dainty white hand
>A full glass, and to drink—it's just grand!
>It's the time when we're all out for fun,
>And the feelings are good all around,
>And the talk isn't just empty sound . . .

(*Working himself up*)

>Let's not spare the bouquets or perfume!
>Or the stuff for the looks of the room!
>And the cooking and all of the rest—
>No need asking: only the best!

(*Breaks off and smiles blissfully. Then continues a little more matter-of-factly.*)

>That's how we spent the rest of the day,
>The boy and I; we were *gai, très gai,*
>When once I'd done my job as planned
>And driven off the enemy band.

(*Gesturing drunkenly toward the wings, stage left*)

>I left them gorging, guzzling, whoring,
> (Left my own girl too), all getting roaring
>Drunk and happy. When I stood up,
>They asked me please to do a dance.

(*Lumbering through a few weird steps*)

>I gave them this, performed, of course,
>With all my usual elegance.
>The steps I did were the very best kinds—
>I've had lessons, you know, in bumps and grinds.

(*More lumbering*)

> Then I put on my coat and gave them one
> That goes like this—but just for fun.
> They stamped, they clapped, they yelled "en-
>   core,"
> And called me back to give them more.

(*Still lumbering*)

> I start again and give them this,
> (Didn't want to do the same thing twice)
> I play it up to the girl I'm with,
> (Make sure that later she'd treat me nice)
> I whirl, I skid—and down I go,
> And that was the swan song for my show.

> So then I try to get on my feet,
>   And—whoops—all over my coat!
> I hand them a laugh with that—and get
>   The jug as antidote.
> I take a drink, I change my coat,
>   I leave the old one there,
> I come out here to clear my head
>   By getting a breath of air.

(*Lurching up to Simo's door*)

I've left the son to see the father, and put a word in his ear
About our deal.

(*Shouting*)

> Open up! Tell Simo, Pseudolus is here!

(*He pounds like a madman, then lurches a few feet away.
A second later the door opens, and Simo appears clutching a
purse.*)

SIMO (*as he comes out*)

> It's the voice of that scoundrel that's brought me out
>   here.

(*Catching sight of Pseudolus advancing boozily*)

> But what's *this* that I see? And how come? Very queer!

PSEUDOLUS *(affably)*

It's your Pseudolus, fresh from a party—and tight.

SIMO

From loose living, by god. Look at that! What a sight!
That your master's right here doesn't scare you one bit.

(To himself)

What's this call for? Sweet reason or throwing a fit?

(Caressing the purse, ruefully)

Ah, but *this* which I'm holding rules out being rough,

(Gesturing contemptuously toward Pseudolus)

If I have any hopes out of *that* for this stuff.

PSEUDOLUS *(in the grand manner)*

Common sinner comes calling on saint nonpareil.

SIMO *(grimly managing a smile and going up to him)*

Hearty greetings, dear Pseudolus—

(As Pseudolus belches resoundingly)

you go to hell!

PSEUDOLUS *(trying hard to keep his balance, as Simo gives him a shove.)*

Hey, what's that for?

SIMO *(snarling)*

Just what do you mean, you disgrace,
By belching your drunken breath in my face?

PSEUDOLUS *(grabbing him for support, reproachfully)*

Take it easy! Hey, hold me and spare me more spills—
Can't you see that I'm tight? I'm soused to the gills!

SIMO *(holding him up, grimly)*

You sure have a nerve going around in this way—
As drunk as a lord in the broad light of day!

PSEUDOLUS *(grinning fatuously)*

I just felt I'd like doing it.

SIMO *(as before)*

Felt like it, eh?

(*As Pseudolus drags up another roaring belch*)

What again? What's all this? You still belching at me?

PSEUDOLUS

Aw, my belches smell sweet, so you *just* let me be.

SIMO (*disgustedly*)

I swear, you could swill in an hour
All the alcohol Italy's manpower,
Using bumper crops only, could press
In four years.

PSEUDOLUS (*grinning*)

Not an hour. Much less.

SIMO (*nodding tight-lipped*)

Guess you're right. Here's a point I've ignored:
At what dock was this load put aboard?

PSEUDOLUS (*carelessly*)

With your son. We've been boozing away.

(*Gleefully*)

I sure gave it to Ballio, eh?
I did what I told you I would!

SIMO (*unhappily*)

You're a model of stinkerhood.

PSEUDOLUS

It's the girl's fault, you know. She's been freed,
And she's there with your son at the feed.

SIMO (*wearily*)

Oh, I've heard a complete résumé.

PSEUDOLUS (*stoutly*)

Then what's holding things up? Where's my pay?

SIMO (*summoning up a ghastly smile, holding out the purse*)

It's your right. I agree. Here you are.

PSEUDOLUS (*unable to believe his eyes*)

You said you'd never come across—and here I get my pay!

(*He grins from ear to ear. Then, like a master ordering his slave, he points to his shoulder.*)

Well, load it on this shoulder, boy, and follow me this way.

SIMO (*shocked*)

You're asking *me* to put this there?

PSEUDOLUS (*grinning*)

You will, and I know why.

SIMO (*to the world at large*)

He takes my money and then gets funny—what can I do
with this guy?

PSEUDOLUS (*as before*)

The victor gets the spoils, they say.

SIMO (*grimly*)

Then bend that shoulder down.

PSEUDOLUS

Okay.

SIMO (*between his teeth*)

I'd never thought I'd see the day
That I'd be on my knees to *you*.
Oh my god, my god!

PSEUDOLUS (*sharply*)

Now that's taboo!

SIMO (*whimpering*)

It hurts!

PSEUDOLUS (*shaking his head feelingly*)

If *you* didn't hurt right now,
Then *I* would have the hurt—and how!

SIMO (*managing to work up an ingratiating smile*)

Now my boy, would you rob your old master of this
treasure?

PSEUDOLUS (*promptly*)

You're darned right. There's nothing would give me more
pleasure.

SIMO (*wheedling*)

Won't you please, as a favor, leave me *some* little part?

PSEUDOLUS

    I will not! Go on, call me a miser at heart,
    But you'll never be richer by a penny from me.
    Had my plans not worked out so successfully, I'd
    Have got damned little pity out of *you* for my hide.

SIMO (*losing control and shaking his stick*)
    Just as sure as I live, I'll get even, you'll see!

PSEUDOLUS (*shrugging*)
    With the hide that I've got, do you think you scare me?

SIMO (*turning away and walking off baffled*)
       All right, then. Good-*by!*

PSEUDOLUS (*calling*)
                     Hey, come back!

SIMO (*in high dudgeon*)
     I come back? And what for?

PSEUDOLUS
                    Just come back.
    I won't fool you.

SIMO (*walking back, suspiciously*)
           I'm back.

PSEUDOLUS (*taking his arm and starting to pull him, gaily*)
                   Well, just think—
    Here's the two of us off for a drink!

SIMO (*trying to hold back as Pseudolus tugs energetically*)
    For a drink?

PSEUDOLUS (*holding up the purse enticingly*)
              You just do as I say
    And I promise you half of this pay—
    Maybe more.

SIMO (*suddenly giving up all resistance*)
          Show the way and I'll go
    Any place that you want.

PSEUDOLUS (*innocently*)
              Is that so?
    You're not angry at me or your son
    On account of these things that I've done?

SIMO (*eying the purse hungrily*)
Not at all.

PSEUDOLUS (*starting to walk off, stage left*)
Come this way.

SIMO (*following him*)
I'm behind.

(*Stopping and pointing to the audience*)
Let's invite the whole crowd. Do you mind?

PSEUDOLUS (*stopping and eying the audience*)
Lord, they and I have never exchanged
A single invitation.

(*To the audience*)
But if you're willing to give a hand,
A loud and warm ovation,
To all our actors and their play—
I invite you all—but not today!

THE ROPE

DRAMATIS PERSONAE

SCEPARNIO, *Daemones' servant* (*slave*)

PLESIDIPPUS, *a wealthy young Athenian residing in Cyrene*

DAEMONES, *an elderly Athenian living in straitened circumstances near Cyrene*

PALAESTRA, *a beautiful young courtesan, the property of Labrax*

AMPELISCA, *an attractive young courtesan, also the property of Labrax*

PTOLEMOCRATIA, *priestess of the shrine of Venus*

FISHERMEN

TRACHALIO, *Plesidippus' valet* (*slave*)

LABRAX, *a slave dealer*

CHARMIDES, *an elderly vagabond who has recently struck up an acquaintance with Labrax*

ROUGHNECK (TURBALIO) ⎱
CUTTHROAT (SPARAX) ⎰ *slaves of Daemones*

GRIPUS, *a fisherman, slave of Daemones*

[DAEDALIS, *wife of Daemones*]

SCENE

A barren shore near Cyrene. In the background are, stage right, Daemones' simple cottage, and, stage left, a shrine of Venus consisting chiefly of a modest temple with an altar in front. The exit near the temple (stage left) leads to Cyrene. That near the cottage (stage right) leads to the beach; sand and rocks and a patch of reeds are visible near it.

PROLOGUE

(The Prologue, dressed in a spangled costume and wearing a glittering star on his forehead, steps forward. He represents Arcturus, the star that, rising in September and setting in November, marks the period of the equinoctial storms.)

ARCTURUS I am from the city of the celestials, fellow citizen of him who holds sway over all peoples, all seas, and all lands. My appearance is as you see: a bright star that glitters and gleams, that rises and sets in heaven and on earth, forever and ever, in its season. My name is Arcturus.

At night I shine among the gods in the sky; by day I walk among men on earth. Other stars, too, come down here from heaven: great Jove, lord of gods and men, assigns us stations, one here and another there, all over the world. We find out for him what men are doing, how they are behaving, particularly which are reverent and honest so that he can show them his favor. If we find people trying to win cases by bearing false witness, or forswearing themselves to deny a debt, we note their names and report them to Jove. From day to day he knows precisely who here on earth is out to do wrong. When rascals go into a trial ready to perjure themselves and trick a judge into awarding them the verdict, *he* reopens the case, reviews it, and passes a sentence so stiff it far outweighs whatever they may have won.

In another set of records he keeps a list of the good. And if the wicked have the idea that they can get on it by winning him over with gifts and offerings, they're wasting their time and money. Why? Because he has no mercy for men who are two-faced. The appeal of the honest man finds favor far more easily than that of the wicked despite all their gifts. And so I advise those of you who are good, who live your lives in reverence and honesty, to go on in this way so that you may reap your reward in time to come.

But now I want to tell you about the play; after all, that's what I'm here for.

(*Gesturing toward the scene behind him*) To begin with, this city is Cyrene; that's the way Diphilus[1] wanted it. This cottage on the seashore and the farm alongside it belong to Daemones. He's an old man who came here as an exile from Athens. He's not a bad man; he didn't leave his homeland because of any wrong he had done. It's simply that, in helping others, he got himself involved and, through his generosity, dissipated a hard-earned fortune. He once had a daughter, and he lost her, too, when she was a little child: she was kidnaped. The kidnaper sold her to a dealer in courtesans, one of the worst men alive.

Now the pimp who bought her brought the girl here to Cyrene. A certain young fellow, an Athenian—which makes him the girl's fellow citizen—happened to see her one day as she was coming home from her music lesson. He fell in love with her, went straight to the pimp, and arranged to buy her for seventy-five hundred dollars. He paid a deposit and had a contract drawn up. But the pimp, true to type, didn't care the least bit either about keeping his word or about the contract he had signed. He happened to have staying with him an old fellow from Agrigentum in Sicily, someone just like himself, a scoundrel who'd sell his own mother. This fellow began to rave about how beautiful the girl was, as well as all the others the pimp owned. And he began to talk the pimp into going to Sicily with him: he kept telling him there were lots of fast livers in Sicily, that courtesans made big money there, and that he could become a rich man there. He convinced him. And so the pimp secretly chartered a vessel and, one night, moved everything out of his house and put it on board. He told the boy who had bought the girl that he was going to the shrine of Venus to make a sacrifice and pay off an obligation—(*pointing*) this is the shrine right here—and even invited the young fellow to share the remains of the animal and have

[1]See pp. xiv and xvii.

lunch with him there. Then he went straight to the ship
and sailed off with his girls. Word reached the boy of what
had happened, that the pimp had left town, but by the
time the young fellow made it down to the waterfront the
ship was already far out at sea.

When I saw that the pimp was carrying the girl off, I
stepped in to help her and hurt him. I raised a storm and
stirred up the waves. You all know that I, Arcturus, am the
fiercest star of all; things get stormy when I rise and worse
when I set. Right now both the pimp and his cohort are
castaways, sitting on a rock; their ship's been shattered.
The girl and one other from the troupe got frightened and
jumped out of the vessel into the ship's boat; at this moment the waves are carrying them to shore near where old
Daemones lives in exile. As a matter of fact, the storm
ripped off his roof with all its tiles. (*As the door of the cottage opens and a figure comes out*) That's his servant there,
coming out. In a minute you'll see the young fellow who
arranged to buy the girl from the pimp. Good-by and good
luck!

ACT I

(*Daemones' servant, Sceparnio, "the wood chopper," comes out of the cottage carrying a spade. Sceparnio, a young fellow in his twenties, is the sort whose face feels more comfortable wearing a scowl than a smile, and his disposition has not been improved by years of work for a penniless master. His expression is even more sour than usual as he looks over the damage done to the cottage during the night.*)

SCEPARNIO (*to the audience*)   God in heaven, what a storm we had here last night! The wind took the roof right off the cottage. Wind? That was no wind; that was a hurricane right out of a play by Euripides! Look how it ripped all the tiles off the roof! It's made the cottage a lot brighter—put in some new skylights for us.

(*Unnoticed by Sceparnio, Plesidippus enters, stage left, followed by three friends; all are wearing coats and carrying swords. Plesidippus is a good-looking young fellow, well and expensively dressed. His face at the moment shows signs of worry and strain. He and his friends are deep in conversation as they come on stage.*)

PLESIDIPPUS (*apologetically*)   And so I rushed you away from your own affairs and all for nothing; I wasn't able to get my hands on that pimp down at the dock. But I didn't want to let up for one minute, I didn't want to give up hope; that's why I've kept you with me all this time. I've come out here to take a look around this shrine of Venus; he told me he was going to make a sacrifice here.

SCEPARNIO (*to himself, eying the spade distastefully*)   If I've got any brains, I'd better start getting some of this blasted clay ready.

PLESIDIPPUS (*overhearing, to his friends*)   Wait—I hear someone talking.

(*The door of the cottage opens and Daemones comes out. Daemones is middle-aged. Though he is dressed in worn work clothes, there is something about his manner and carriage that indicates he was not born a peasant.*)

DAEMONES (*calling*)   Hey, Sceparnio!

SCEPARNIO (*as he turns around*)   Who wants me?

DAEMONES   The man who paid good money for you.

SCEPARNIO (*sourly*)   Why don't you come right out with it and call me your slave?

DAEMONES   We're going to need lots of clay, so there's lots of digging for you to do. It looks as if we'll have to reroof the whole cottage. Daylight's coming through everywhere; there are more holes up there than in a sieve.

PLESIDIPPUS (*to Daemones*)   Good morning, Dad. (*Noticing Sceparnio*) Good morning to you both.

DAEMONES   Good morning.

SCEPARNIO   What do you mean by calling him "Dad"? You his— (*Eying his rather dandified dress distastefully*) What are you anyway, male or female?

PLESIDIPPUS (*astonished*)   I? I'm a man.

SCEPARNIO   Well, my man, go find your father farther on.

DAEMONES (*sorrowfully*)   I once did have a little daughter, but I lost her. She was the only child I had; I never had a son.

PLESIDIPPUS (*politely*)   God will give you one.

SCEPARNIO (*snarling*)   And he'll give you, whoever you are, what you won't want. Bothering busy people with your blabbering!

PLESIDIPPUS (*pointedly ignoring him, to Daemones; gesturing toward the cottage*)   Do you live here?

SCEPARNIO   What do you want to know for? What are you doing, casing the place? Looking for someone to rob?

PLESIDIPPUS (*turning on him*)   You must be one important and trusted slave to be able to answer for your master when he's present—and insult a gentleman.

SCEPARNIO   And you must be one nervy boor to be able to come up to the house of a total stranger who doesn't owe you the time of day and make a nuisance of yourself.

DAEMONES   Keep quiet, Sceparnio. (*To Plesidippus*) What would you like, my boy?

PLESIDIPPUS (*testily*)   I'd like to see that slave of yours get what's coming to him for taking it on himself to do the talking when his master's around. (*Politely*) If you don't mind, there are a few questions I'd like to ask you.

DAEMONES   Well, I'm busy right now, but I'll be glad to help even so.

SCEPARNIO (*to Daemones, quickly*)   Why don't you go down to the swamp and cut some canes for the roof while the weather's still clear?

DAEMONES (*curtly*)   Quiet! (*To Plesidippus*) Now, what can I do for you?

PLESIDIPPUS (*eagerly*)   Tell me, have you seen a fellow around here with curly gray hair? A sneaking, wheedling, lying—

DAEMONES (*interrupting, grimly*)   Lots of them. It's because of men like that that I live the way I do.

PLESIDIPPUS   I mean right here, at the shrine. Fellow with two girls with him, coming to make a sacrifice? Yesterday or maybe this morning?

DAEMONES (*shaking his head*)   No, my boy, I haven't seen anyone come here to make a sacrifice for a good many days now. And when they do, I see them all right—they always drop in to get water or fire or borrow dishes or a knife or a spit or a cooking pot or something. You'd think I kept a kitchen and a well for Venus and not myself. But they've left me alone for quite a while now.

PLESIDIPPUS (*in anguish*)   You know what you've just done? Pronounced my death sentence!

DAEMONES   Believe me, if I had my way, you'd be alive and healthy.

SCEPARNIO (*to Plesidippus*)   Listen you, if you're hanging around this shrine to beg some scraps to fill your belly, you'll do a lot better having lunch at home.

DAEMONES (*to Plesidippus*)   What happened? Someone invite you to lunch and not show up?

PLESIDIPPUS   Exactly.

SCEPARNIO   It's all right; *we* don't mind if you go home from here with your belly empty. Why don't you try Ceres' shrine instead? She handles the commissary; Venus only deals with love.

PLESIDIPPUS (*half to himself, bitterly*)   The way that man put one over on me is a crying shame!

DAEMONES (*happening to look off, stage right*)   Good god! Sceparnio, what are those men doing there in the surf?

SCEPARNIO   If you ask me, they're going to a fancy breakfast.

DAEMONES   Why?

SCEPARNIO   Because they took a bath last night.

DAEMONES (*gazing intently*)   They've been wrecked at sea!

SCEPARNIO   Sure. Take a look at the roof of our cottage— we've been wrecked on land.

DAEMONES   Poor fellows! Tossed overboard and having to swim for it.

PLESIDIPPUS (*trying to follow the direction of his gaze*)   Where do you see these men, anyway?

DAEMONES (*pointing*)   There, toward the right. See? Near the beach.

PLESIDIPPUS   I see them now. (*To his friends*) Follow me. I only hope one of them is that blasted crook I'm after. (*To Daemones and Sceparnio*) Well, take care of yourselves. (*They rush off, stage right.*)

SCEPARNIO (*calling after him*)   We've got it in mind; we don't need any reminders from you. (*Watches them go off, then suddenly gives a start*) Oh, my god in heaven, what's that I see?

DAEMONES   What is it?

SCEPARNIO (*excitedly*) Two girls in a boat, all by themselves. Look at the way the poor things are being tossed
about! (*Gazes intently in silence for a moment.*) Good,
good! The waves just carried the boat away from the rocks
and toward the shore; there isn't a helmsman alive who
could have done better. I don't think I've ever seen the
surf this bad in my life! If they can only get clear of those
breakers they'll be all right. Now's the moment they have
to watch out for—oh, a wave just hit them and one fell overboard—wait, it's shallow there—she can swim out easily.
Good work! She's on her feet—she's coming this way—she's
safe! (*Turning his head as if looking in a slightly different
direction*) The other's just jumped out of the boat to get on
shore—oh, she lost her nerve, she's fallen in the water, she's
on her knees—no, she's safe! She's wading out—now she's on
the beach—oh, oh, she turned to the right, she's going off in
that direction. Damn! That poor girl's going to do a lot of
hiking today!

DAEMONES What do you care?

SCEPARNIO (*still gazing intently*) If she falls off that cliff
she's heading toward, she'll finish her hike in a hurry.

DAEMONES (*with some asperity*) If you were going to eat at
their expense tonight, Sceparnio, I think you should worry
about them. But if you're going to eat at mine, you'd better
pay attention to me.

SCEPARNIO True. You're absolutely right.

DAEMONES Follow me.

SCEPARNIO I'm right behind.

(*The two enter the cottage. A moment later Palaestra, "the
struggler," enters, stage right. Her face is haggard, her hair
dripping, her clothing drenched, and she barely has the energy to drag herself along. Despite all this, we can see that
she is a remarkably fine-looking young girl. She makes her
way downstage and addresses the audience.*)

SONG

PALAESTRA

> The tales they tell of men's mishaps are mild,
> Compared to actual experience.
> It seems that Heaven's pleased to leave me thus—
> A frightened castaway in lands unknown.
> Oh, god, what can I say? That I was born
> For this? Have I received this as reward
> For all my honest and devoted prayer?
> For me to undergo such hardships would
> Be understandable if I had sinned
> Against my parents or, perhaps, my god.
> But when I've striven so to lead a life
> That's free of all such blame, this treatment is,
> O god, unfair, unjust, and undeserved.
> What mark hereafter will you place on guilt
> If such is the reward for innocence?
> If I were conscious that I'd done you wrong,
> Or that my parents had, then I would be
> More reconciled to all this misery.

(Pauses a moment, then resumes with bitterness and passion.)

> But the crimes of my owner are the cause of my grief.
> It is *his* sins I suffer for—his, and not mine!
> All he owned has gone down with his ship in the sea;
> I am all that is left of his worldly possessions.
> And that girl who escaped in the boat at my side,
> Even she has been lost; I'm alone, all alone.
> If she'd only been saved! Then at least, with her help,
> This sad blow would have been a bit lighter to bear.
> For what hope have I now or whose help can I seek?
> I'm deserted, alone in a desolate spot
> Where there's nothing but rocks and the sound of the sea,
> Where there isn't a chance of my meeting a soul.
> All I own in this world are the clothes on my back,
> And I've no idea where to find shelter or food.

Oh, it's hopeless! Why try to go on with my life?
I don't know where I am; it's a place strange to me.
How I wish that some person would come and point out
Where a road or a path is! I'm so at a loss
I can't make up my mind to go right or go left;
It's all wild—not a sign of a field can I see.
All the horrors of cold and distraction and fear
Have me now in their grasp. Poor dear parents of mine,
You can have no idea of your daughter's despair!
I was born a free girl, but my birth was in vain—
At this moment how more of a slave could I be
Had I been one from birth? Oh, what good have I been
All these years to the parents who cherished me so!

(*She staggers back to the rocks on stage right, sinks down on them, and buries her face in her arms. The next moment there enters, stage right, the companion she thought had been lost. Ampelisca, "tender grape," is a pretty girl with an attractive, gay, vivacious manner. Right now she is as bedraggled and forlorn as Palaestra. She makes her way downstage and addresses the audience.*)

AMPELISCA

Oh, what act could be better or more suitable now
    Than to sever my soul from my body?
For my life is a torment and my breast is beset
    By an army of cares that destroy me!
In the face of all this I've no stomach for life,
    All the hope that once buoyed me is ended:
For I've roamed everywhere, used my voice, eyes, and
        ears,
    Crept through thorns, to track down my companion;
She's been lost without trace, and I have no idea
    Where to turn, in what place to go searching.
And I haven't been able to meet anyone
    I could speak to and ask for directions.
Why, this region's a desert—in all of the world
    There's just no place so lonely and barren.

Yet as long as I live—granted she's alive too—
I'll persist in the search till I find her.

PALAESTRA (*to herself, raising her head in alarm*)
　　　　　Whose voice is that I hear?
　　　　　Was that a sound nearby?
　　　　　Oh, god, I'm so afraid!

AMPELISCA (*to herself*)
　　　　　Did I hear someone speak?

PALAESTRA (*in desperation*)
　　　　　O god of hope! Please help!

AMPELISCA (*to herself, hopefully*)
　　　　　Does this mean my release
　　　　　From misery and fear?

PALAESTRA (*to herself, listening intently*)
　　　　　I'm absolutely sure
　　　　　I heard a woman's voice.

AMPELISCA (*to herself, listening intently*)
　　　　　A woman's somewhere here—
　　　　　I heard a woman's voice.

PALAESTRA (*dubiously*)
　　　　　It can't be Ampelisca!

AMPELISCA (*calling uncertainly*)
　　　　　Palaestra! Is that you?

PALAESTRA (*jumping to her feet, excitedly*)
　　Oh, I *must* make her hear me—I'll call out her name!
　　Ampelisca!

AMPELISCA (*calling*)
　　　　　Who's there?

PALAESTRA
　　　　　　　　It's Palaestra! It's me!

AMPELISCA (*looking about without seeing her*)
　　I can't see where you are.

PALAESTRA
　　　　　　　　I'm in all sorts of trouble.

AMPELISCA

    I've a share in it too—one as big as your own.
    But I'm dying to see you.

PALAESTRA

                And I to see you.

AMPELISCA

    Let's both talk and we'll follow the sounds. Where are
      you?

PALAESTRA

    Over here. Come this way. Now walk up to me. Come!

AMPELISCA (*walking slowly and hesitantly toward her*)
    This is the best I can do.

PALAESTRA (*as she comes near*)
              All right, give me your hand.

AMPELISCA (*doing so*)
    Here it is.

PALAESTRA (*grabbing it, pulling her near, and embracing her*)
        Ampelisca! You're safe! You're alive!

AMPELISCA (*tearfully*)
    Yes—and now that I'm able to touch you, Palaestra,
    You've restored the desire to go on with my life.
    But I scarcely believe that you're here in my arms!
    Oh, my dear! Hold me tight! How you make me forget
    All my troubles!

PALAESTRA

           You've taken the words from my mouth!
    But we ought to get out of this place.

AMPELISCA

                  And go where?

PALAESTRA

    Shall we follow the beach?

AMPELISCA

             Go wherever you like;
    I'll be right at your heels. But we're both sopping wet—
    Are we going to tramp up and down in these clothes?

PALAESTRA

Yes, we must. We just have to take things as they come.

(*Starts trudging off with Ampelisca close behind and then suddenly stops and points.*)

What is that, do you think?

AMPELISCA

What is what?

PALAESTRA

Don't you see?

There's a shrine over there.

AMPELISCA

Over where?

PALAESTRA

On the right.

AMPELISCA (*following the direction of her hand*)
I can make out a spot that would serve for a shrine.

PALAESTRA

It's so pleasant a place that I'm sure we shall find
There are people about. Now let's pray that the god
Dwelling here will have pity on us in our plight,
And will come to the rescue and bring to a close
All these torments and terrors, these worries and woes!

(*As the two girls slowly make their way toward the little temple that marks the shrine, the door opens and Ptolemocratia, the priestess, comes out. She is an elderly woman dressed in flowing white robes that, although spotlessly clean, have obviously seen better days. Her face is kindly and serene.*)

PTOLEMOCRATIA (*to herself*)
The sound of prayer just roused me now
To step outside. But who has come
To ask my mistress for a favor?
The goddess they implore is quick
To yield, and loath to hide, her grace,
A patroness both kind and good.

PALAESTRA (*timidly*)
> Good morning, Mother.

PTOLEMOCRATIA (*responding perfunctorily*)
>   Morning, girls.

(*Suddenly aware of their appearance*)
> Tell me, where have you come from, my dears?
> You're in rags! And you're both sopping wet!

PALAESTRA
> Well, right now from a place that's nearby.
> But our homeland is far, far away.

PTOLEMOCRATIA (*in mock-tragic style*)
> Then you came o'er the blue of the sea
> On a charger of canvas and wood?

PALAESTRA
> Yes, we did.

PTOLEMOCRATIA (*reproachfully*)
>   But you should have come here
> Dressed in white and prepared to give gifts.
> This is simply unheard of, my dears—
> Coming into this shrine in this way.

PALAESTRA (*taken aback*)
> From two castaways fresh from the sea?
> Tell me, where would you have us find gifts?

(*The two girls drop to the ground and embrace Ptole-mocratia's knees.*)
> Here we are on our knees at your feet.
> We need help! We don't know where we are,
> We don't know what's in store for us next.
> Oh, I beg you, please pity our plight.
> Give us shelter and save us, please do!
> We are homeless and hopeless, and all
> That we own you can see on our backs!

PTOLEMOCRATIA (*gently*)
> Now I want you to give me your hands
> And get up from your knees, both of you.

There's no woman alive with a heart
That's as tender as mine, I am sure.
But this shrine's very humble, my girls.
I can barely keep living myself.
And the offerings for Venus come from me.

AMPELISCA

Then is this one of Venus' shrines?

PTOLEMOCRATIA

Yes, it is, dear. And I am in charge.
We'll make do. You will both be put up
Just as well as my means will permit.
Come with me.

PALAESTRA

We're most grateful to you
For a welcome so friendly and kind.

PTOLEMOCRATIA

It's a duty I've always in mind.

(Ptolemocratia and the girls enter the temple, and the stage is now empty.)

ACT II

(A group of fishermen, dressed in rags and carrying tackle, enters, stage left.)

FISHERMEN *(to the audience)*

The poor in every single way
    Find life a sad progression
Of miseries, especially men
    Without a trade or profession.
Their living's strictly limited
    To things in their possession.
What *our* financial status is,
    You see by this here get-up.
These hooks and rods we have are our
    Sole economic set-up.
Each day we hike from town to beach
    To forage for our rations.
(It's our substitute for wrestling, gym,
    And other sporting passions.)
We grub for limpets, oysters, clams,
    Sea urchins, scallops, mussels.
And then to try our luck with fish,
    With rod to rock each hustles.
We fill our bellies from the sea;
    But when the sea's defaulted,
We take a swim—if not the fish,
    The fishers get cleaned and salted—
Then sneak back home and climb in bed
    Without a thing for dinner.
With seas as rough as they are right now,
    Our hopes are getting thinner;
Unless we find a clam or two,
    We've had today's collation.
To get some help, let's proffer to
    Kind Venus veneration.

(*Trachalio, "bull-necked," Plesidippus' servant, enters, stage left. He's a burly young fellow, honest and good-natured at heart, and gay in temperament. He rather fancies himself as a man of importance, and with—or without—provocation often begins orating instead of talking.*)

TRACHALIO (*to himself, worriedly*) And I watched so carefully all the way so's not to miss that master of mine on the road! When he left the house he said he was going to go to the waterfront, and gave me orders to meet him here at the shrine of Venus. (*Catching sight of the fishermen*) Now, that's convenient: there are some fellows over there I can ask. (*Calling*) Hail, heroes of the hook and half shell, despoilers of the deeps, members of the Honorable Order of the Empty Belly, how're you doing? How're you dying?

FISHERMAN The way fishermen always do—of optimism followed by starvation.

TRACHALIO Did you happen to see a young fellow come along while you've been standing here? Husky, red-faced fellow looking as if he meant business? He had three others with him; they were all wearing cloaks and daggers.

FISHERMAN Nobody answering to that description's come along, so far as we know.

TRACHALIO How about an old guy, pretty big, with a bald forehead like an old satyr, a fat belly, bushy eyebrows, and a dirty look? A low-down, filthy, lying, thieving, swindling crook? Had two good-looking girls with him?

FISHERMAN Anyone with those sterling virtues ought to be headed for a town jail, not a temple of Venus.

TRACHALIO But did you see him?

FISHERMAN No. He hasn't been here. So long. (*They leave, stage right.*)

TRACHALIO (*calling after them*) So long. (*To himself*) I thought so; I had a suspicion this would happen. They've put one over on that master of mine: that damned pimp skipped town. Took passage on a ship and took the girls away. I'm a prophet, that's what I am. The lousy liar! He even invited Plesidippus for lunch out here. Well, the best thing I can do is wait around here until Plesidippus shows up. And while I'm at it, if I see the priestess, I'll quiz her and find out if she knows anything more about all this. She'll tell me.

(*The door of the temple opens and Ampelisca comes out, carrying a pitcher. Her first words are addressed to the priestess inside.*)

AMPELISCA (*through the doorway*) Yes, I understand. I'm to go to the cottage right next door to the shrine, knock, and ask for water.

TRACHALIO (*pricking up his ears, to himself*) Now whose voice is that the wind has wafted to mine ears?

AMPELISCA (*turning at the sound*) Who's that talking out there, please? (*Seeing him*) Look who's here!

TRACHALIO (*turning, to himself*) Isn't that Ampelisca coming out of the temple?

AMPELISCA (*to herself*) Isn't that Trachalio, Plesidippus' valet, I see?

TRACHALIO (*to himself*) That's who it is, all right.

AMPELISCA (*to herself*) That's who it is, all right. (*Calling*) Trachalio! Hello there!

TRACHALIO (*going up to her*) Hello, Ampelisca. What have you been doing with yourself?

AMPELISCA (*bitterly*) Spending the best years of my life in the worst possible way.

TRACHALIO Don't say things like that!

AMPELISCA (*as before*) Sensible people should tell the truth —and listen to it. But where's Plesidippus?

TRACHALIO (*looking at her blankly*) What a question! He's inside with you people, isn't he?

AMPELISCA (*emphatically*) He is not. He hasn't been here today.

TRACHALIO Hasn't been here?

AMPELISCA   You never said a truer word.

TRACHALIO   (*grinning*)   Rather unusual for me. Well, when will lunch be ready?

AMPELISCA   (*taking her turn at looking blank*)   What lunch are you talking about?

TRACHALIO   You people are making a sacrifice here, aren't you?

AMPELISCA   My dear boy, will you please wake up?

TRACHALIO   But I know for certain our masters were getting together for lunch here. Labrax invited Plesidippus.

AMPELISCA   (*bitterly*)   I'm not at all surprised. Exactly what you'd expect of a pimp—as ready to cheat a goddess as a man.

TRACHALIO   You mean you people and Plesidippus *aren't* making a sacrifice here?

AMPELISCA   (*scornfully*)   You're a prophet.

TRACHALIO   What are you doing around here, then?

AMPELISCA   (*breathlessly*)   We were in terrible trouble, scared to death, in danger of losing our lives, with not a thing to our name and not a soul to help us. And the priestess here took us in. The two of us—me and Palaestra.

TRACHALIO   (*excitedly*)   You mean Palaestra's here? His sweetheart's here?

AMPELISCA   Of course.

TRACHALIO   (*as before*)   Ampelisca, that's the best possible news you could have brought me. But what was this danger you were in? I'm dying to hear about it.

AMPELISCA   Trachalio, last night our ship was wrecked!

TRACHALIO   What ship? What are you talking about?

AMPELISCA   Didn't you hear what happened? The pimp wanted to move all of us to Sicily without anybody knowing about it. So he loaded all his belongings on board a ship. And now he's lost everything!

TRACHALIO   (*exulting*)   Good work, Father Neptune! Congratulations! Nobody can play the game better than you:

you hit the jackpot; you gave that liar his lumps. But where is our pimping friend Labrax now?

AMPELISCA Probably died of drink. Neptune was serving in the big glasses last night.

TRACHALIO (*chuckling*) And he probably insisted on bottoms up, every round. Ampelisca, I love you! You're so sweet! What honeyed words you have for me! (*Suddenly becoming serious*) But how were you and Palaestra rescued?

AMPELISCA I'll tell you just how it happened. We saw that the ship was being carried toward the rocks, and we both got so scared we jumped into the ship's boat. Then, while everybody on board was busy having the shakes, I hurried and cast off the rope. The storm carried us away from them, to the right. And then we were tossed about by the wind and waves in the worst way imaginable, all night long. Finally, just this morning, the wind drove us up on the beach. We were half dead!

TRACHALIO I know. That's what Neptune always does. (*Grinning*) Most meticulous purser in the business: any bad merchandise around, and he heaves it right overboard.

AMPELISCA Oh, go to the devil!

TRACHALIO You almost did, Ampelisca, my girl. (*Becoming serious*) I knew that pimp would do something like that; I said so all along. You know what I really ought to do? Grow a beard and be a prophet.

AMPELISCA (*tartly*) Considering that you knew all about it, you and that master of yours certainly took good care not to let him get away.

TRACHALIO (*defensively*) What should he have done?

AMPELISCA (*angrily*) If he really loved her, you wouldn't have to ask such a question! He should have kept his eyes open night and day, been on his guard every minute. My god! That Plesidippus of yours certainly took fine care of her! Shows how much she mattered to him!

TRACHALIO (*reproachfully*) Why do you say that?

AMPELISCA (*severely*)   It's plain as day, isn't it?

TRACHALIO   Can't you understand? Why, you take a fellow who goes to a public bath: he watches his clothes like a hawk and still he gets robbed. There are so many people around, he doesn't know which one to keep an eye on. It's easy enough for the crook to spot the man *he* wants to keep his eye on, but it's tough for the fellow who's on guard to spot the crook. (*Quickly changing the subject*) But how about taking me to Palaestra?

AMPELISCA   Just go inside the temple here. You'll find her sitting there crying her eyes out.

TRACHALIO   Crying? That I'm sorry to hear. What's she crying about?

AMPELISCA   I'll tell you what she's crying about: she's all broken up because the pimp took away a little jewel box she had in which she kept some things that were her only means of identifying her parents. She's afraid it's lost.

TRACHALIO   Where was this box?

AMPELISCA   On board with us. He kept it locked up in a satchel. He wanted to make sure she'd never be able to find her parents.

TRACHALIO   What a criminal thing to do! A girl who ought to be free and he wants to keep her a slave!

AMPELISCA   It must have gone down to the bottom with the ship. The pimp had all his money in the same satchel.

TRACHALIO (*comfortingly*)   Oh, someone's probably dived down and rescued it.

AMPELISCA   The poor girl is simply miserable at the thought of having lost those things.

TRACHALIO   All the more reason for me to go in and cheer her up. I don't want her to go on tormenting herself that way. I know for a fact there are lots of people whose affairs turned out much better than they ever expected.

AMPELISCA   And I know for a fact there are lots who expected their affairs to turn out well and they never did.

TRACHALIO   When you come down to it, the best medicine
for trouble is a level head. Well, if there's nothing more I
can do for you, I'll run along inside. (*Enters the temple.*)

AMPELISCA   Go ahead. (*To herself*) And I'll do that errand
for the priestess and ask them next door for some water.
She told me they'd give it to me right away if I said it was
for her. (*Walking toward the cottage*) I don't think I've
ever met anyone nicer than that old lady. I think she deserves every kindness god or man can do for her. There we
were, castaways, frightened to death, drenched to the skin,
helpless, half alive, and she took us in and was so sweet
and generous and open and unbegrudging—just as if we
were her own daughters! She even tucked up her robe and
heated the water herself so that we could take a bath.
Well, I don't want her to be held up on my account, so
I'll go where she told me right now and get some more
water. (*Knocking on the door of the cottage*) Hello there!
Anyone inside? Anyone there to open this door? Will someone please come out?

SCEPARNIO   (*throwing the door open and looking past her as
he does*)   Who's the wild animal trying to break this door
down?

AMPELISCA   Here I am.

SCEPARNIO   (*breaking into a pleased smile as he sees her, to
himself*)   Hey, here's a piece of luck. Damn it all, that's
one good-looking girl there!

AMPELISCA   Good morning, mister.

SCEPARNIO   Good morning to *you*, miss.

AMPELISCA   I've come here to—

SCEPARNIO   (*interrupting with a leer*)   It's a little too early in
the morning for me to entertain you, my girl. Come back
later this evening and I'll really take care of you. (*Putting
his arm around her*) Well, how about it, baby?

AMPELISCA   (*deftly fending him off*)   Hey, don't you get so
familiar with those hands!

SCEPARNIO   (*aside*)   Lord in heaven, this is Lady Venus herself! Look at those eyes—this girl's the lively type. And those cheeks! Like silt—silk, I mean. And those breasts! And that mouth calls for a kiss. (*Makes another pass at her.*)

AMPELISCA (*as before*) Can't you keep your hands off me? I'm for your betters, boy!

SCEPARNIO Come on, little one, just one little hug, nice and gentle, like this. (*Tries to get an arm around her again.*)

AMPELISCA Later on, when I'm not busy, you and I'll have time to play around, but right now I have a favor to ask and please just tell me yes or no.

SCEPARNIO All right, what do you want?

AMPELISCA (*holding up the pitcher*) If you had any brains, this would show you what I want.

SCEPARNIO (*making an obscene gesture*) And if you had any, this would show you what *I* want.

AMPELISCA (*remembering her instructions, importantly*) The priestess of the shrine of Venus sent me to ask you for some water for her.

SCEPARNIO (*tapping his chest*) *I'm* lord and master around here. Unless you ask me for it, you don't get a drop. We risked our own necks to dig this well, and we did it with our own tools. (*Leering*) And no one gets a drop without asking me nicely.

AMPELISCA What's the matter? You won't give me some water? What any stranger would give to another?

SCEPARNIO What's the matter? You won't give me what any friend would give to another?

AMPELISCA (*enticingly*) I? Of course I will. I'll do anything you want, honey.

SCEPARNIO (*aside*) Congratulations, old boy, you're in; she just called you "honey." (*To Ampelisca*) Sure I'll give you the water. I don't want you to fall in love with me and get nothing for it. Give me the pitcher.

AMPELISCA Here it is. And please hurry.

SCEPARNIO (*taking the pitcher*)   You wait here. I'll be right back—honey. (*Enters the cottage.*)

AMPELISCA (*worriedly*)   What should I tell the priestess took me so long? (*Gazes about abstractedly, and her eye falls on the sea.*) Ugh! When I look at that water, I get frightened even now. (*Starting*) Oh, my god, what's that I see on the beach? It's the pimp and his friend from Sicily! And I, like a poor fool, thought the two of them had drowned! That means more trouble in store for us than we had thought. But what am I waiting for? I've got to hurry into the temple and tell Palaestra so that we can throw ourselves on the altar before that filthy pimp comes here and catches us. I'd better run—every minute counts!

(*She hurries into the temple. A second later Sceparnio comes out carrying the pitcher.*)

SCEPARNIO (*smiling fatuously, to himself*)   Lord, oh, lord, I never thought water had so much happiness to offer. It was a sheer pleasure to draw it—the well never seemed that shallow before. Practically no work at all to haul it up. Sceparnio, knock on wood, you're quite a guy. Got yourself a love affair going today, eh, boy? (*Calling*) Where's my pretty girl? Here's your water. (*Putting the bucket on his head and mincing about*) See? This is the way I want you to carry it, like a lady. Want me to like you? Then do it just like this. (*Calling*) Sweetie-pie, where are you? Come on and get your water. Where are you? (*Grinning even more fatuously*) Well, what do you know—the little devil's playing hide-and-go-seek. Boy, did she fall for me! (*Calling*) Where are you? (*After waiting a moment in silence*) Hey, are you going to come and get this pitcher? Where are you? Come on, no more games, I'm serious. How about taking this here pitcher? (*Removes the pitcher from his head and starts searching in earnest.*) Where the devil are you? Good god, I don't see her anywhere. Is she playing a trick on me? (*Slamming the pitcher down, angrily*) I'll just leave the blasted pitcher right in the road. (*Starts

walking away, then stops abruptly.) Wait a second—what
if someone walks off with it? That's no ordinary pitcher;
it belongs to the shrine. I'll get into trouble. (*Excitedly*)
I think that girl framed me—wanted me to get caught with
a holy pitcher on me. If anyone sees me with this thing, the
judge'll have every right to throw the book at me. Look—it's
even got its name on it—it practically shouts to high heaven
whose it is. Holy god, I'm going to call the priestess out
here right now to get her pitcher. I'm heading right for her
door! (*Rushes up to the door and starts shouting frantically.*) Hey! Ptolemocratia! Come on out and get your
pitcher! Some blamed girl brought it to me. (*Waits a moment; then, getting no reply, disgustedly*) I'll have to carry
it in. Fine business if, on top of everything else, I've got to
deliver the water right to the house!

(*Sceparnio goes into the temple. A second later Labrax,
"the shark," enters, stage right. He is wet, bedraggled, and
shivering.*)

LABRAX (*to himself*)   If anyone wants to become a beggar,
just let him trust himself, body and soul, to Father Neptune. Believe me, whenever you do business with him, this
(*indicating his appearance*) is the way he sends you home.
I remember a story about a girl who always refused to set
foot on a ship with Hercules—she was a smart one, all right.
But where's that guest of mine who's been my ruination?
Oh, there he is. Look at him taking his time!

(*Charmides enters, stage right, in the same condition as
Labrax.*)

CHARMIDES (*sourly*)   What the devil's the hurry, Labrax?
I can't keep up when you go that fast.

LABRAX (*bitterly*)   I wish to god you had gone to the gallows
in Sicily before I ever set eyes on you. You're to blame for
getting me into this!

CHARMIDES   And I wish to god I had spent the night in the
town jail rather than let you take me home with you that

day. There's only one favor I want from heaven—that from now on till the end of your days, your guests be the same breed as yourself, every one of them.

LABRAX The day I took you in I let Bad Luck walk right in the front door. Why did I ever listen to a good-for-nothing like you? Why did I ever leave here? Why did I get aboard that ship? (*Thinking of the money he took from Plesidippus*) I've lost even more than I owned!

CHARMIDES I'm not surprised that ship went down—not when it was carrying a crook like you and all that crooked stuff you had.

LABRAX You ruined me, you and that slick talk of yours.

CHARMIDES How about that filthy meal you served me? Believe me, Thyestes and Tereus[2] didn't get worse.

LABRAX (*holding his stomach*) Oh, god, I feel sick. Hold my head, will you?

CHARMIDES Damn you, I hope you puke up your lungs while you're at it.

LABRAX Poor Palaestra and Ampelisca. I wonder where they are now.

CHARMIDES Probably feeding the fish down in the drink.

LABRAX It's all your doing that I'm a beggar now. I had to listen to that big talk of yours!

CHARMIDES (*grinning maliciously*) You ought to be grateful to me. You never knew how to get along before. I taught you how to get along swimmingly.

LABRAX Why don't you go straight to hell and leave me alone?

CHARMIDES That's just what I was going to invite you to do.

LABRAX God, there isn't a man alive worse off than I am.

CHARMIDES Oh, yes there is. One lots worse off—me.

LABRAX How so?

CHARMIDES Because you deserved what you got. I didn't.

---

[2] Mythological characters who had been served their own sons.

LABRAX   Look at those bulrushes. I envy them. Always nice and dry.

CHARMIDES   I'm practicing to be a Spanish dancer. I'm shivering so much, every time I speak I clack like a castanet.

LABRAX   That Neptune sure runs a cold bathing establishment. I leave the place, have all my clothes on, and I'm still freezing. And he doesn't even have a hot-drink counter. Only drinks he serves are cold and salty.

CHARMIDES   The fellows I envy are the blacksmiths. Around a fire all day. Always nice and warm.

LABRAX   What I'd like to be right now is a duck. Come straight out of the water and still be dry.

CHARMIDES   I think I'll get me a job playing a ghost in a theatrical troupe.

LABRAX   Why?

CHARMIDES   Listen to the terrific clatter I can make with my teeth. (*Shaking his head ruefully*) If you ask me, being cleaned out of everything I owned was just what was coming to me.

LABRAX   Why?

CHARMIDES   How could I have had the nerve to get aboard a ship with someone like you? I'll bet you made all those waves yourself, just to spite me.

LABRAX   I listened to you, that's what I did. You kept telling me girls made big money where you came from. You promised I'd rake in the cash there.

CHARMIDES   And you expected to swallow up the whole island of Sicily in one gulp, like a damned vulture.

LABRAX   Talk about swallowing, I wonder what whale got my satchel. I had all my money in it.

CHARMIDES   Probably the same one that got my wallet. The inside pocket was full of cash.

LABRAX   Do you know that all I've got left to my name is this shirt and this rag of a coat? I'm done for!

CHARMIDES You and I could set up a perfect partnership. We'd hold identical shares.

LABRAX If only my girls were still alive, there'd be some hope. If that young fellow Plesidippus sees me now, the one I took a down payment from for Palaestra, he's going to make real trouble for me—and soon.

CHARMIDES What are you crying about, stupid? So long as that tongue of yours is alive, you've got what it takes to get you out of any debts you owe.

(*The door of the temple opens, and Sceparnio comes out, looking puzzled.*)

SCEPARNIO (*to himself*) What's going on here, anyway? Two girls inside the temple, holding on to the altar and crying their eyes out. The poor things are scared to death of someone but I don't know who. They said they'd been shipwrecked last night and tossed up on the beach this morning.

LABRAX (*to Sceparnio, eagerly*) Say there, mister, where are these girls you're talking about?

SCEPARNIO Here, in the temple.

LABRAX How many of them are there?

SCEPARNIO Two.

LABRAX (*half to himself*) I'll swear they're mine.

SCEPARNIO And I'll swear I don't know about that.

LABRAX What do they look like?

SCEPARNIO Not bad. I could go for either one of them—if I was good and drunk.

LABRAX They're pretty young, aren't they?

SCEPARNIO You're pretty much of a nuisance, aren't you? Go on in and take a look if you want.

LABRAX (*to Charmides, excitedly*) Charmides! Those girls in there must be mine!

CHARMIDES Whether they are or they aren't, you can go to hell for all I care.

LABRAX   I'm going into that temple this minute. (*Rushes into the temple.*)

CHARMIDES   (*calling after him*)   I wish you were going straight to hell this minute. (*To Sceparnio*) Say, how about playing host and giving me a place where I can stretch out and get some sleep?

SCEPARNIO   Stretch out wherever you want. No one's stopping you. It's a free country.

CHARMIDES   But look at me—these clothes I'm wearing are wringing wet. How about putting me up in your house and giving me some dry clothes until these get dry? I'll make it up to you sometime.

SCEPARNIO   (*pointing to a homely coverall of rushes hanging up alongside the cottage*)   See that mat there? That's all I've got. It's dry, and if you want it you're welcome to it. It's my coat, and it doubles as umbrella when there's rain. Here, give me your things and I'll dry them out.

CHARMIDES   (*backing away suspiciously*)   Oh, no. Isn't the cleaning out I got at sea enough for you? Do you have to put me through it all again on land?

SCEPARNIO   I don't give a damn whether you get cleaned out or rubbed out. I'm not trusting you with anything of mine without security. Go ahead—freeze to death or sweat to death, get sick or get well. Who cares? I don't want any foreigners around the house, anyway. And that's that. (*Stomps into the cottage.*)

CHARMIDES   (*calling after him*)   Hey, where are you going? (*To himself*) Whoever he is, the man must be a slave dealer—doesn't know what it is to feel pity. But what am I standing around here in these wet clothes for? Why don't I go into this temple here and sleep off last night's party? Drank too much; lots more than I wanted. You'd think we were cheap wine, the way Neptune watered us. Maybe he was figuring on giving us a salt-water laxative. When you come right down to it, if he had kept on serving drinks much longer we'd have gone to sleep then and there; this way he let us go home—half alive, but alive. Well, I'll see what my fellow drunk is doing inside here now.

(*Enters the temple, and the stage is now empty.*)

ACT III

(Daemones comes out of the cottage shaking his head wonderingly.)

DAEMONES *(to the audience)* It's amazing the way heaven plays tricks on us mortals. The amazing dreams heaven sends you when you're asleep! A person's not left in peace and quiet even in bed. Last night, for example, I had an incredible dream, something unheard of. I dreamed that an ape was trying to climb up to a swallow's nest and get his hands on the swallows, but couldn't quite make it. After a while it came to me to ask for the loan of a ladder. I refused, pointing out that swallows were descended from Philomela[3] and Procne, and I pleaded with it not to do any harm to what were, in effect, my fellow countrymen. That just made it more belligerent than ever, and it threatened to beat me. It hauled me into court. There I lost my temper and, somehow or other, managed to grab the filthy creature around the middle and chain it up. *(Scratching his head perplexedly)* Now, what does it all mean? I've thought all morning but I just can't figure it out. *(A clamor is heard in the temple.)* What's that? Noise in the shrine next door? That's queer.

(The door of the temple flies open and Trachalio bursts out.)

TRACHALIO *(at the top of his lungs—and at his oratorical best)* Citizens of Cyrene! Farmers! Anyone who lives in the area! In god's name, help for the helpless! Harm for the harmful! Are the merciless to be mightier than the meek who shrink at the very name of crime? Then help right a wrong, give the righteous their reward and the dastards their deserts. Fight the good fight to let us live by law and order and not by fists and force. Everyone here, everyone who hears my

[3] A mythological princess of Athens.

voice, in god's name, into this shrine of Venus as fast as
you can! Help the poor souls who have entrusted life and
limb to the protection of Venus and her priestess in accord-
ance with our ancient custom! Wring the neck of wrong
before it reaches *you!*

DAEMONES (*impatiently*)   What's this all about?

TRACHALIO (*throwing himself on the ground and embracing
Daemones' knees*)   My dear sir, by these knees, I call upon
you, whoever you are—

DAEMONES (*interrupting, as before*)   Let go of my knees and
tell me what this yelling's about. And make it short!

TRACHALIO (*not budging*)   I beg you, I implore you! Do you
want a good crop on your farm this year? Do you want to
see it arrive at an overseas market safe and sound? Do you
want to get rid of what ails you? Do you—

DAEMONES (*interrupting*)   Are you in your right mind?

TRACHALIO (*unabashed*)   Do you want an ample supply of
seed for sowing? Then, my dear sir, please don't refuse to
do what I'm asking you to.

DAEMONES (*testily*)   And I call upon *you* by that back of
yours and those legs and heels. Do you want a good harvest
of birch-rod welts? Do you want a bumper crop of trouble
this year? Then you'd better tell me what's going on here
and what this shouting's all about.

TRACHALIO (*getting up, reproachfully*)   You're not fair: I
asked only for nice things for you.

DAEMONES (*promptly*)   I am so fair: I asked only for what
you deserve.

TRACHALIO   Please! Listen to me!

DAEMONES   What is it?

TRACHALIO   There are two innocent girls in there. They need
your help. The treatment they've had—and are getting this
minute—is a blot on the escutcheon of justice and law. Right
in the temple of Venus, too! Even the priestess is being
manhandled.

DAEMONES (*finally aroused*)   Who would have the gall to lay
hands on a priestess? Who are these girls? How are they
being mistreated?

TRACHALIO   If you'll listen to me for a minute, I'll tell you.
(*Breathlessly*) They ran to Venus' altar for safety. Now
this fellow has the colossal nerve to want to pull them away.
And both of them by rights ought to be free.

DAEMONES   Who's the man who's so free and easy with
priestesses and temples? And no speeches!

TRACHALIO   A swindler, a crook, a murderer, a liar, a lawbreaker; a foul, filthy, unprincipled—in a word, a pimp.
Need I say more?

DAEMONES   You've said enough. Perfect material for a flog-
ging.

TRACHALIO   He even tried to strangle the priestess.

DAEMONES   By god, he's going to pay for that, and pay
plenty. (*Shouting to his servants inside*) Hey! Roughneck
and Cutthroat! Come on out here! Where are you, anyway?

TRACHALIO   Please, I beg you. Go in the temple and rescue
them.

(*Two husky slaves rush out of the house and stand at attention before Daemones.*)

DAEMONES (*to Trachalio, reassuringly*)   One word from me
will be enough. (*To the slaves*) Follow me! (*They charge
toward the temple.*)

TRACHALIO (*remaining prudently behind and calling to Daemones*)   Give it to him! Tell those boys to make believe
they're cooks scaling fish and have them scratch his eyes
out!

DAEMONES (*to the slaves*)   Drag him out here by the feet,
like a stuck pig.

(*The three enter the temple. Trachalio stands near the
door, listening intently.*)

TRACHALIO (*to the audience*) I hear a racket: the pimp's getting a going-over. I hope they knock every tooth out of the rascal's mouth. (*Stepping back as the door opens*) Here come the girls. They look scared to death.

(*Palaestra and Ampelisca come out and rush past Trachalio without noticing him.*)

SONG

PALAESTRA (*to the audience*)
    The dread moment's at hand; now we're utterly helpless.
    There's just no one to come to our aid or defense,
    No release from our danger, no way to find safety.
    And we're both so afraid we can't think where to run.
    Oh, the vicious and brutal ordeal that that pimp
    Put us through just a moment ago in the shrine!
    Why, the monster attacked the old priestess, poor thing,
    Shoved her this way and that—it was dreadful to see—
    And then dragged us by force from the innermost altar.
    In the state that we're in, we'd be better off dead.
    In the depths of despair what is dearer than death?

TRACHALIO (*to himself*)
    Hey, what's this? What a way for a young girl to talk!
    I must swing into action—they need cheering up.
    (*Calling*)
    Hey, Palaestra!

PALAESTRA (*too frightened to turn around*)
               Who's there?

TRACHALIO (*calling*)
                    Ampelisca!

AMPELISCA (*clutching Palaestra*)
                     Who wants me?

PALAESTRA (*as before*)
    Who's that calling our names?

TRACHALIO
                Turn around and you'll see.

PALAESTRA (*turning and seeing him, fervently*)
Oh, some hope for our safety at last!

TRACHALIO (*walking over to them, importantly*)
                                        Now be calm.
Take it easy. Trust me.

PALAESTRA
                                Yes—if you'll give your word
We need fear no more violence and force. Otherwise
I'll be brought to a violent act on myself!

TRACHALIO (*as before*)
Now you're just being silly. No more of this talk.

PALAESTRA (*dully*)   Don't try to console me in my misery
with mere words. If you don't have some real help to offer,
Trachalio, it's all over with us.

AMPELISCA (*wildly*)   I've made up my mind to die rather
than suffer at the hands of that pimp any longer. (*Hesitat-
ingly*) But I'm just a woman, after all; every time I even
think of death I get paralyzed with fright. Oh, what a night-
mare this day is!

TRACHALIO (*heartily*)   Courage, girls!

PALAESTRA (*dully*)   Courage? Where am I going to find it?

TRACHALIO (*as before*)   Take my word for it, there's no reason to be afraid. (*Pointing to the altar outside the shrine*)
Come, sit down on this altar.

AMPELISCA   Why should this one do us any more good than
the one in the shrine? We were clutching it just now when
they pulled us away by brute force.

TRACHALIO (*leading them to the altar and seating them on it*)
You just sit down. I'll stand guard over here. See? The altar's your fort, here are the walls, and I'm the garrison.
With Venus at my side I'm ready to counter the pimp's
sneak attacks.

AMPELISCA   All right, we'll do whatever you say. (*Falling on
her knees and praying*) Dear Venus, here we are, both of
us, on our knees, in tears, before your altar. We beg of you:

guard us, watch over us. Give us our revenge on those criminals who had so little respect for your shrine. Be gracious and let us find safety by this altar. Thanks to Neptune we had a bath last night; please don't be offended or hold it against us if you feel such a washing isn't all that your ritual requires.

TRACHALIO (*looking up toward heaven, importantly*) Venus, if you ask me, that's a perfectly valid request and they deserve to have it granted. You should make allowances for them: the scare they had forced them into this informality. They tell me that you were born from a sea shell; don't leave these poor shells abandoned on the beach! (*As the door of the temple opens*) Look! Here's your savior and mine—the old man's coming out. He couldn't have picked a better time.

(*Daemones comes out followed by the two slaves, who are unceremoniously shoving Labrax ahead of them.*)

DAEMONES (*to Labrax*) Get out of that shrine, you scum of the earth! (*Turning to address the girls*) And you two sit down on the altar—where are they?

TRACHALIO Over here.

DAEMONES Perfect. Exactly what I wanted. Just let him try to get near them now. (*To Labrax*) So you thought you could get away with your lawbreaking inside a temple while we were around, eh? (*To one of the slaves*) Give him a sock on the jaw.

LABRAX (*blustering*) This is an outrage—and you'll pay for it!

DAEMONES What's that? You've got the nerve to make threats?

LABRAX (*as before*) You're depriving me of my rights. These are my girls and you took them from me without my consent.

TRACHALIO You go right down to City Hall here at Cyrene and pick yourself a judge—anyone you want, the most influential you can find. Let *him* decide whether these girls should be yours or should go free—and whether you shouldn't be clapped into jail and stay there until you wear the place out.

LABRAX (*turning on him*)   I'm in no mood today for conversation with a blasted slave. (*To Daemones*) It's you I want to talk to.

DAEMONES (*gesturing toward Trachalio*)   First you'll have it out with this fellow here. He knows you.

LABRAX (*curtly*)   My business is with you.

TRACHALIO   But you're going to take it up with me whether you like it or not. So these girls are yours, eh?

LABRAX   That's right.

TRACHALIO   Well, you just try touching either one of them with the tip of your little finger.

LABRAX (*belligerently*)   And what'll happen if I do?

TRACHALIO (*very brave with the odds four to one in his favor*)   So help me, I'll make a punching bag out of you, that's what'll happen. I'll tie you up and knock the stuffings out of you, you damned liar.

LABRAX (*to Daemones*)   You mean I can't take my own girls away from that altar?

DAEMONES   That's what I mean. That's the law around here.

LABRAX (*scornfully*)   Your laws have nothing to do with me. I'm taking both those girls out of here right now. (*Leering*) If you're so much in love with them, you old goat, you're going to have to come across with hard cash. And if they're such favorites with Venus, she's welcome to them—if she pays me.

DAEMONES   Pay you! There's something you'd better get straight: if you try the least bit of rough stuff, even as a joke, on these girls, I'll send you away from here in such a state you won't recognize yourself. (*To the slaves*) Listen, you two. The minute I give the signal, knock the eyes out of his head. If you don't, I'll wrap a whip around you like twine on a spool.

LABRAX   So you're going to use force on me, eh?

TRACHALIO (*exploding*)   Look who's talking about force! You stinking hypocrite!

LABRAX (*shouting*)   No blasted slave can talk to me like that!

TRACHALIO   Sure, I'm a blasted slave and you're a saint—but that doesn't change the fact that these girls should be free.

LABRAX   What do you mean, free?

TRACHALIO   What's more, damn it, you ought to be their slave. They come from the heart of Greece. (*Pointing to Palaestra*) This one was born in Athens. Her parents were respectable Athenians.

DAEMONES (*eagerly*)   What's that you say?

TRACHALIO   I said this girl is an Athenian and was no slave when she was born.

DAEMONES   You mean she's from my own city?

TRACHALIO (*surprised*)   You weren't born here in Cyrene?

DAEMONES   Oh, no. I'm a native Athenian, born and raised in Athens.

TRACHALIO   Then I implore you to defend your fellow citizens.

DAEMONES (*sighing*)   How I'm reminded of my own daughter when I look at this girl! The very thought stirs up old sorrows. Three years old she was, when I lost her, and if she's alive she'd be just that tall, I'm sure of it.

LABRAX   I paid their owner good money for both of them. What do I care whether they come from Athens or Thebes so long as I'm satisfied with the way they slave for me.

TRACHALIO (*confident enough now to assume his orator's manner*)   So, you sneaking cradle snatcher, you think you're going to get away with snatching infants from their mother's breast and grinding them to nothingness in your foul trade? I admit I don't know where this other girl comes from. But I know one thing: she's far above scum like you.

LABRAX (*sneering*)   I suppose they belong to you?

TRACHALIO   All right. Let's you and I take a back test to see which of us tells the truth. First I'll inspect you. And if that back of yours hasn't more welts from the whip than a ship's hull has nails, *I'm* the world's worst liar. Then you look at me. And if my hide isn't so smooth and unblemished that any leatherworker would classify it as absolutely top grade, give me one good reason why I shouldn't tan yours until I get tired of it. (*As Labrax glances toward the altar*) What are you staring at those girls for? You lay a hand on them and I'll gouge your eyes out!

LABRAX (*belligerently*) You know what? Just because you say I can't do it, I'm going to take them both away with me right now.

DAEMONES (*scornfully*) And just how do you propose to do that?

LABRAX You've got Venus on your side? I'll use Vulcan. (*Rushing toward the door of the cottage*) I'm going for fire.

TRACHALIO (*alarmed*) Where's he going?

LABRAX (*as he nears the door*) Hey! Anybody inside? Hey, there!

DAEMONES (*calling*) You touch that door and I'll fill that face of yours with fists for you. (*Nods to the two slaves, who run over and haul Labrax back.*)

SLAVE (*to Labrax, grinning*) We don't use fire. All we eat is dried figs.

TRACHALIO I'll give you fire all right—I'll light one on your head.

LABRAX Damn it, I'll get fire from somewhere else then.

DAEMONES And just what are you going to do with it when you get it?

LABRAX (*gesturing toward the altar*) I'll start a bonfire right here.

DAEMONES Funeral pyre for yourself, eh?

LABRAX No, sir. I'm going to burn the both of them alive right here on the altar, that's what I'm going to do.

TRACHALIO The minute you try it, I'll heave you in the fire

by that beard of yours, haul you out just as you begin to brown, and feed you to the vultures.

DAEMONES (*to himself*)   Now it comes to me! This is the ape I saw in my dream, the one I wanted to keep from pulling the swallows out of their nest.

TRACHALIO (*to Daemones*)   Would you please do me a favor? Would you keep an eye on these girls and see that no harm comes to them while I go get my master?

DAEMONES   Go ahead. Find him and bring him here.

TRACHALIO (*gesturing toward Labrax*)   But don't let him—

DAEMONES (*interrupting*)   If he lays a hand on them, or even tries to, he'll be sorry.

TRACHALIO   Be careful now.

DAEMONES   I'm being careful. You go along.

TRACHALIO   But keep an eye on him too, so's he doesn't get away. We agreed to forfeit fifteen thousand dollars to the hangman if we didn't produce him today.

DAEMONES   Just run along. I'll take care of everything until you get back.

TRACHALIO   I'll be back right away. (*Exits, stage right.*)

DAEMONES (*to Labrax*)   Hey, pimp! I'll give you your choice: you prefer a beating to keep you quiet or will you stay still without one?

LABRAX   I don't give a damn what you say. These girls are mine, and I'm going to drag them off this altar by the hair whether you or Venus or god almighty himself likes it or not.

DAEMONES   Just try to touch them.

LABRAX   Sure I'll touch them.

DAEMONES (*with elaborate cordiality*)   Go right ahead. Step right this way. (*Points toward the altar.*)

LABRAX   You just tell those boys of yours to step back that way. (*Points away from the altar.*)

DAEMONES   Oh, no. Any stepping they do will be toward you.

LABRAX (*belligerently*)   Oh, yeah? I don't think so.

DAEMONES   What'll you do if they step closer? (*Nods to the slaves, who advance on Labrax.*)

LABRAX (*taking a hasty step backward*)   I'll move back. Listen, you old goat, if I ever catch you back in town, believe me, I'll have my fun out of you before I let you go, or I'm no pimp.

DAEMONES (*grimly*)   You do that. But, in the meantime, if you lay a hand on these girls I'll let you have it—and hard.

LABRAX   Yeah? How hard?

DAEMONES   Hard enough for a pimp.

LABRAX   I don't give a damn for your threats. I'm dragging those girls out of here right now whether you like it or not.

DAEMONES   Just try to touch them.

LABRAX   Sure I'll touch them.

DAEMONES   So you'll touch them, will you? And do you know what's going to happen? (*To one of the slaves*) Roughneck! Hurry into the house and bring out two clubs.

LABRAX (*taken aback*)   Clubs?

DAEMONES (*to the slave*)   Be sure they're thick ones. Quick! On the double! (*The slave dashes off. He turns back to Labrax.*) I'll see that you get the reception you deserve.

LABRAX (*to himself*)   And I had to lose my helmet in the wreck! If I still had it, now's the time I could use it. (*To Daemones*) Look, can't I at least talk to them?

DAEMONES   No, you can't. (*As the slave hurries back carrying two hefty clubs, jovially*) Look who's here—my clubman. Couldn't have come at a better time.

LABRAX (*to himself*)   Look what's here—an earache. Couldn't have come at a worse time.

DAEMONES (*to the slaves*)   Cutthroat, take one of those clubs. (*Pointing to either side of the altar*) Now one of you stand there, and one here. Take your positions. (*Nodding with satisfaction as they do*) That's the way. Now listen to me. If he lays a finger on them and you don't lay those clubs on

him until he doesn't know which way is up, so help me,
I'll murder you both. If he tries to talk to either one of them,
stay just where you are and answer instead. And the minute he tries to get away from here, wrap those clubs around
his shins as fast as you can.

LABRAX You mean they're not even going to let me leave
here?

DAEMONES (*distastefully*) I've got no more to say to you.
(*To the slaves*) And when that servant who went for his
master gets back here with him, you come right home.
Mind you—do exactly what I told you. (*Goes into the cottage.*)

LABRAX (*to himself*) Amazing how quickly shrines change
around here. A minute ago this one belonged to Venus;
now it's Hercules'—that's what it looks like with these two
statues, clubs and all, that the old man just set up. God
almighty, I don't know where I can run to now. Storms
everywhere: first on sea, and now on land. (*Calling*) Palaestra!

SLAVE What do you want?

LABRAX Hey, must be some mistake; this Palaestra isn't the
one I know. (*Calling*) Ampelisca!

SLAVE Watch yourself or I'll let you have it.

LABRAX (*to himself*) Not bad advice, even though it comes
from a pair of clods like this. (*To the slaves*) Hey, you two,
I'm talking to you. No harm in my going a little closer to
them, is there?

SLAVE Not at all—for us.

LABRAX How about for me?

SLAVE None for you either—if you can keep your eyes open.

LABRAX Keep my eyes open for what?

SLAVE (*brandishing the club*) See this? For a good hard
wallop.

LABRAX For god's sake, please just let me get out of here!
(*Takes a tentative step away.*)

SLAVE   Go right ahead, if you want. (*The two take a step toward him.*)

LABRAX (*backing away in a hurry*)   Very kind of you; thanks very much. No, I think I'll stick around—and you fellows can stand right where you are. (*To himself*) God damn it, I'm not doing well at all. (*Settling himself for a long wait*) Well, I'll get those girls yet. I'll stay put and starve them out.

(*Plesidippus and Trachalio enter, stage right, deep in conversation.*)

PLESIDIPPUS (*shocked*)   You mean that pimp wanted to drag my girl away from Venus' altar by brute force?

TRACHALIO   Exactly.

PLESIDIPPUS   Why didn't you kill him on the spot?

TRACHALIO (*glibly*)   I didn't have a sword.

PLESIDIPPUS   You should have picked up a stick or a rock.

TRACHALIO (*as if appalled at the suggestion*)   What? Chase a man with stones like a dog?

PLESIDIPPUS   That scum? Of course!

LABRAX (*catching sight of them, to himself*)   Oh, lord, now I'm in for it! Here comes Plesidippus. By the time he gets done, there won't be a speck of me left.

PLESIDIPPUS   Were the girls still sitting on the altar when you left to get me?

TRACHALIO (*looking toward the altar*)   They're there right now.

PLESIDIPPUS   Who's minding them?

TRACHALIO   Some old fellow who lives next door to the shrine. He gave us all the help you could ask for. He and his servants are standing guard. (*Importantly*) I ordered him to.

PLESIDIPPUS   Take me right to that pimp. Where is he?

LABRAX (*ingratiatingly*)   Good morning, Plesidippus.

PLESIDIPPUS   Don't you good-morning me! You're getting a

rope around your neck: do you prefer to be carried or dragged? Make up your mind while you still have the chance.

LABRAX (*gulping*) Neither, thanks.

PLESIDIPPUS (*to Trachalio*) Trachalio, get down to the beach on the double. You know those fellows I brought out here with me to help me hand this creature over to the hangman? Tell them to go back to town and meet me down at the docks. Then come back here and stand guard. I'm hauling this godforsaken good-for-nothing into court. (*As Trachalio dashes off, stage right, Plesidippus goes up to Labrax and ties a rope around his neck.*) Come on, get moving. We're heading for the courthouse.

LABRAX (*with injured innocence*) What did I do?

PLESIDIPPUS (*exploding*) What did you do? I suppose you didn't take a deposit from me for the girl and then carry her off?

LABRAX I did *not* carry her off.

PLESIDIPPUS How can you say a thing like that?

LABRAX I only carried her on board. It was my damned luck that I wasn't able to carry her off. Look—I told you I'd meet you at the shrine of Venus. Didn't I do just what I said? I'm here, ain't I?

PLESIDIPPUS (*grimly*) Tell it to the judge. There's been enough talk around here. Follow me. (*Starts walking off, jerking Labrax after him at the end of the rope.*)

LABRAX (*shouting*) Charmides! Help! They've tied a rope around my neck and they're hauling me off!

CHARMIDES (*appearing in the doorway of the temple*) Who's calling me?

LABRAX (*frantically*) See the way they're hauling me off?

CHARMIDES (*coolly*) I sure do. And I'm delighted to see it.

LABRAX (*unbelievingly*) You mean to say you're not going to help me?

CHARMIDES (*disinterestedly*) Who's hauling you off?

LABRAX   That young fellow Plesidippus.

CHARMIDES *(grinning)*   You were out to get him, now keep him. You ought to creep into jail happy as a lark. You've just had happen to you what most people in the world wish for.

LABRAX   What's that?

CHARMIDES *(as before)*   Getting what they've been looking for.

LABRAX *(desperately)*   Please, Charmides, stick with me! *(Grabs hold of him.)*

CHARMIDES *(disgustedly)*   Just like you to ask a thing like that. You're being hauled off to jail, so you want me to go along too. Come on, let go of me! *(Brushes Labrax's arm away.)*

LABRAX   I'm sunk!

PLESIDIPPUS   I hope to god you're right. *(Turning to the girls)* Palaestra, dear, and you, Ampelisca, stay right here until I get back.

SLAVE   I think they'd be better off in our house until you come back for them.

PLESIDIPPUS   Good idea; thanks very much. *(The two slaves lead the girls into the cottage.)*

LABRAX *(shouting at them)*   You're a bunch of robbers!

SLAVE   What's that? Robbers? *(To Plesidippus)* Haul him out of here.

LABRAX *(calling)*   Palaestra, please, I beg you—

PLESIDIPPUS *(jerking the rope)*   Damn you, follow me!

LABRAX *(to Charmides)*   My friend—

CHARMIDES *(distastefully)*   I'm no friend of yours. You and I are quits.

LABRAX   So you're throwing me over, eh?

CHARMIDES   That's exactly what I'm doing. One drinking session with you was enough.

LABRAX (*as Plesidippus hauls him off, stage left*) God damn you to hell!

CHARMIDES (*calling after him*) Same to you! (*To the audience*) I'm a believer in the theory that men get turned into different kinds of animals. If you ask me, that pimp is being turned into a bird—a jailbird. He's going to build a nest in the town lockup right now. But I'm going to stand by him in court. Maybe I can help convince the judge to let him go—to jail.

(*Exits, stage left, and the stage is now empty.*)

ACT IV

(Daemones comes out of the cottage.)

DAEMONES *(to the audience)*   That was a good turn I did today, helping those girls, and a very pleasant one to do. Now I have a pair of devoted followers—young ones, too, and not bad looking. But that shrew of a wife of mine is watching me like a hawk to make sure I don't start anything with either one of them. *(Looking off, stage right, toward the sea)* I wonder how my servant Gripus is doing? He took the boat out last night for some fishing. Believe me, he'd have shown more sense if he had stayed in bed. With the weather we had last night, and are having right now, he's wasting his time, his energy, and his nets. Look how rough that water is! I'll be able to fry what he catches on my fingers. *(A call is heard from inside.)* There's my wife calling me for lunch. *(Heaving a sigh)* I'd better go in; it's time for my earful of her gabble.

(Daemones goes into the cottage. A second later Gripus, "the fisherman," enters, stage right. He is hauling mightily at his net, dragging along in it a satchel that, to judge by the effort it takes to move it, is no light weight; a rope, tied to the satchel, trails loosely behind. Gripus is by nature sour and uncommunicative, very much like his fellow slave Sceparnio; at the moment, however, his face is wearing an expression that is almost beatific.)

SONG

GRIPUS *(to the audience)*
> I'm sending many thanks down to
> My benefactor Neptune, who
> Resides where salt and fish abound.
> When I left his bailiwick, you see,
> He sent me off decked royally:
> A load of loot and my boat still sound.

Through heavy seas it had carried me
To a rich, new type of fishing ground.

(*Breathlessly*)

It's a marvel, a freak, to have made such a haul!
Best fishing I've ever done yet.
Though I didn't pull in one more ounce of fresh fish
Than what I've got here in my net.

(*Pauses, then resumes less excitedly*)

At 1:00 A.M. I jumped from bed—
I felt a chance to get ahead
Was better than a good night's sleep.
I had in mind, though the seas were steep,
To see if I could somehow ease
This hard-up family's miseries.
(And help myself as well, I'll add.)
I gave the project all I had.

(*Vehemently*)

Any man who is lazy is not worth a damn;
The whole bunch of them makes me see red.
If a man wants to finish his work in good time,
He should know when to get out of bed
And not wait for his master to call him to work.
If a man likes to sleep or to sun, he
Will get plenty of rest, but he'll find there's a quirk:
It pays off—but in trouble, not money.

(*Rapturously*)

I, who've never lazed a day,
Now have found the means for a
Life of lazing, if I like.
On the sea this lucky strike
Came my way. Who knows just what
This contains—but it weighs a lot!

(*Excitedly*)

Do you know what I think? That there's gold inside
here!

Not a soul knows about it but I.
Now's your chance, Gripus boy, to be free as a bird.
            Here's my plan, here's the scheme that I'll try.
I'll go up to the master, and, playing it smart,
            Make a very low bid for my head.
I'll keep upping the price till he lets me go free.
            Once I'm free of this life that I've led,
I'll go buy me a farm and a house and some slaves.
            I'll invest next in shipping, that's what.
I'll be rolling in money and known far and wide.
            Then I'll build me a luxury yacht,

(*Working himself up*)

            And I'll do what the millionaires do,
            Take a round-the-world cruise, maybe two.
            When I get enough fame and renown,
            I'll erect a big fortified town,

(*Reaching his climax*)

            A metropolis named Gripopolis,
            A memorial to Gripus, the hero renowned,
            The capital of a nation, one that I'll found!

(*Pauses for a moment transfixed, then comes to*)

            I'm standing here with big ideas
                    Of the things I'll do some day,
            When I'd better take this satchel here
                    And hide it right away.
            And then, King Gripus, soon you'll munch
            The bread and beans you'll get for lunch!

(*As he starts walking toward the cottage, Trachalio enters, stage left, sees him and his catch—and immediately becomes extremely interested.*)

TRACHALIO (*calling*)
        Hey, wait.
GRIPUS (*suspiciously*)
                        What for?

TRACHALIO (*casually reaching down to pick up the trailing rope, cheerily*)

                        Your rope is dragging, see?
I'll coil it up for you.

GRIPUS (*curtly*)

                              Just let it be.

TRACHALIO (*holding on, brightly*)

    Please let me help. No matter what the cost,
    To do good folks good turns is never lost.

GRIPUS (*uneasily*)

    That windstorm yesterday just wouldn't end.
    Don't get ideas—I've got no fish, my friend.
    Why, can't you see I'm dragging back a net
    With nothing scaly in it, only wet?

TRACHALIO (*heartily*)

    It's not your fish I want, oh no indeed.
    Your charming conversation's what I need.

GRIPUS (*pulling on the net and trying to walk away*)

    You bore me to tears, whoever you are. Let go!

TRACHALIO (*pulling in the opposite direction and bringing him to a halt*)

    Now, *I'm* not letting you leave this place. So, whoa!

GRIPUS

    Hey, what's the big idea of holding me back?
    You watch your step or that jaw will get a smack.

TRACHALIO

    Now, listen here—

GRIPUS (*interrupting*)

                      I won't.

TRACHALIO (*grimly*)

                    You won't right now,
    But later on you'll listen, boy, and how!

GRIPUS (*trying, without much success, to sound indifferent*)

    Oh, speak your piece.

TRACHALIO

> What I want to tell to you,
> You'll find well worth your while to listen to.

GRIPUS (*as before*)

> All right, start talking, you. What's on your mind?

TRACHALIO (*looking around warily*)

> First look and see if anyone's behind.

GRIPUS (*looks around and turns back; nervously*)

> Is it something to do, say, with me?

TRACHALIO

> Well, of course! What I'm after, you see,
> Is your view on a matter in doubt.

GRIPUS

> You just tell me what this is about.

TRACHALIO

> Just keep quiet. You'll hear. But I must have fair play—
> Do you give me your word you won't give me away?

GRIPUS (*anxiously*)

> Whoever you are, here's my word. It's okay.

TRACHALIO (*confidentially*)

> Now then, listen. I happened to see
> A thief rob a man known to me.
> So I later go up to the crook,
> And I give him this deal, I say, "Look,
> As it happens, I know whom you robbed.
> He'll hear nothing about it at all
> If you'll hand over half of the haul."
> Now, I've not heard a word from him yet.
> Well, how much of a share should I get?
> I expect you'll say half. Am I right?

GRIPUS (*blurting*)

> God, I'd ask even more! You're all set:
> If he won't come across, don't think twice,
> Turn him in to his victim on sight!

TRACHALIO (*promptly*)

> Now I'm ready to use your advice.

(*Pointing a finger at him*)

> Listen carefully now. It's all true—
> And the crook it applies to is *you!*

GRIPUS (*startled*)   What do you mean?

TRACHALIO   That satchel there—I've known all along whose it is—

GRIPUS (*interrupting, defensively*)   What are you talking about?

TRACHALIO   —and how it was lost.

GRIPUS (*heatedly*)   But *I* know how it was found and *I* know who found it and *I* know who owns it now. What you know is none of my business, any more than what I know is yours. You know whose it used to be. I know whose it is now. (*Grimly*) There isn't a man alive who can take it away from me, so don't get your hopes up that you can.

TRACHALIO   You mean you won't give it up if the owner comes for it?

GRIPUS   The owner? Make no mistake about it, my friend, there's only one man in this world who owns this thing— me. I caught it when I was fishing.

TRACHALIO   You did, eh?

GRIPUS (*argumentatively*)   You won't deny my right to the fish in the sea, will you? If, as, and when I catch any, they're mine. I keep them; they're my property. No one else lays a hand on them or puts in any claims for any share. They're my goods and I sell them as such in the fish market. The sea is absolutely public domain; everybody shares it in common.

TRACHALIO (*promptly*)   Agreed. So then, my friend, why shouldn't I share this satchel in common? It came from the sea—public domain, you know.

GRIPUS   Don't be a wise guy. If the law was the way you put it, fishermen would be finished. The minute any fish went up for sale in the market, everyone would start claiming a share; no one would buy a thing. Everyone'd say they were caught in the public domain.

TRACHALIO   Who's the wise guy now? Compare a satchel to a fish? What a nerve! Are you trying to tell me you think they're the same?

GRIPUS (*shrugging*)   That's no problem of mine. When I throw over a net or a line, whatever gets caught there I pull up. And what my nets or lines catch is mine, absolutely and positively mine.

TRACHALIO   Oh, no, it isn't. Not if you pulled up some pot, say.

GRIPUS (*scornfully*)   What are you, a lawyer?

TRACHALIO   Listen, you stinker, did you ever in your life see a fisherman catch a satchel-fish or peddle one in the market? You can't take over just any trade you want, not by a long shot. Damn you, you want to be a fisherman and a satchel-maker all in one. Either you show me exactly how a satchel is a fish or you don't walk off with something that doesn't have scales and certainly wasn't born in salt water.

GRIPUS (*affecting incredulity*)   What? You never heard of a satchel-fish before?

TRACHALIO   Cut it out. There's no such thing.

GRIPUS (*assuming the air of an expert*)   Oh, yes there is. I'm a fisherman, I know. But you don't often catch them. Isn't a fish around landed less often.

TRACHALIO   You're wasting your time. You can't kid me, you crook. All right, what color is it?

GRIPUS (*as before, pointing to the satchel*)   Very few are like this one here. Some of them have a dark red skin. Then there are some that are big and black.

TRACHALIO   Oh, sure. (*Savagely*) If you want my opinion, you better watch out or you'll turn into a satchel-fish yourself: that skin of yours is going to get dark red, and then wind up black—and blue.

GRIPUS (*half to himself*)   The god-damned trouble I had to run into today!

TRACHALIO (*impatiently*)   This argument's getting us nowhere. We're wasting time. Come on, my friend, who do you want to pick as judge to settle this for us?

GRIPUS (*eying him balefully*)   Judge? The satchel.

TRACHALIO   Oh, yeah?

GRIPUS   Yeah.

TRACHALIO (*exasperated*)   God, you're stupid!

GRIPUS (*scornfully*)   Well, listen to the professor!

TRACHALIO (*getting a firm grip on the rope*)   You're not moving an inch with this thing today—not unless you agree to a third party to hold it or a judge to judge the matter.

GRIPUS   Look here, are you in your right mind?

TRACHALIO (*scornfully*)   I'm as mad as a hatter.

GRIPUS (*tightening his grip on the net*)   Then I'm as crazy as a loon—but I'm not letting go.

TRACHALIO   You say one more word and I'll sink my fists in your skull. You know what they do to a new sponge? If you don't let go, that's the way I'll squeeze the juice out of you.

GRIPUS   You know how I slam the ink out of an octopus? You lay a finger on me and that's what I'll do to you. (*Sticking his chin in Trachalio's face*) So you want to fight, eh?

TRACHALIO (*abruptly losing his belligerence*)   Why do we have to fight? Why don't you and I just split the swag?

GRIPUS   Don't get any ideas: the only thing you'll be able to get for yourself out of all this is a sock on the jaw. (*Starts pulling the net toward the cottage*) I'm getting out of here.

TRACHALIO (*running ahead and yanking the rope so that the net—and Gripus—are spun about*)   No, you're not getting out of here—I'm putting this ship about. You stay where you are.

GRIPUS (*between his teeth*)   If you're going to play deck

hand on this ship, I'll be skipper. (*Roaring*) Damn you, let go that rope!

TRACHALIO   Sure I'll let go. You let go that satchel.

GRIPUS   By god, you're not going to get one single solitary square inch of this satchel.

TRACHALIO (*standing his ground*)   You can't get around me just by saying no. Either you cut me in, or you put up security, or you let a judge decide.

GRIPUS   What do you mean? Something *I* caught in the sea—

TRACHALIO (*interrupting*)   But *I* saw it from the shore.

GRIPUS (*disregarding him*)   —with my own hands, my own net, and my own boat?

TRACHALIO   I saw you get it from the shore, right? So, if the owner should come along, then I'm in this thing just as deep as you are, I'm an accomplice, right?

GRIPUS   Right.

TRACHALIO   All right, you stinker, you just prove to me how I can be an accomplice and not be entitled to a cut. Come on, show me how!

GRIPUS (*baffled and confused*)   I don't know. I don't know anything about that legal stuff you city boys do. All I say is that this satchel is mine.

TRACHALIO   And I say it's mine.

GRIPUS (*switching suddenly to affability*)   Wait a second. I just figured out how you don't have to be an accomplice— or get a cut.

TRACHALIO   Yeah? How?

GRIPUS   First you let me leave here. Then you go your own way—and keep your mouth shut. You don't say a word about me to anybody—and I don't give you anything. You stay mum, and I keep my trap shut. That's the fairest and squarest way to do it.

TRACHALIO   You mean you're not going to offer me a deal?

GRIPUS (*promptly*)   I already did: that you let go that rope, go away, and stop bothering me.

TRACHALIO Wait a second. I've got a counteroffer to make.

GRIPUS Yeah? Well offer to get the hell out of here.

TRACHALIO (*disregarding the last remark, with elaborate casualness*) Do you know anybody hereabouts?

GRIPUS (*evasively*) My own neighbors, naturally.

TRACHALIO (*as before*) Whereabouts do you live?

GRIPUS (*waving vaguely*) Farther on. Lots farther on. 'Way off at the end of those fields out there.

TRACHALIO (*concealing his satisfaction at the answer, even more casually than before*) How'd you like the fellow who lives in this cottage to be judge?

GRIPUS (*concealing his satisfaction at the suggestion*) Suppose you give me a little slack on that rope so I can step off to the side and think it over?

TRACHALIO Sure. (*Slacks off the rope, letting Gripus lug the net a few feet off to the side.*)

GRIPUS (*to the audience, jubilantly*) Hooray! I'm in! The swag's mine for keeps. He's inviting me to call in my own master as judge, right here on my own home grounds. Good old Daemones wouldn't judge anyone in his household out of a penny. This fellow here has no idea what kind of deal he's offering me. Sure I'll take a judge!

TRACHALIO Well, what do you say?

GRIPUS (*as if grudgingly*) Even though I know for sure that by rights this thing is mine, rather than have a fight with you, I'll do it your way.

TRACHALIO (*heartily*) That's what I like to hear.

GRIPUS (*as before*) And even though you're bringing me up before a judge I don't know, if he turns out honest, I may not know him but I want to; if he doesn't, I may know him but he's the last man in the world I want to. (*The door of the cottage opens and Daemones and the two girls come out.*)

DAEMONES (*to the girls*) Much as I want to do what you want me to, girls, I'm afraid that wife of mine will kick me out of the house on account of you. She'll say I'm bringing in a pair of mistresses right under her nose. I'd rather have you two running to that altar for help than me.

PALAESTRA   Oh, my god! This is the end!

DAEMONES (*reassuringly*)   Don't be afraid. I'll make sure you're safe. (*Noticing that the two slaves with the clubs are tagging along after the girls*) What are you following them outside for? No one's going to hurt them with me around. All right, guards, off guard and into the house, both of you. (*They go back into the cottage.*)

GRIPUS   Hello, master.

DAEMONES   Why, Gripus! Hello! How did things go?

TRACHALIO (*startled, to Daemones*)   Is he your servant?

GRIPUS (*grinning*)   His servant, and proud of it.

TRACHALIO (*glaring at him*)   I've got nothing to say to you.

GRIPUS   Yeah? Then get out of here.

TRACHALIO (*to Daemones*)   Please, mister, tell me: is he your servant?

DAEMONES   Yes, he is.

TRACHALIO (*jubilantly*)   Oh, boy! If he's yours, that's the best thing that could have happened! I'll say it for the second time today: I'm mighty glad to meet you.

DAEMONES (*cordially*)   Glad to meet you too. Aren't you the one who left here to get your master a little while ago?

TRACHALIO   I'm the one.

DAEMONES   Well, what can we do for you?

TRACHALIO   So he's yours, eh?

DAEMONES   Yes, he is.

TRACHALIO (*grinning broadly*)   If he's yours, that's the best thing that could have happened.

DAEMONES   What's this all about?

TRACHALIO (*pointing to Gripus, vehemently*)   That devil there is a damned crook!

DAEMONES (*patiently*) And just what has the "damned crook" done to you?

TRACHALIO I want him drawn and quartered!

DAEMONES Now what is this you two are making such a case about?

TRACHALIO I'll tell you.

GRIPUS (*quickly*) Oh, no you don't. I'll tell him.

TRACHALIO (*with elaborate formality*) If I'm not mistaken, I have the right to open this action.

GRIPUS If you had any decency, you'd get into action and get out of here.

DAEMONES (*sharply*) Gripus! Shut up and listen.

GRIPUS (*unbelievingly*) You mean he's going to speak first?

DAEMONES (*nodding curtly*) You listen. (*To Trachalio*) And you start talking.

GRIPUS (*as before*) You're going to let an outsider talk ahead of one of your own household?

TRACHALIO (*eying him balefully*) Isn't there any way to handle this fellow? (*Turning to Daemones*) What I started to tell you was this. Remember that pimp you kicked out of the temple? Well, this fellow has his satchel. (*Pointing*) See? There it is.

GRIPUS (*trying to edge in front of the net*) I haven't got it.

TRACHALIO What do you mean you haven't got it? I'm not blind.

GRIPUS (*aside.*) I only wish you were! (*To Trachalio*) I have it, I don't have it—what are you sticking your nose into my affairs for?

TRACHALIO (*doggedly*) What's more important is how you got it, whether legally or illegally.

GRIPUS (*to Daemones, heatedly*) You can string me up by the neck this minute if I didn't find this satchel while I was fishing. (*To Trachalio*) And if I fished it up from the sea with my own net, how do you figure it's yours instead of mine?

TRACHALIO (*to Daemones*) He's trying to pull the wool over your eyes. What I just told you are the facts.

GRIPUS (*menacingly*) What did I hear you say?

TRACHALIO (*to Daemones*) He's yours, isn't he? Can't you handle him somehow? Get him to shut up until his betters finish speaking?

GRIPUS (*leering and making an obscene gesture*) So you want me to get what your master gives you, eh? Well, yours may "handle" you, all right, but ours doesn't pull that stuff with us.

DAEMONES (*to Trachalio, smiling*) He got the better of you there, my boy. Now, what is it you want? Speak up.

TRACHALIO For myself, nothing. I don't want any part of that satchel there, and I never once said it was mine. But there's a little jewel box in it that belongs to this girl here (*gesturing toward Palaestra*). She's the one I was telling you earlier was no slave.

DAEMONES (*nodding*) You mean the one you said came from the same city I did?

TRACHALIO Exactly. Well, the birth tokens she wore when she was a child are there in that box, and the box is there in that satchel. (*Nodding scornfully in Gripus' direction*) It's no earthly use to him, but he'll be doing this poor girl a real service if he gives her the only means she has for finding her parents.

DAEMONES Say no more. I'll have him hand it over.

GRIPUS So help me, I'm not giving him a thing!

TRACHALIO (*to Daemones*) All I'm asking for is the jewel box and birth tokens.

GRIPUS Oh, yeah? What if they're gold?

TRACHALIO What difference should that make to you? (*Loftily*) Any gold or silver will be bought and paid for in cash.

GRIPUS All right, my friend, you let me see that cash and I'll let you see the box.

DAEMONES   Gripus, shut up or you'll be sorry. (*To Trachalio*) Finish what you started to say.

TRACHALIO (*earnestly*)   I have just one favor to ask of you: have pity on this girl—I mean, if the satchel really is that pimp's, as I suspect it is. (*Pointedly*) You see, at this moment I can't say anything for sure, I can only guess.

GRIPUS (*to Daemones, excitedly*)   Don't you see? That good-for-nothing's trying to lay a trap for us!

TRACHALIO (*to Gripus*)   Will you let me finish talking? (*To Daemones*) I say the satchel belongs to that filthy pimp. Now, if it does, the girls will be able to recognize it. So will you please make him show it to them?

GRIPUS (*spluttering*)   What's that? Show it to them?

DAEMONES (*mildly*)   There's nothing wrong with his suggestion, is there, Gripus? Just to show it to them?

GRIPUS (*roaring*)   I should say there is! A hell of a lot wrong!

DAEMONES   How so?

GRIPUS   Because the minute I show it to them, naturally they'll say they recognize it.

TRACHALIO (*heatedly*)   Damn you, you think everybody's as big a liar as you are!

GRIPUS (*gesturing toward Daemones*)   So long as he's on my side, you can say anything you like; it won't bother me in the least.

TRACHALIO   He may be standing on your side, but he's going to take his testimony from this side (*pointing to the girls*).

DAEMONES (*sharply*)   Gripus, you listen. (*To Trachalio*) And you explain what you want—and make it short.

TRACHALIO (*patiently*)   I already did. But if you didn't follow me, I'll do it again. As I've already told you, neither of these girls should be slaves. (*Gesturing toward Palaestra*) This one here was kidnaped from Athens when she was a child.

GRIPUS   Suppose you explain to me just what their being slaves or not has to do with this satchel?

TRACHALIO (*angrily*) Damn you, you want me to tell the story all over again just to waste the whole day.

DAEMONES (*to Trachalio, sharply*) Cut out the cursing and do what I asked you.

TRACHALIO It's just as I told you before. There should be a little jewel box in that satchel. It contains the birth tokens she can use to identify her parents. She was wearing them when she was snatched from Athens as a child.

GRIPUS (*savagely*) I wish to god someone'd put the snatch on you! What the hell's going on here? (*Gesturing angrily toward the girls*) What's the matter with them? Are they dumb? Can't they talk for themselves?

TRACHALIO Sure. But they're keeping quiet because they know that's what makes a good woman—knowing how to keep quiet and not talk.

GRIPUS So help me, by that token you don't make either a good man or a good woman.

TRACHALIO Why?

GRIPUS Because you're no good whether you talk or keep quiet. (*To Daemones*) Please! Am I going to get a chance to speak today?

DAEMONES (*turning on him*) One more word out of you today and I'll have your head!

TRACHALIO (*to Daemones*) As I was saying, would you please make him give the box back to the girls? If he insists on some sort of reward, he can have one: let him keep whatever else is in the satchel for himself.

GRIPUS Finally you said it! And you know why? Because you know very well what my rights in the matter are. A few minutes ago you were out to get half for yourself.

TRACHALIO You know what? I still am.

GRIPUS I once saw a vulture out to get something, and you know what? He didn't get away with a thing.

DAEMONES (*to Gripus, angrily*) Do you need a beating to keep you quiet?

GRIPUS (*stubbornly*)   If he shuts up, I'll shut up. But if he's going to talk, let me talk too, and give my side of the story.

DAEMONES   Gripus, hand me that satchel.

GRIPUS   I'll trust you with it if you promise that, if there's nothing of theirs in it, I get it back.

DAEMONES   You'll get it back.

GRIPUS (*taking the satchel out of the net and handing it over*) Here it is.

DAEMONES   Now, Palaestra, and you too, Ampelisca, listen to me. Is this the satchel you say has your box in it?

PALAESTRA (*without hesitation*)   Yes, it is.

GRIPUS   Oh, my god in heaven, I haven't got a chance! She said it was hers before she even got a good look at it!

PALAESTRA (*earnestly*)   I know it's confusing, so let me clear things up for you. There should be a little wicker box in that satchel. Now, without your showing me a thing, I'll name every article that's in it. If I make a mistake, then I've wasted my breath and you people keep whatever's in there for yourselves. But if I don't, then please, please let me have my things back.

DAEMONES   Agreed. In my opinion, what you're asking for is plain and simple justice.

GRIPUS   And in mine, damn it all, plain and simple injustice. Supposing she's a witch or a fortuneteller and reels off the name of whatever's in there perfectly? Are we going to let some fortuneteller walk off with everything?

DAEMONES (*sharply*)   She's not walking off with a thing unless she names every item without a mistake. Fortune-telling won't get her anywhere. Now, unstrap that satchel so that I can find out who's right and who's wrong without wasting another minute.

TRACHALIO (*watching Gripus unstrap the satchel, aside with satisfaction*)   And that settles *his* hash.

GRIPUS (*to Daemones*)   The straps are off.

DAEMONES   Now open it.

PALAESTRA (*excitedly*)   I see the box!

DAEMONES (*taking it out and holding it*)   Is this it?

PALAESTRA   That's it! (*Extending her hand and touching it almost caressingly, to herself*) Dear parents, all I have of you I carry locked up here. Here are stored all my hopes, the only means I have of ever finding you.

GRIPUS (*to himself, growling*)   You deserve the wrath of god on your head, whoever you are, for squeezing your parents into something that small.

DAEMONES (*pointing to a spot at his side*) Gripus, you stand here; this concerns you now. (*To Palaestra*) You stand over there and call off all the things in the box and tell us what each looks like. Mind you, don't leave anything out. And, believe me, if you make the slightest mistake, don't get any ideas about correcting it later. It'll be a sheer waste of time, my girl. (*Palaestra nods and steps a few paces away.*)

GRIPUS (*nodding approvingly*)   You're asking only for what's fair.

TRACHALIO   God knows he wouldn't ask anything like that of you. You don't know what it is to be fair.

DAEMONES (*to Palaestra*)   All right, my girl, you can start now. (*As Gripus opens his mouth*) Gripus! Shut up and pay attention.

PALAESTRA (*with her back to Daemones and Gripus*)   The box has my birth tokens.

DAEMONES (*holding the box open before him*)   I see them.

GRIPUS (*to himself*)   Knocked out in the first round! (*Grabbing Daemones' arm to bring the box closer to his chest*) Wait a second! Don't show them to her!

DAEMONES   Now tell me what each one of them looks like.

PALAESTRA   First there's a miniature gold sword. It's inscribed.

DAEMONES   What's the inscription say?

PALAESTRA   My father's name. Next, alongside the sword is

a miniature two-headed ax, also of gold and inscribed; this time it's my mother's name.

DAEMONES Wait a second. What is your father's name? I mean the one on the sword?

PALAESTRA Daemones.

(*Daemones holds the trinket in his hand and stares at the letters in amazement. Slowly he lifts his head to look toward the sky.*)

DAEMONES (*to himself, hoarsely*) God in heaven! What is happening to all my hopes!

GRIPUS (*aside*) You mean what's happening to all mine!

TRACHALIO (*to Palaestra and Daemones, eagerly*) Please! Go on, don't stop!

GRIPUS (*turning on him*) Either you take it easy or go straight to hell!

DAEMONES (*in a voice so full of emotion it is barely audible*) Tell me, what's the name on the little ax, your mother's name?

PALAESTRA Daedalis.

DAEMONES (*to himself, choking with emotion*) It was heaven's will to rescue me!

GRIPUS (*aside*) And throw me overboard!

DAEMONES (*sotto voce to Gripus*) Gripus! This girl! She must be my daughter!

GRIPUS (*not exactly overcome by the news, sotto voce*) It's all right with me. (*Looking toward Trachalio, under his breath*) God damn you to hell for having gotten a look at me today—and me for being damned fool enough not to have looked around a hundred times to make sure no one was watching before I pulled that net out of the water!

PALAESTRA (*unaware of the excitement she is causing*) Next a miniature silver sickle, and two clasped hands, and a miniature windlass—

GRIPUS (*aside*) Windlass? I wish to hell you were windless.

PALAESTRA   —and a gold medallion my father gave me on my birthday.

DAEMONES (*to himself, ecstatically*)   It's she! I must take her in my arms! (*Rushing to her and taking her hands*) My daughter! I'm you own father! I'm Daemones! Daedalis —your mother—is right inside!

PALAESTRA (*throwing herself into his arms*)   Oh, my father, my father! Who ever imagined this could happen!

DAEMONES (*holding her tightly*)   What a joy it is to have you in my arms!

TRACHALIO (*beaming on them*)   It's a joy to see how heaven has rewarded you both for being as good as you are.

DAEMONES   Trachalio, pick up the satchel if you can and bring it inside. Hurry!

TRACHALIO (*to Gripus, grinning broadly*)   See where all your dirty tricks got you? My heartiest congratulations on your bad luck.

DAEMONES (*to Palaestra*)   Come, my daughter, let's go in to your mother. She'll be able to test you further about all this. She used to be with you more, and she's more familiar with these trinkets of yours.

PALAESTRA   Let's all go in. Then we can do it all together. (*Turning to Ampelisca*) Follow me, Ampelisca.

AMPELISCA (*tearfully*)   I'm so happy that god has been so good to you!

(*Daemones, Trachalio, and the two girls enter the cottage.*)

GRIPUS (*to himself*)   Why the hell did I have to fish that satchel up today? Or, rather, why the hell didn't I stash it away in a safe spot after I fished it up? So help me, it was so rough out there when I found the thing, I knew I'd have a rough time with it. God, I'll bet that satchel's full of money. The best thing for me to do now is just sneak off and hang myself—at least for a while until the ache goes away! (*Exits, stage right.*)

(*The door of the cottage opens and Daemones emerges. He is radiant. He walks downstage and addresses the audience.*)

DAEMONES I swear I'm the luckiest man in the world! Suddenly, like a bolt from the blue, I found my daughter. (*Shaking his head wonderingly*) You know, when heaven wants to do well by a man, somehow he ends up getting his fondest wish—if he's been decent and god-fearing. Take me —today, like a bolt from the blue, I found my daughter, something I had given up hoping for, no longer believed could happen. And I'm going to marry her to a fine young fellow from one of the best families in Athens. What's more, I find that he's a relative of mine. I want him to come out here and see me just as soon as possible, so I've told his servant to step outside; I want to send him to town right away. (*Looking toward the door*) He hasn't come out yet. I wonder what's keeping him? I think I'd better take a look inside. (*Walks back to the entrance and peers in.*) What's this? My wife hanging on to my daughter's neck? All this hugging and loving is getting to be a silly nuisance. (*Calling through the doorway*) My dear wife, it's time to stop the kissing and start getting things ready for me. As soon as I come in I want to give a thank offering to our guardian angel for having added to our family the way he has. The lambs and pigs for the sacrifice are all ready. (*Impatiently*) What are you women keeping Trachalio for? (*Stepping back from the door*) Good. He's coming out now.

TRACHALIO (*as he hurries out the door, breathlessly*) I don't care where he is, I'll track him down and bring him back here with me. Plesidippus, I mean.

DAEMONES (*nodding approval*) And tell him what happened about my daughter. Ask him to drop everything and come right out here.

TRACHALIO Right.

DAEMONES Tell him he has my permission to marry her.

TRACHALIO Right.

DAEMONES   And that I know his father; he's a relative of mine.

TRACHALIO   Right.

DAEMONES   And hurry.

TRACHALIO   Right.

DAEMONES   Bring him here right away, so we can start preparing dinner.

TRACHALIO   Right.

DAEMONES (*somewhat irritated*)   Everything I say is "right," eh?

TRACHALIO   Right. But do you know what I'd like from you? That you remember the promise you made about my getting my freedom today.

DAEMONES   Right.

TRACHALIO   You get Plesidippus to agree to set me free.

DAEMONES   Right.

TRACHALIO   And get your daughter to ask him; she'll get it out of him without any trouble.

DAEMONES   Right.

TRACHALIO   And arrange to have Ampelisca marry me as soon as I'm free.

DAEMONES   Right.

TRACHALIO   I want to see some tangible appreciation for all I've done for you.

DAEMONES   Right.

TRACHALIO   Everything I say is "right," eh?

DAEMONES   Right—I'm just returning the favor. Now, off to the city this minute, on the double, and then come back here.

TRACHALIO   Right. I won't take long. In the meantime you get everything ready that we need.

DAEMONES   Right. (*To himself as Trachalio dashes off, stage left*) The devil take him with his "rights"! My ears are ringing: whatever I said, it was nothing but "right," "right," "right."

(*Enter Gripus, stage right.*)

GRIPUS (*determinedly*) Daemones, when will it be all right to have a word with you?

DAEMONES (*wincing at still another "right"*) What's on your mind, Gripus?

GRIPUS It's about that satchel. If you've got any sense, you'll have the sense to hold onto something heaven's dropped right in your lap.

DAEMONES (*reproachfully*) Do you think it's right for me to claim somebody else's property as my own?

GRIPUS (*exasperated*) But it's something I found in the sea!

DAEMONES So much the better for the man who lost it. But that doesn't make it any more your satchel.

GRIPUS (*disgustedly*) That's why you're so poor. It's that sanctified goodness of yours.

DAEMONES (*gently*) Gripus, Gripus, there are so many traps set for men during their lifetime to trick and fool them! What's more, the traps are often baited; if a man's avaricious and goes after the bait greedily, he gets trapped by his own greed. The man who's careful and experienced and astute in watching his step can live a long and honest life on what he's honestly earned. If you ask me, this prize you're so wedded to will fall prize to its owner—and the divorce will cost us money. (*In shocked tones*) I hide something brought to me that I know isn't mine? None of that for your old master Daemones, no, sir! The one thing any man of intelligence is always on guard against is consciously taking part in wrongdoing. I'll have nothing whatsoever to do with making any gains by collusion.

GRIPUS (*eying him pityingly*) I've often seen actors in a play deliver themselves of gems of wisdom of this sort—and seen them get a round of applause for having mouthed for the audience all these·rules of good behavior. Then, when the audience left and everybody was back in his own home, there wasn't a one who behaved the way he had been told to.

DAEMONES (*impatiently*)   Oh, go inside and stop bothering me. And watch that tongue of yours. Make no mistake about it—I'm not going to give you a thing.

(*Gripus, without a word, marches up to the door, opens it, then turns to deliver a parting shot.*)

GRIPUS (*bitterly*)   I hope to god whatever's in that satchel— gold or silver or what not—turns into ashes! (*Ducks into the cottage, slamming the door.*)

DAEMONES (*to the audience, shaking his head sadly*)   See that attitude? That's the reason we have such bad servants. Now if that Gripus of mine had gotten together with some other servant, he'd have involved the two of them in grand larceny. He'd have been thinking he had his hands on a prize, and he'd have turned out to be the prize himself. What he caught would have caught him. Well, I'll go in now and attend to the offering. And then I'll give orders to have dinner ready immediately.

(*Daemones goes into the cottage. A moment later Trachalio and Plesidippus enter, stage left. One glance at the latter is enough to reveal that he has gotten the news.*)

PLESIDIPPUS (*ecstatically*)   Trachalio, my friend, my freedman-to-be, no, my patron—more than that, the founder of my household! Tell me that whole story over again. So Palaestra found her mother and father?

TRACHALIO (*smiling indulgently*)   Yes, she did.

PLESIDIPPUS   And she's an Athenian like me?

TRACHALIO   I think so.

PLESIDIPPUS   And she's going to marry me?

TRACHALIO   I suspect so.

PLESIDIPPUS   What do you think, will we become engaged today?

TRACHALIO (*pretending, indulgently, to be under formal interrogation*)   Yes, Mr. Chairman.

PLESIDIPPUS   What do you say, should I congratulate her father on having found her?

TRACHALIO   Yes, Mr. Chairman.

PLESIDIPPUS   How about her mother?

TRACHALIO   Yes, Mr. Chairman.

PLESIDIPPUS   Have you anything to tell the chair?

TRACHALIO   Yes, Mr. Chairman: yes to whatever the chair asks.

PLESIDIPPUS (*slyly*)   All right, can you estimate the chair's net worth?

TRACHALIO (*taken aback*)   Me? (*Recovering*) Yes, Mr. Chairman—

PLESIDIPPUS (*interrupting*)   Look, I'm standing; forget about this "chair" business.

TRACHALIO   Yes, Mr. Chairman.

PLESIDIPPUS   Should I rush up to her?

TRACHALIO   Yes, Mr. Chairman.

PLESIDIPPUS   Or should I go up to her quietly, like this? (*Demonstrates.*)

TRACHALIO   Yes, Mr. Chairman.

PLESIDIPPUS   Should I shake her hand when I go up to her?

TRACHALIO   Yes, Mr. Chairman.

PLESIDIPPUS   Her father's too?

TRACHALIO   Yes, Mr. Chairman.

PLESIDIPPUS   And then her mother's?

TRACHALIO   Yes, Mr. Chairman.

PLESIDIPPUS   Should I embrace her father when I go up to him?

TRACHALIO   No, Mr. Chairman.

PLESIDIPPUS   How about her mother?

TRACHALIO   No, Mr. Chairman.

PLESIDIPPUS (*eagerly*) How about her?

TRACHALIO No, Mr. Chairman. (*Starts walking toward the cottage.*)

PLESIDIPPUS Oh, lord! He votes Nay just when I want Aye —and walks out on the meeting.

TRACHALIO (*calling*) You're crazy. Come on!

PLESIDIPPUS Lead on, my patron, whither thou will.

(*The two enter the cottage, and the stage is now empty.*)

ACT V

(*Enter Labrax, stage left.*)

LABRAX (*to the audience*) Is there another man alive right now who's worse off than I am? I've just come from court; Plesidippus got them to condemn me, and they made me give Palaestra up. I'm ruined! (*Bitterly*) If you ask me, pimps were put on this earth just to make people laugh— that's the way it looks, judging from the general hilarity whenever a poor pimp has to suffer. (*Turning and walking toward the shrine*) I'm going to see to that other girl of mine in the shrine here. At least I'll take her away with me —the only remnant left of all my property.

(*The door of the cottage opens and Gripus comes out. He is holding a spit encrusted with rust—eloquent testimony as to how long it's been since Daemones last held a party. He turns to speak to those inside.*)

GRIPUS (*through the doorway*) By god, you're not going to lay eyes on me alive after tonight—unless I get that satchel back!

LABRAX (*to himself*) Oh, god! Whenever I hear anyone mention a satchel, it's like the stab of a sword through my heart.

GRIPUS (*as before*) That damned Trachalio gets his freedom and you refuse to give a single thing to the man who fished the satchel up in his net!

LABRAX (*his attention arrested, to himself*) So help me, what this fellow is saying sounds very, very interesting.

GRIPUS (*as before*) I'm going right out and post notices everywhere in letters a foot and a half high: "Found. One satchel full of gold and silver. For information see Gripus." You think you're going to get away with my satchel, don't you? Well, you're not.

LABRAX (*to himself*)   By god, I think this fellow knows who has my satchel! I'd better have a talk with him. Lord in heaven, help me now!

GRIPUS (*as someone calls him to come back inside*)   What are you calling me back for? I want to clean this outside here. (*Turns away from the door and starts scraping the spit; to himself*) My god! You'd think this spit's made of rust instead of iron. The more I scrape it, the redder and skinnier it gets. I think there's a curse on it: the thing's dying of old age right in my hands.

LABRAX (*in his most affable manner*)   Hello there.

GRIPUS (*eying him distastefully*)   Hello yourself, dirty face.

LABRAX (*as before*)   What are you doing with yourself these days?

GRIPUS (*scraping away industriously*)   Cleaning a spit.

LABRAX   Business good around here?

GRIPUS   What's it to you? You a broker?

LABRAX   Oh, no. I'm one letter short of that.

GRIPUS   Broke, eh?

LABRAX   You hit the nail on the head.

GRIPUS   I know. You look it. What happened to you?

LABRAX   My ship was wrecked last night. Lost everything I had in it.

GRIPUS   What did you lose?

LABRAX (*pointedly*)   A satchel full of gold and silver.

GRIPUS (*his attention caught*)   Do you remember any of the things in this satchel you lost?

LABRAX (*evasively*)   What difference does it make? It's lost, isn't it? Forget it. Let's talk about something else.

GRIPUS   What if I know who found it? I just want to see if you can prove it's your property.

LABRAX   Well, there were eight hundred gold pieces in a pouch. Then another hundred gold eagles in a separate leather sack.

GRIPUS (*aside*) God almighty, what a haul! I'm in for a fat reward. There is a providence after all: I'm going to get a load of loot out of this fellow. It's his satchel, no question about it. (*To Labrax*) Go on, tell me what else was in it.

LABRAX Thirty thousand dollars in silver in a sack, all good coin. And some silverware—a bowl, a bucket, a pitcher, a jug, and a cup.

GRIPUS. Wow! That's quite a fortune you had there.

LABRAX I "had"; now I don't have a thing. Saddest and worst word in the language, "had."

GRIPUS (*eying him narrowly*) What are you willing to pay the fellow who brings you information about its whereabouts? (*As Labrax hesitates*) Come on, speak up!

LABRAX Fifteen hundred dollars.

GRIPUS (*snorting*) Stop kidding.

LABRAX Two thousand.

GRIPUS That's a laugh.

LABRAX Two thousand, five hundred.

GRIPUS Peanuts.

LABRAX Three thousand.

GRIPUS Chicken feed. ▪

LABRAX I'll give you three thousand, five hundred.

GRIPUS What's the matter? Your mouth hot and you want to air it out?

LABRAX I'll give you five thousand dollars.

GRIPUS Wake up.

LABRAX Not another cent.

GRIPUS All right then, beat it!

LABRAX Listen—

GRIPUS (*heading for the door*) Once I leave here, my friend, I'm gone for good.

LABRAX Will you take five thousand, five hundred?

GRIPUS (*walking away*) You're dreaming.

LABRAX (*calling after him*)   Name your price.

GRIPUS (*stopping*)   Fifteen thousand dollars and you don't have to give me a penny more. But not a penny less! That's it; take it or leave it.

LABRAX (*shrugging*)   What can I say? I've got to take it. All right, I'll give you fifteen thousand.

GRIPUS (*walking over to the altar*)   Come on over here; I want Venus to be a party to this deal.

LABRAX (*following him*)   Anything you want; just tell me what it is.

GRIPUS   Put your hand on this altar.

LABRAX   It's on.

GRIPUS (*grimly*)   You've got to swear by Venus here.

LABRAX   What should I swear?

GRIPUS   What I tell you to.

LABRAX   You say it; I'll swear it. (*Aside, sardonically*)   The old master being told what to swear!

GRIPUS   Got hold of the altar?

LABRAX   Right.

GRIPUS   Give me your solemn oath you'll pay me the money the day you get your satchel back.

LABRAX   So be it. (*Raising his eyes to heaven and intoning*)   I solemnly swear in the name of Venus of Cyrene that, if I find the satchel I lost in the shipwreck and regain possession of it with the gold and silver safe inside, I will pay to this man—

GRIPUS (*interrupting*)   Say "I will pay to this man Gripus" and touch me at the same time.

LABRAX (*sardonically*)   To make it absolutely clear to you, Venus, I will pay to this man Gripus fifteen thousand dollars on the spot.

GRIPUS   Now say that, if you should welsh, Venus should ruin your body, your soul, and your business. (*Aside*)   And once you've done swearing it, I hope she does it to you anyway.

LABRAX (*intoning*)   If I go back on anything I have sworn, may all pimps suffer a life of misery.

GRIPUS   Don't worry, that'll happen even if you keep your word. (*Walking toward the door*) You wait there. I'll bring the old man outside right away. As soon as I do, you ask him for your satchel. (*Hurries into the cottage.*)

LABRAX (*looking after him scornfully, to himself*)   Even if he gets the satchel back for me, I don't owe him a dime. *I'm* the one who decides what I· do about what I swear. (*The door opens and Gripus and Daemones come out lugging the satchel.*) Here he comes with the old man. I'd better shut up.

GRIPUS (*to Daemones*)   Follow me. This way.

DAEMONES   Where is that pimp of yours?

GRIPUS (*calling to Labrax*)   Hey, you! (*Pointing to Daemones*) Here he is. This fellow's got your satchel.

DAEMONES (*to Labrax*)   Yes, I have it and I don't mind telling you that I do. What's more, if it's yours, you're welcome to it. You'll find everything that was in it still there, safe and sound. Here, take it if it's yours.

LABRAX (*unable to believe his eyes*)   Well, what do you know! My satchel! (*Going up to it and fingering it lovingly*) Greetings, old satchel, greetings!

DAEMONES   Is it yours?

LABRAX (*getting a firm grip on it*)   What a question! I don't care if it belonged to god almighty himself; it's mine now.

DAEMONES   Everything in it is safe and sound—with one exception: I took out a little box of trinkets I used in finding my daughter today.

LABRAX   Who's that?

DAEMONES   Palaestra, the girl you used to own. I found out she's my daughter.

LABRAX (*assuming his heartiest manner*)   Well, that's just fine! Things have turned out beautifully for you. Just what you hoped for. I'm delighted.

DAEMONES (*dryly*)   I find it a little hard to believe that.

LABRAX (*as before*)   It's the god's honest truth. (*Slyly*) And just to prove my feelings are genuine, you don't have to pay me a cent for her. She's a gift.

DAEMONES (*as before*)   So kind of you.

LABRAX   Oh, no, nothing at all, really.

GRIPUS (*pointedly*)   All right you, you have your satchel now.

LABRAX   That's right.

GRIPUS   Well, let's get on with it.

LABRAX (*producing his blankest look*)   Get on with what?

GRIPUS   Paying me my money.

LABRAX   I'm not paying you any money. I don't owe you a cent.

GRIPUS   Hey, what's going on here! (*Disbelievingly*) You don't owe me a cent?

LABRAX   That's right. Not a cent.

GRIPUS   But you gave me your oath.

LABRAX (*blandly*)   I know I did. I'll give you another right now if I feel like it. This oath business is strictly for holding on to property, not letting it go.

GRIPUS (*shouting*)   You hand over that fifteen thousand dollars, you dirty liar!

DAEMONES (*to Gripus*)   Gripus, what's this fifteen thousand you're asking him for?

GRIPUS   He gave me his oath he'd pay it to me.

LABRAX (*to Gripus, as before*)   I get fun out of giving oaths. What are you, the chief justice? Going to try me for perjury?

DAEMONES (*to Gripus*)   What did he promise you the money for?

GRIPUS   He swore he'd give me fifteen thousand dollars if I got his satchel back for him.

LABRAX (*to Gripus, scornfully*)   Pick some free man to rep-

resent you and let's go to court. (*Grinning*) I'll prove you
made me a party to a fraudulent contract, (*the grin widening*) and that I'm still a minor.

GRIPUS (*pointing to Daemones*)   He'll represent me.

LABRAX (*losing his grin*)   No. You'll have to get someone
else.

DAEMONES (*to Labrax, firmly*)   I'm not going to let you take
a penny away from this boy—unless I find he's done something wrong. Now then, did you promise him the money?

LABRAX (*unabashed*)   Sure I did.

DAEMONES (*promptly*)   What you promised a servant of
mine is by rights mine. (*As Labrax opens his mouth*)
Don't get the idea you can pull any of your pimp's tricks
on me; you won't get away with it.

GRIPUS (*to Labrax, jubilantly*)   So you thought you had
gotten your hands on some poor devil you could swindle,
eh? You'll pay—and in good money, too. And the minute I
get it I'm giving it to this man here (*pointing to Daemones*) to pay for my freedom.

DAEMONES (*to Labrax, reproachfully*)   When you think of
how well I've treated you and that it was all because of me
this money was kept safe for you—

GRIPUS (*interrupting angrily*)   None of that—all because of
me, not you.

DAEMONES (*turning on him*)   If you've got any brains, you'll
keep your mouth shut! (*To Labrax*) —the least you could
do is act decently and reciprocate for all I've done for
you.

LABRAX (*softened by Daemones' conciliatory tone*)   I take
it you're asking me this because you recognize my rights?

DAEMONES   I'm not exactly asking you to use them against
me, you know.

GRIPUS (*his eyes fixed on Labrax' face, aside*)   I'm in! The
pimp's weakening! My freedom's just around the corner!

DAEMONES (*gesturing toward Gripus*)   First of all, this boy who found that satchel of yours is my servant. Secondly, I kept it safe for you, money and all.

LABRAX (*nodding his head in agreement*)   I'm really very grateful to you. About that fifteen thousand I swore to give that boy of yours—I see no reason why you shouldn't have it.

GRIPUS (*to Labrax, shouting*)   Hey, you! You give it to me, not him! Haven't you got any brains?

DAEMONES (*turning on him*)   Will you please shut up!

GRIPUS (*wildly*)   You're just pretending to be working for my interests; you're really out for yourself. I may have lost all the rest of the swag in that satchel, but, by god, you're not going to screw me out of this!

DAEMONES (*angrily*)   If you say another word, I'll have you whipped!

GRIPUS (*as before*)   Go on, kill me! I'll only keep quiet if you gag me with fifteen thousand dollars. There's no other way to shut me up.

LABRAX (*to Gripus, disgustedly*)   Oh, pipe down. He certainly is working for your best interests.

DAEMONES (*beckoning Labrax off to the side*)   Step over here, will you?

LABRAX   Sure.

GRIPUS (*calling to them as they move to one side*)   Hey, let's keep it in the open! I don't want any of this whispering business.

DAEMONES (*sotto voce*)   How much did you pay for that other girl? Ampelisca, I mean.

LABRAX (*sotto voce*)   Five thousand dollars.

DAEMONES (*sotto voce*)   How'd you like me to make you a good offer for her?

LABRAX (*sotto voce*)   I sure would.

DAEMONES (*sotto voce*)   I'll split that fifteen thousand with you.

LABRAX (*sotto voce, with pleased surprise*)   Thanks!

DAEMONES (*sotto voce*)　You take half for letting Ampelisca go free, and give me half.

LABRAX (*sotto voce*)　It's a deal.

DAEMONES (*sotto voce*)　The half I get will pay for Gripus' freedom. After all, it was because of him that you found your satchel and I my daughter.

LABRAX (*sotto voce*)　Thanks very much. I'm much obliged to you.

GRIPUS (*calling*)　Hey, how soon am I going to get my money?

DAEMONES　It's all settled, Gripus. I've got it.

GRIPUS　Damn it all, I want me to have it!

DAEMONES　Well, damn it all, you're not getting it, so don't start getting your hopes up. And I want you to let him (*gesturing toward Labrax*) off his oath.

GRIPUS (*roaring*)　Damn it all, that's the end of me. I'm a goner—unless I hang myself. And, damn it all, I'll do it right now—you won't get a second chance to swindle me, no sir!

DAEMONES (*to Labrax*)　How about joining us for dinner?

LABRAX　Thanks. Be glad to.

DAEMONES　Follow me in, both of you. (*Walks downstage and addresses the audience.*) Ladies and gentlemen, I'd invite you to dinner too—except that I'm not serving anything, and there's nothing decent to eat in the house anyway; besides, I know you've all got other invitations to eat out tonight. But, if you'd care to give a hearty round of applause to our play, you can all come to a big party at my house—sixteen years from now. (*Turning to Labrax and Gripus*) You two come to dinner.

LABRAX AND GRIPUS　Thank you.

DAEMONES (*to the audience*)　Your applause, please.